ET  IE

The 2008 crisis in the financial industry, precipitated by the bursting of a bubble in the housing sector, brought the U.S. economy to the brink of a major depression. Government officials, economists and financial executives intervened to implement measures to mitigate the damage, applying their expertise and using their best judgments to rescue the economy. The actions they took required technical competence, pragmatic judgments and controversial decisions. As events played out in the autumn of 2008, there was little time to reflect on how immoral conduct contributed to the crisis and how financial recovery needs to be built on an ethical foundation. But now, in the aftermath of the economic crisis of 2008, it is important to ask what ethics has to say to the many stakeholders in the U.S. economy. The purpose of this book is to examine the role of ethics in setting things right.

This book discusses the conditions that contributed to the financial collapse that began in 2008 and continues today, parsing what went wrong ethically and drawing from this financial meltdown any lessons that can be learned. Featuring eighteen short case studies alongside a detailed examination of the financial crisis that is still at the forefront of many academic and political minds, it is a valuable contribution to the business ethics literature.

Eileen P. Flynn is a professor in the Department of Theology at Saint Peter's College, New Jersey. She obtained a Ph.D. in Moral Theology from Fordham University, and is the author of fifteen books. She was awarded *bene merenti* status in 2001 in recognition of her outstanding service of twenty years.

ETHICAL LESSONS OF THE FINANCIAL CRISIS

Eileen P. Flynn

Routledge
Taylor & Francis Group

NEW YORK AND LONDON

First published 2012
by Routledge
711 Third Avenue, New York, NY 10017

Simultaneously published in the UK
by Routledge
2 Park Square, Milton Park, Abingdon, Oxon OX14 4RN

Routledge is an imprint of the Taylor & Francis Group, an informa business

Library of Congress Cataloging in Publication Data
Flynn, Eileen P. (Eileen Patricia)
Ethical lessons of the financial crisis/Eileen Flynn.
    p. cm.
    Includes bibliographical references and index.
    1. Global Financial Crisis, 2008–2009–Moral and ethical aspects. 2. Financial
    crises–United States–Moral and ethical aspects. 3. Financial services industry–
    United States–Moral and ethical aspects. 4. Financial institutions–United
    States–Moral and ethical aspects. I. Title.
    HB37172008.F59 2012
    174–dc23   2012003276

ISBN: 978-0-415-51674-7 (hbk)
ISBN: 978-0-415-51675-4 (pbk)
ISBN: 978-0-203-12404-8 (ebk)

Typeset in Baskerville
by Wearset Ltd, Boldon, Tyne and Wear

Printed and bound in the United States of America
by Edwards Brothers, Inc.

To Luke, Julia, Erin, Brendan and James

CONTENTS

INTRODUCTION

In the aftermath of the economic crisis of 2008 it is important to ask what ethics has to say to the many stakeholders in the U.S. economy. The crisis in the financial industry, precipitated by the bursting of a bubble in the housing sector, brought the U.S. economy to the brink of a major depression. Government officials, economists and financial executives intervened to implement measures to mitigate the damage, applying their expertise and using their best judgments to rescue the economy. The actions they took required technical competence, pragmatic judgments and controversial decisions. They worked through a crisis to try to prevent a very bad situation from becoming a catastrophe. As events played out in the fall of 2008, there was little time to reflect on how immoral conduct contributed to the crisis and how financial recovery needs to be built on an ethical foundation. The purpose of this book is to examine the role of ethics in setting things right. In taking a close look at the events of 2008 this book makes an important contribution to business ethics.

We begin in Chapter 1 by discussing the question "What went wrong?" and follow in Chapter 2 with a sober reflection on who was affected by the meltdown and subsequent recession. Given the complex and technical nature of the financial crisis, this will be a daunting task, but it is a necessary preliminary step. We need to define the problem before we can grasp what needs to be done to solve it. A large part of the problem is that there were deeply rooted flaws in the interconnected systems in which financial transactions take place; these flaws were structural in nature and require systemic change. We need to understand this reality in order to gain sufficient insight to engage in meaningful and relevant ethical reflection. It is not sufficient to indict the greed of mortgage brokers and those who profited from selling mortgage-backed securities as the cause of the crisis. The *system* that facilitated the sale of mortgages and the *system* that encouraged short-term profit at the expense of long-term viability also need to be critiqued. The authors of the *Report* of the Financial Crisis Inquiry Commission make this point well when they say that to pin this crisis on moral flaws like greed and hubris would be simplistic. Failure to account for human weakness set the stage for the crisis.[1] Chapters 1 and 2 stand as a case study of the financial crisis. All the chapters in this book are followed by case studies which encourage the reader to examine how human conduct can contribute to or detract from economic stability.

In Chapter 3 we consider steps that need to be taken to put the U.S. economy back on a solid footing. In Chapters 4, 5 and 6, we concentrate on ethics and consider how input from individual and social ethics should inform the process of recovery. Two tasks are at the core of this undertaking: comprehending what ethics requires and committing ourselves to observing ethical standards. These preconditions must be met in order to build a strong economic future.

Reading a book like this and engaging with its interactive elements requires effort. Why should an individual expend this effort? Quite simply, because people have been profoundly affected by the financial crisis and they need to understand that things have changed and that they face hard times. Generation Y, for example, is confident and achievement-oriented. They have high expectations and want meaningful work and a prosperous life. In easier times members of Generation Y assumed that the youthful behaviors they had taken for granted would continue in the years after college graduation. Life would continue to hold lots of pleasant, expensive activities. The financial crisis destroyed this assumption. Jobs are hard to come by; unemployment is pervasive and long-lasting; people don't have money for discretionary spending or calendars marked with costly outings. It is difficult to get a job interview and really hard to get a job, any job. Student loans go unpaid, and interest and late fees accumulate. Parents are stretched thin and unable to help. Most alarming of all, parents are beginning to turn to their college graduate offspring and ask *them* for help.

The financial crisis has made for hard times and it is not an understatement to call these hard times a *crisis*. Motivational speakers who frequently cite the fact that the Chinese word for crisis is made up of the characters for danger and opportunity provide us with a means to move beyond the negativity that could overwhelm us and enable us to acknowledge the positives that could occur. One such positive is that we could learn from history and we could avoid making the same (or similar) mistakes in the future. Another positive is that we could take the time to understand that ethical conduct by each of us is important because being good will bring us contentment and acting rightly will result in the kind of corporations, government and society that function to promote the well-being of everyone.

1

WHAT WENT WRONG?

On September 15, 2008, with the collapse of Lehman Brothers, the fourth largest investment bank in the United States, and an avalanche of alarming financial news, the U.S. economy faltered, and a severe recession, perhaps a depression, loomed on the immediate horizon. The problems had been building for a few years, but it was only after Lehman's collapse that most people became acutely aware of the perilous state of the economy. People did not know that a complicated host of systemic and structural factors came together to cause the mess that dominated headlines and brought them fear and confusion. Their questions were pointed: what caused this crisis? Who is affected? What needs to be done to set things right? We address the first question in this chapter; subsequent chapters respond to the second and third questions. While there is no question that moral failure contributed to the perfect storm, we will hold off on ethical analysis for now and concentrate on what went wrong in the marketplace.

What Caused the Economic Crisis?

The financial crisis began with the issuance of mortgage loans to people who were not able to repay them, followed by the bundling of mortgages and packaging them into securities, which were sold to investors all over the world. Insurance was written to cover losses if mortgage-backed securities defaulted and this insurance was sometimes purchased by investors to speculate that there would be a crash in the housing market.

Issuance of insurance on mortgage-backed securities made the crisis complex and far-reaching.

Let us begin by considering the role mortgages played in the crisis. Problematic mortgage loans were made during the boom years of 2001 to 2005, a time when home prices were rising rapidly. By 2007, housing prices stopped rising, many borrowers lacked the ability to sell their homes or make mortgage payments, and it was apparent that there were major problems in the housing sector. The combination of few home buyers, many houses for sale, and homeowners unable to make mortgage payments deflated the housing bubble.

Mortgages. Most people do not have enough money to buy a house with cash so they borrow money to buy the house. The money to buy a house comes from a lender and a borrower uses these funds to purchase the property. At the time of purchase the borrower *gives* a mortgage to the lender and the mortgage entitles the lender to take possession of the property in the event that the borrower does not repay the loan. The property stands as collateral against the loan.

In the vernacular, however, people think of mortgages as loans secured by properties and given by lenders to borrowers. They consider a mortgage to be an agreement requiring that money borrowed from a lender to buy a house should be repaid by the borrower. It is in this vernacular sense that we will use the term *mortgage*.

For most people, a mortgage is the largest and most serious financial obligation they ever undertake.[1] How do people get a mortgage? Mortgage brokers often arrange for borrowers to obtain financing in order to buy residential real estate. Alternatively, a prospective buyer can go directly to a bank or other lender to procure a mortgage. After borrowers pay off their mortgages, they own their homes. Until the mortgage loan is repaid, the house stands as collateral; if the borrower does not make payments, the lender can take steps to evict the borrower and sell the house in order to satisfy the loan. Should this occur, the process is known as foreclosure.

In the early years of the new millennium a housing bubble developed during which housing prices rose higher and higher in an over-inflated market. The bubble was created by rising home prices along with the assumption that prices would continue to increase. Both prospective homeowners and speculators who were seeking gains on real estate investments thought that it was important to buy now because tomorrow the house would cost more. There were more buyers than sellers and scarcity contributed to the bubble. In this environment many people who already owned homes borrowed against the equity in their homes and used the borrowed money to make purchases. (These loans were called home equity loans.) Both those who financed their homes with mortgages and those who borrowed money with home equity loans assumed that, if they were ever in a situation of financial distress, their homes would have appreciated in value and they could sell their property for more than they owed and pay off the mortgage and home equity loan.

In regard to appreciation in home prices, consider statistics released by the Federal Deposit Insurance Corporation in February 2005 at the height of the market:

> U.S. home prices have boomed in recent years. Average U.S. home prices rose 13 percent in the year ending September 2004, and are up almost 50 percent over five years. In December 2004, the Office of Federal Housing Enterprise Oversight (OFHEO) noted, "The growth in home prices over the past year surpasses any increase in 25 years."[2]

While the figures just cited relate to the nation as a whole, in some markets the increase was even higher. Hyper-inflated markets included Washington, D.C., Boston, San Diego, Las Vegas, Phoenix and South Florida. In the so-called *sand states* of California, Nevada, Arizona and Florida, builders borrowed money and constructed developments in anticipation of housing demand.

During the housing boom the mortgage brokerage industry thrived. Mortgage brokers were kept busy securing mortgages for first-time home buyers who were eager to buy a house and for people who wanted to trade up. A broker is an intermediary between a lender and a borrower. The broker brings the two together and arranges financing for a home purchase in the form of a mortgage. The broker gets paid a salary and/or commission for performing this service. In an ideal situation, a borrower would have a dependable source of income and would be able to afford reasonable mortgage payments and a lender would have enough capital to continue to operate even if a significant number of borrowers did not repay their loans. Both lender and borrower would be well served by the broker if the broker ascertained that the borrower's employment and credit history were acceptable and that borrowers could meet their debt obligations.

Given the tenor of the times, however, many mortgage brokers sidestepped established protocols and obtained financing for borrowers who lacked the ability to repay their loans. These types of mortgages were called *subprime* mortgages. The term subprime is often misunderstood by people who think that the loan itself is somehow less than reasonable or ideal. This is not the meaning of subprime. Subprime means that borrowers likely lack the ability to repay the amount they owe. Certain classes of borrowers are subprime, such as those with poor credit scores, insecure employment, or wages so low that they cannot make payments. The mortgages that they procure may or may not be reasonable loans.

During the course of the housing bubble, novel types of mortgages were introduced to borrowers and some of these were unsound. Each of these mortgages differs from a so-called *prime mortgage*. A prime mortgage is obtained by a borrower with a dependable source of income and a good credit score; this mortgage typically has a term of fifteen, twenty or thirty years and a fixed rate of interest. Prime mortgages are issued to borrowers with substantial down payments of approximately

20 percent. Unsound mortgages included interest-only loans in which the borrower would pay only the interest for a specified number of years and then, at the conclusion of the term, the principal would be due in full. (In a traditional mortgage, a borrower pays down the principal over the course of the loan; interest is included along with principal in each payment.) Adjustable rate mortgages (ARMs) were also issued in which the rate of interest the borrower paid was linked to changes in the market. Typically, the rate would be low at the outset and would reset to higher rates down the road, as interest rates fluctuated in the economy. There was also a product known as a balloon mortgage which typically came due in five to seven years. With a balloon mortgage, a consumer's payments are roughly comparable to what a person would be required to pay monthly on a thirty-year mortgage but, at the end of the term of five or seven years, the entire principal amount comes due. The most novel type of mortgage that was marketed was termed *pick-a-pay*. With this the borrower was allowed to choose each month from among options: make a predetermined minimum payment; pay the interest only; pay the principal only; or make a traditional payment of interest and principal. However, if the payment that was picked was for an amount that was less than the required traditional payment, the difference would be added to the principal of the loan so that the total amount owed would increase.

Alt-A is another type of mortgage. Alt-A mortgages may be somewhat risky in that the borrower may be a self-employed individual whose income varies, the borrower may have a troubled credit history, or the borrower may want the mortgage for investment property; mortgages that are of an amount larger than the amount that Fannie Mae and Freddie Mac will guarantee ($417,000 in 2010) are also placed in the category Alt-A. Alt-A mortgages are not bought on the secondary mortgage market by Fannie and Freddie. The mortgages that are bought by Fannie and Freddie are referred to as *agency paper*. Alt-A mortgages are an alternative to agency paper; hence the name,

Alt-A. (The missions of Fannie Mae and Freddie Mac will be explained below.)

Peter Wallison, an attorney and Counsel to the U.S. Treasury Department from 1981 to 1985, was a member of the Financial Crisis Inquiry Commission. Mr. Wallison answers the important questions of how much money and what percent of mortgages were subprime and Alt-A:

> I've spent several years examining and writing about the activities of Fannie Mae and Freddie Mac and the housing policies of the U.S. government. In this work, I have found that there are approximately 25 million subprime and other non-prime loans, known as Alt-A loans, that are now on the books of banks and financial institutions in this country and abroad. These weak loans, which total over $4 trillion, constitute almost 50 percent of all mortgages in the United States. They began to default at very high rates in 2007, when housing prices leveled off.[3]

When subprime mortgages were issued the tendency was to ignore the downside and the assumption was that if people could not make payments they could refinance or sell their homes and settle their debts. When the housing market collapsed, however, it was impossible to sell homes at inflated prices and the option of refinancing ceased to exist. This led to high numbers of foreclosures as well as many homeowners owing more on their mortgages than they could reasonably expect to receive from the sale of their property. There were more homes for sale than buyers and prices were declining. The U.S. housing market was in crisis and its repercussions would be felt throughout the global economy. (Owing more than the property is worth is known as being *underwater.*)

The foundation of the economic crisis was laid when mortgage brokers did not properly examine their client's credit and employment information and, lacking this data, arranged for mortgages that could not be repaid. This failure was abetted by consumers who did not understand or agree with the basic tenet that money borrowed should be paid back and that income sufficient to repay a loan is required of a borrower. The unfounded assumption that housing prices would continue to rise prompted lenders and borrowers not to worry about a worst-case scenario. Precisely such a scenario occurred when large numbers of borrowers became delinquent in their payments and lenders moved to foreclose record numbers of properties.

Mortgage brokers arranged mortgages. Mortgage lenders provided funds for borrowers. Mortgage lenders, such as mortgage companies and community banks, did not hold on to individual mortgages on specific properties. Instead, they sold these mortgages to large banks, or firms such as Fannie Mae and Freddie Mac. Buyers of mortgages bundled these mortgages and then sold shares in these so-called *securities* to investors. Investors bought the securities, known as mortgage-backed securities (MBS) and collateralized debt obligations (CDOs), in order to receive regular payments generated from interest and principal paid by borrowers. Since mortgage brokers and lenders were transferring repayment risk to investors, as long as they were able to pass subprime loans on to investors, they did not stand to lose money if the housing sector faltered. In view of the fact that the issuance of large numbers of unconventional subprime mortgages during a housing bubble was a first, lenders might have thought that it represented a viable new reality or they might not have cared about the stability of the market because they were not at risk on the downside. As far as mortgage brokers were concerned, they earned more from arranging unconventional mortgages than from traditional mortgages and, therefore, they had no financial incentive to question the wisdom of arranging subprime mortgages for their clients.

By carrying large numbers of subprime mortgage loans on their books and also owning mortgage-backed securities, major mortgage corporations like IndyMac and Countrywide were in a precarious position when the housing market crashed. On the brink of collapse, Countrywide was acquired by Bank of America on July 1, 2008 and IndyMac was closed by the U.S. Office of Thrift Supervision on July 11, 2008. The market for mortgage-backed securities had disintegrated, neither of these financial institutions could collect from large numbers of subprime borrowers, some of their mortgage holders who were underwater on their homes walked away instead of repaying, and foreclosures were at a record high. The mortgage lending industry was in disarray and the implications of this fact were unsettling financial markets.

Before its collapse, IndyMac specialized in making Alt-A mortgages, which were too big to be sold to Fannie Mae or Freddie Mac. (As noted above, at the time Fannie and Freddie did not purchase mortgages for more than $417,000 and Indy-Mac's Alt-A mortgages were for larger amounts than this.) In addition to problems related to mortgages, IndyMac also had approximately 10,000 depositors[4] who had more than $1 billion on deposit. When these depositors became aware of IndyMac's exposure to subprime mortgages, they went in large numbers to withdraw their deposits and this run on the bank contributed to its failure.

Before it imploded under the weight of subprime mortgages, Countrywide was the largest mortgage lender in the United States. As its fortunes declined, so did its stock price, from approximately $30 a share in August 2007 to less than $6 a share when it was taken over by Bank of America in July 2008. Bankrate.com explains why Countrywide's insolvency was a major shock to the mortgage industry:

> Countrywide is the nation's biggest mortgage lender. It funded $39 billion in mortgage loans in July (2007). It's also the largest or next-largest loan servicer. The servicer is the company you send your monthly mortgage payment to. It then distributes the money to pay the principal, interest, taxes and insurance. Americans owe about $13 trillion in mortgages, and Countrywide services about $1.4 trillion

of that. So a significant percentage of mortgage-paying homeowners send a check to Countrywide every month.[5]

(Bank of America bought Countrywide to expand its operations and make money. As it turned out, however, the bad mortgages issued by Countrywide wound up costing Bank of America more than $20 billion in settlement costs in the second quarter of 2011 alone, with future costs hard to estimate. In view of this fact, the $2.5 billion that Bank of America paid to acquire Countrywide cannot seem like a good deal.[6])

In retrospect, it is easy to understand that subprime mortgages should not have been issued and more attention should have been paid to the qualifications of borrowers who procured subprime mortgages. The false assumptions that fueled the housing bubble should have been recognized. Hindsight is 20/20 but, while the stage was being set for an implosion, the facts we now comprehend did not inform the practices of mortgage brokers, mortgage lenders, mortgage securitizers, investors or subprime borrowers. Common sense was obscured by the euphoria of the bubble psychology that had taken hold. However, the cause of the crisis entailed more than this: it involved financial deal making on an international scale that attempted to game the system and generate profits for investors who had nothing to do with procuring or issuing mortgage loans. Faulty analyses by credit rating agencies contributed to a sense of false optimism and exploitation of regulatory loopholes allowed the creation of problematic financial products to go undetected until several major U.S. financial firms teetered on the brink of bankruptcy.

Credit rating agencies. Credit rating agencies evaluate the strengths and weaknesses of corporations, nonprofit organizations and federal, state and local governments and render analyses of the financial soundness of these entities or the investment products issued by them. When ratings on mortgage-backed securities (MBS) are issued these ratings are used by prospective buyers to evaluate whether or not the security is likely to meet its scheduled payments. The advice given by credit rating agencies lets investors know the probability that the borrowers (or securities) being evaluated will repay as scheduled. When a rating is issued on a mortgage-backed security, both the issuer and the collateral that backs it should be taken into account. Consider, for example, a collateralized debt obligation (CDO) packaged by an investment bank consisting partly of subprime mortgages: in determining a rating, the agency needs to evaluate both the dependability of the warrants and representations of the investment bank and the soundness of the subprime, other mortgages and other debts that make up the security.

The principal credit ratings agencies in the United States are Moody's, Standard & Poor's and Fitch. During the housing boom years, Moody's and Standard & Poor's, which issued the vast majority of ratings for mortgage-backed securities, experienced tremendous growth in business because of the large volume of securities they were hired to rate. From 2000 to 2007, 42,625 MBS were rated AAA by Moody's. In 2006, Moody's rated $869 billion in MBS AAA; 89 percent were later downgraded.[7] Because inaccurate ratings were issued for mortgage-backed securities, individual and institutional investors and financial institutions which took the ratings at face value bought products that were of poor quality. This resulted in catastrophic losses to individual investors as well as financial firms such as mortgage lenders, banks, hedge funds, pension funds and endowments. The situation became so dire in September 2008 that Lehman Brothers declared bankruptcy and Merrill Lynch had to be taken over by Bank of America. The two remaining U.S. investment banks, Goldman Sachs and Morgan Stanley, were in a precarious position. So, too, were large commercial banks such as Wachovia, Washington Mutual, Citibank and Bank of America. A grave and far-reaching financial crisis had erupted.

Sheila Bair, former Chairperson of the Federal Deposit Insurance Corporation, set out a clear explanation of how mortgage-backed securities are assembled and rated:

A typical private-label MBS might issue six tranches or securities to fund the mortgage pool of assets it purchases. Each tranche has an associated par value and yield and all except, perhaps, the most junior tranches will be rated by a credit rating agency. The cash flows from the mortgage pool owned by the MBS flow through a "waterfall" created by the terms of the different tranches. The most senior mortgage investments (typically AAA-rated) have the highest priority claim on the mortgage-pool cash flows and are paid first. The remaining cash flows are then allocated to fill the terms of the next highest priority tranche and so on through the priority structure. When all the mortgages in the pool are performing, each tranche in the MBS structure will receive the promised cash flows. As mortgages default, the lowest priority tranche suffers losses first. If the mortgage pool losses are large enough, the claims of the lowest tranche could be wiped out completely and the second-lowest priority tranche would begin to bear losses. As losses grow, they are spread to sequentially higher priority tranches.[8]

Nicholas Weill, the Chief Credit Officer of Moody's, speaking in defense of his employer and in response to Moody's critics who laid a big share of the blame for the financial crisis on credit rating agencies, said that Moody's acted in good faith in issuing AAA ratings to MBS because Moody's, like the other agencies, did not anticipate the speed and severity of the housing downturn. In arriving at its ratings Moody's assumed that, if there were a downturn in housing, the decline in housing prices would be similar to what happened during the recession of 2001–2002, which was short in duration and moderate in intensity.[9] As it turned out, of course, this assumption was incorrect.

The U.S. Senate report on the financial crisis explained how ratings downgrades by Moody's and Standard & Poor's contributed to the financial implosion:

In July 2007, as mortgage defaults intensified and subprime residential mortgage backed securities and collateralized debt obligation securities began incurring losses, both companies (Moody's and S & P) abruptly reversed course and began downgrading at record numbers hundreds and then thousands of their RMBS and CDO ratings, some less than a year old. Investors like banks, pension funds, and insurance companies were suddenly forced to sell off their RMBS and CDO holdings, because they had lost their investment grade status. RMBS and CDO securities held by financial firms lost much of their value, and new securitizations were unable to find investors. The subprime RMBS market initially froze and then collapsed, leaving investors and financial firms around the world holding unmarketable subprime RMBS securities plummeting in value. A few months later, the CDO market collapsed as well.[10]

Mortgage-backed securities-Collateralized debt obligations (MBS-CDOs). Mortgage-backed securities (MBS) are financial products made up of thousands of individual mortgages which are bundled into securities and sold to investors. It is fairly standard to convert a large package of MBS into perhaps 80 percent investment-grade bonds, 10 percent mezzanine and 10 percent equity.[11] The process involved in bundling a large number of individual mortgages into MBS and then dividing the MBS into tranches is called *securitization.* Borrowers execute mortgages; lenders lend borrowers the amount of the mortgage, with the house as collateral; the lenders then sell the mortgages to investment or commercial banks or government agencies that subsequently package the mortgages into MBS and sometimes repackage the MBS into CDOs; the packager, known as a securitizer, pays a fee to a servicer to collect from borrowers and deal with delinquencies and/or defaults on the mortgages in the package; the servicer also delivers payments to CDO owners; investors buy one of three kinds of MBS: investment grade, which is composed of the highest rated mortgages, stands the best chance of being repaid, and pays the lowest rate of interest; mezzanine grade, which contains less than the best mortgages in the bundle, but stands a fair chance of being repaid, and pays a higher rate of interest than investment grade; or equity grade, which provides the highest yield (payment) but which is made up of the lowest grade of mortgages (subprime) and which has the lowest chance of being repaid.

Because the majority of mortgages in the bundles were investment grade, credit ratings agencies rated these products AAA, inspiring investor confidence. The first signs of problems with MBS occurred when the bottom tranches were hit by defaults from subprime mortgage borrowers. Since the instruments were bundled, mortgages which had a better chance of being repaid were part of a bundle and were not easily separated from it. Lack of confidence in the bundled product made the market for them dry up. Commercial and investment banks and other institutions that wanted to sell MBS or repackage MBS into CDOs wound up holding these securities on their books. There was a scarce supply of buyers for mortgage-backed securities and a large, illiquid inventory, causing economic instability. Just as there is no appetite for beef after E. coli is isolated in a few dozen hamburgers, so there was no demand for MBS after awareness of defaulting subprime borrowers entered the national consciousness. When the market dried up, financial firms stopped creating mortgage-backed securities. MBS ceased to exist as quickly as they had come into being. Their lifespan was roughly six years, from 2001 to 2007.

Collateralized debt obligations (CDOs), made up partly of mortgage-backed securities, started to be assembled, traded and sold on a small scale in the early years of the new millennium; they reached their peak in the years between 2005 and 2007. Collateralized debt obligations differ from mortgage-backed securities in that they are made up of mortgages and other types of debt, such as credit card debt, car payments and other loans. By buying CDOs containing residential mortgages investors around the world owned shares in the U.S. housing market and, they thought, were participating in a prosperous market. Positive ratings by credit rating agencies contributed to the confidence investors placed in these securities. Little did investors suspect that when the U.S. housing market crashed the investments they owned would be worth little or nothing because there would be no buyers. And, even if there were buyers, in the absence of a functioning market, there would not be agreement as to how to price a particular CDO. To the extent that mortgage companies such as Countrywide and IndyMac, Fannie Mae, Freddie Mac and banks had MBS or CDOs on their books, they were in jeopardy. So, too, were investors who held these securities. If these firms held subprime mortgages, which had not yet been bundled into securities, they were similarly in jeopardy.

Mortgage-backed securities and collateralized debt obligations are financial products; investors who own them own debt obligations. People buy these securities in order to generate income from pools of mortgage loans or other debts. Those who obtain loans are expected to pay their debts and those who purchase CDOs expect a predictable income flow. Instead of making payments to a bank or a mortgage lender, those paying off mortgages which have been bundled into securities are two or more steps removed from the original lender. They do not make mortgage payments to the originator of the mortgage or the entity that subsequently bought the mortgage, such as Fannie Mae or Freddie Mac. Instead, they make payments to the firm that arranged the bundling or to an agent of that firm who services the security. This is the entity that processes payments.

When housing prices fell, mortgage-backed securities lost value because subprime mortgage holders were unlikely to make payments. As delinquencies increased, the optimism driving the market quickly changed to pessimism.

As housing prices declined, major global financial institutions that had borrowed and invested heavily in subprime

MBS reported significant losses. Defaults and losses on other loan types also increased significantly as the crisis expanded from the housing market to other parts of the economy. Total losses are estimated in the trillions of U.S. dollars globally.[12]

A new reality was taking hold: people did not or could not pay their bills; unemployment was rising; and confidence in the U.S. economy was souring.

In the early months of 2008, at the beginning of the financial collapse, collateralized debt obligations composed wholly or partly of subprime mortgages represented tens of trillions of dollars of investments. Mortgage-backed securities that were in existence prior to the crisis still exist but the tens of trillions of dollars of value that these products once held has dramatically diminished. What are they worth today? This is a question to which no one is currently prepared to give a definitive answer.

When they purchased mortgage-backed securities, investors anticipated little risk and high rates of return. This was because they were relying on projections that came from the formula that was used in constructing the instruments. In time financial analysts realized that these calculations, based on the Gaussian Copula formula, were invalid and, therefore, so were analyses of the MBS-CDOs constructed using the formula.[13] The Gaussian Copula formula was devised in 2000 by David X. Li who worked at JPMorgan Chase. Li used a mathematical schema that correlated the risks associated with pools of residential mortgages with default data from credit default swaps (CDS). The data Li relied upon were generated in the prosperous 1990s when credit default swaps did not pay off because the underlying bundled products the CDS insured were debts such as credit card debts and auto loans, which, for the most part, were repaid by borrowers. When he made his calculations there was no data on residential subprime mortgages so he decided to construct his formula using credit data from credit cards and auto loans. Li did not take into account the possibility of a rapid and pervasive decrease in the price of residential real estate along with the existence of a large number of subprime mortgages in the securities that were being marketed. In other words, the collateralized debts of the 1990s were of a different kind from home loans and the features of subprime mortgages did not correspond to features in pooled debts assembled from credit cards or auto loans. Therefore, the Gaussian Copula formula was not a valid instrument to use in forecasting the future of the market in mortgage-backed securities and should not have been used. Nevertheless, even though the Gaussian Copula formula analysis was inherently flawed and should not have led Li to conclude that MBS-CDOs were sound, this was precisely what happened. In 2005, Li told the *Wall Street Journal*, "Very few people understand the essence of the model."[14] Even David Li, it seems, did not understand it should not have been applied to the MBS-CDO market. While the mathematics of the model are relatively simple by Wall Street standards, the fact that so few people on Wall Street or Main Street understood its central flaw goes a long way in explaining how securities made up in whole or in part of residential mortgages could have seemed like a good investment when, in fact, they were not.

It is important to understand that issuers of subprime mortgages actually created the perfect storm. Many subprime mortgages that were issued in 2005 and 2006 reset in 2007. The years 2005 and 2006 represent the top of the housing bubble when residential real estate prices were at their peak. Since subprime borrowers obtained mortgages at teaser interest rates or with other features that permitted low payments or even no payments at the outset, it took time before their inability to make payments became apparent. In 2007 and 2008 this became obvious but, by then, the genie was out of the bottle. If a financial firm had few MBS-CDOs on its books, it did not have to deal with huge losses. If, however, a firm had billions of dollars of MBS-CDOs on its books, this represented a huge liability and a threat to the continued existence of the firm.[15] Regarding firms with major exposure, Anna Katherine Barnett-Hart summarizes the sad story:

Once the conveyor belt stopped, it turned out that the hot potato, which had so efficiently been passed along the chain from mortgage broker to Wall Street and beyond, had been leaving pieces of itself along the way. Once investors no longer wanted to buy CDOs, Wall Street banks were left holding the excess of unsold CDOs and yet-to-be securitized CDO assets. And once Wall Street no longer wanted to buy subprime mortgages, mortgage originators were left holding a huge number of mortgage loans they knew had little chance of ever being repaid. And once mortgage companies no longer wanted to originate risky mortgages, homebuyers were left holding the subprime mortgages they had planned to refinance. And once home-buyers began to default on their mortgages in mass, it became clear that the credit rating agencies had made a colossal mistake, and Moody's, Fitch, and S&P were left holding the burden of a shattered reputation in a business built on the necessity of trust.[16]

When the U.S. economy was on the brink of implosion in September 2008, so-called *toxic assets* on the books of banks and other businesses were the issue that required resolution. These toxic assets were subprime mortgages and the little understood mortgage-backed securities-collateralized debt obligations that had gone viral and spread an economic plague.

Toxic assets. Addressing the Financial Crisis Inquiry Commission, Dr. Kenneth Scott of Stanford University explained how mortgage-backed securities became toxic assets when the contagion from the lower tranches affected the middle and top layers. Dr. Scott also explains that debt obligations other than from residential mortgages were sometimes included in CDOs:

The bulk of toxic assets are based on residential mortgage-backed securities (RMBS), in which thousands of mortgages were gathered into mortgage pools. The returns on these pools were then sliced into a hierarchy of "tranches" that were sold to investors as separate classes of securities. The most senior tranches, rated AAA, received the lowest returns, and then they went down the line to lower ratings and finally to the unrated "equity" tranches at the bottom. But the process didn't stop there. Some of the tranches from one mortgage pool were combined with tranches from other mortgage pools, resulting in Collateralized Mortgage Obligations (CMO). Other tranches were combined with tranches from completely different types of pools, based on commercial mortgages, auto loans, student loans, credit card receivables, small business loans, and even corporate loans that had been combined into Collateralized Loan Obligations (CLO). The result was a highly heterogeneous mixture of debt securities called Collateralized Debt Obligations (CDO). The tranches of the CDOs could then be combined with other CDOs, resulting in CDO squared.

Each time these tranches were mixed together with other tranches in a new pool, the securities became more complex. Assume a hypothetical CDO squared held 100 CLOs, each holding 250 corporate loans – then we would need information on 25,000 underlying loans to determine the value of the security. But assume the CDO squared held 100 CDOs each holding 100 RMBS comprising a mere 2,000 mortgages – the number now rises to twenty million!

Complexity is not the only problem. Many of the underlying mortgages were highly risky, involving little or no down payments and initial rates so low they could never amortize the loan. About 80% of the $2.5 trillion subprime mortgages made since 2000 went into securitization pools. When the housing bubble burst and house prices started declining, borrowers began to default, the lower tranches were hit with losses, and higher tranches became more risky and declined in value.[17]

As government and financial leaders of the United States confronted the realities of an imploding economy in the fall of 2008, toxic assets were the primary subject to be confronted and resolved.

Credit default swaps (CDS). A credit default swap is like an insurance policy; it is bought in order to hedge against a loss from a security. The buyer of a CDS, thinking that a security such as a CDO may not pay off, purchases insurance that will pay off if the CDO defaults. The credit default swap is an agreement between two parties whereby one party pays the other a fixed amount over a specified term. The party that issues the CDS "makes no payment unless a specified credit event such as a default occurs, at which time a payment is made and the swap terminates."[18]

As we have seen, the market for mortgage-backed securities and collateralized debt obligations began after the year 2000 and accelerated between 2005 and 2007. The buying and selling of credit default swaps related to this market reached a high point between 2005 and 2007. Why would investors want to buy insurance against defaults? The answer is obvious: because they were concerned that the subprime mortgages in MBS and CDOs might not be paid, or because they had large investments and wanted to hedge their bets so that if the MBS market faltered they would be able to collect money from an insurer. People who did not own MBS or CDOs could also purchase CDS. In essence, they were betting that mortgage-related securities would fail and that they would profit from the failure.

Michael Lewis, in his book *The Big Short*,[19] details how some investors understood the flaws in MBS-CDOs and made large amounts of money by purchasing credit default swaps. (These few were the minority; the majority of people did not see problems ahead.) Lewis also details the entry of investment banks into the CDS market before the collapse of mortgage-backed securities; these banks were simultaneously selling MBS to their customers and hedging against the soundness of these securities on their balance sheets. American International Group

(AIG), a huge insurance company, was brought to the brink of bankruptcy because of credit default swaps it issued to clients.

In June 2008 the combined market for MBS-CDOs and CDS was in excess of $680 trillion. According to Brooksley Born, Chairperson of the Commodity Futures Trading Commission from 1996 to 1999:

> Through rampant speculation and excessive leverage, over-the-counter derivatives spread and multiplied risk throughout the economy and played a major role in the financial crisis. They include the credit default swaps disastrously sold by AIG and many of the toxic assets sold by our biggest banks. Warren Buffett has appropriately dubbed them "financial weapons of mass destruction."[20]

American International Group (AIG). In 2008, American International Group was the seventeenth largest corporation in the world. AIG was a successful global insurance company until the issuance of credit default swaps by one of its units, AIG FP (Financial Products), undermined its viability. During the years when mortgage-backed securities seemed to be a good investment, selling insurance to be paid in the event of default was a lucrative business, bringing in large fees with little apparent risk. When the market went bad the situation changed dramatically and, in September 2008, AIG's viability was threatened because it held $440 billion of credit default swaps on its books;[21] its credit rating was downgraded; counterparties demanded payments of money owed to them by the corporation; it was undercapitalized; and the reality was that it was on the verge of bankruptcy. AIG's stock declined 90 percent on September 16, 2008. Fearing that the bankruptcy of AIG "could very well trigger a global panic,"[22] on September 16, 2008 the U.S. Federal Reserve Bank lent AIG $85 billion to stabilize it; in exchange, the Fed assumed a 79.9 percent equity share in the company. Over the next nine months the total amount of government assistance to AIG would increase to $182.5 billion. The conditions that the U.S. government attached to its loans were that AIG would be run by a government-appointed CEO and that the company would sell profitable units in order to repay the government. The plan was that most or all of AIG's divisions would cease to exist as part of the parent organization and, looking ahead, the possibility was that the entire corporation might disappear. The rationale that prompted U.S. government assistance to AIG was that the corporation was too big to fail, meaning that its failure would cause such severe financial repercussions that the entire global economy would be threatened.

Fannie Mae and Freddie Mac (The Federal National Mortgage Association and Federal Home Mortgage Corporation). Before their takeover by the U.S. Treasury Department in September 2008, both Fannie Mae and Freddie Mac were stockholder-owned private corporations which were also government-sponsored enterprises (GSEs). Technically, they were private companies but they were unique in that they were implicitly backed by the federal government. The mission of Fannie Mae and Freddie Mac was to make home ownership possible to ordinary Americans by purchasing mortgage loans from banks and mortgage lenders, guaranteeing those mortgages and then issuing mortgage-backed securities, known as agency paper. When Fannie and Freddie buy mortgages from originators, originators obtain the money to make more mortgage loans, thus expanding home ownership. What do Fannie and Freddie do with the mortgages they buy? They securitize these mortgages and sell them to investors; the term for their products is agency paper, and this traditionally has been a viable business for the GSEs. During 2006 and 2007, however, these agencies bought $294 billion[23] in mortgage-backed securities. Many of the mortgages in the MBS did not meet the GSE's criteria and would not have been guaranteed had Fannie and Freddie purchased them to securitize in-house. Not all of the $294 billion in mortgage-backed securities was toxic, but enough to bring Fannie and Freddie to the brink of bankruptcy.

These two government-sponsored enterprises faltered when subprime borrowers defaulted on their mortgages.[24] On September 7, 2008 Fannie Mae and Freddie Mac were placed into conservatorship by the Federal Housing Finance Agency, in effect putting the U.S. government in charge of running the companies. This extraordinary action was necessary because the liabilities associated with mortgage-backed securities on their books threatened the firms' survival. Such a large amount of MBS-CDOs owned by the GSEs was worthless that the stock in both companies fell 90 percent, fears of bankruptcy were expressed, and the sentiments of panic that were building in the financial markets spilled over onto the GSEs. The terms offered by the U.S. Treasury and accepted by the boards of directors of both institutions were that the U.S. government

would acquire $1 billion of new preferred senior shares in each company, which would give it 79.9 percent of the common shares of each. The government would contribute as much as $200 billion into both companies if necessary. The terms were nonnegotiable.[25]

The U.S. Treasury bailed Fannie and Freddie out because of the government's sponsorship of these two corporations.

Banks. The banking business is not simple. People may approach banking simplistically, thinking that banks hold deposits and make loans, and this is as far as it goes. The interest paid to the bank for borrowed money is greater than the interest paid by the bank to depositors, enabling banks to make money. Banks also profit by charging fees on credit cards; they may charge fees for maintaining customers' checking accounts and the use of ATMs; banks charge fees on overdue credit card accounts and for overdrawn checks. This is traditional banking. What else could banks do with the money people deposit or pay in fees or interest? Financial problems began when banks issued subprime mortgages, expecting high interest payments, and retained these mortgages on their books. Banks were also at risk if they owned MBS-CDOs; when the MBS-CDO market collapsed, banks holding these toxic assets suffered losses. If the mortgages they held went into default, banks stood to lose part of the money they had lent to borrowers. If insufficient capital reserves were on hand to meet the requirements of depositors, bank failures followed. In the United States during 2008, there were twenty-five bank failures; 140 in 2009; and 157 in 2010,[26] the largest number since the Savings and Loan crisis in 1992. There were ninety-two bank failures in 2011, signaling a leveling off.[27]

Four large banks, Washington Mutual, Wachovia, Citibank and Bank of America, were badly damaged by the toxic assets on their books. Washington Mutual was seized on September 26, 2008 by the Office of Thrift Supervision and most of its assets were sold to JPMorgan Chase. Its depositors were made whole but its stockholders were wiped out. Wachovia, the fourth largest bank in the United States by assets, was taken over by Wells Fargo Bank on October 3, 2008. In November 2008, the U.S. government announced a plan to assist Citigroup by taking a $20 billion share in the firm as well as guaranteeing hundreds of billions of dollars in toxic assets. Citi held subprime mortgages in its portfolio and this exposure put the giant bank in jeopardy. Bank of America was assisted by the U.S. government on January 16, 2009 through a $20 billion loan and a guarantee for almost $100 billion of potential losses on toxic assets. The deteriorating balance sheet from Merrill Lynch & Co, the brokerage firm acquired by Bank of America (September 15, 2008) as well as losses on mortgage loans issued by Countywide (acquired January 11, 2008), forced Bank of America to turn to the U.S. government for assistance.[28] (As it turned out, the investment banking and wealth management operations of Merrill Lynch became profit centers for Bank of America in 2011.)

Investment banks. The phenomenon of the failure of a modest-sized bank or a large savings bank like Washington Mutual is easier to understand than the financial instability experienced by large multinational investment banks. Investment banks undertake different functions from commercial banks. They help companies come into existence by arranging for initial public offerings of stock (IPOs); they create issues of preferred stock to raise capital for corporations; they raise debt capital through issuing bonds; they engage in proprietary trading in which traders make trades using the bank's capital in order to make profits; and, in the years 2002–2007, investment banks bundled, traded and held MBS-CDOs and they also issued and traded credit default swaps. At first these activities were lucrative and resulted in profits. By September 2008, however, the miscalculations of investment banks were obvious and the viability of Western capitalism was in doubt.

In April 2011 a subcommittee of the U.S. Senate, the Permanent Subcommittee on Investigations, issued a more than 600-page report that consisted of case studies intended to illustrate how particular financial sectors contributed to the crisis. In regard to investment banking, the report focused on Goldman Sachs and stated that six specific practices of Goldman Sachs imperiled financial markets. First, the report charged that from 2004 to 2007, in exchange for lucrative fees, Goldman Sachs helped mortgage lenders like Long Beach, Fremont and New Century securitize high risk, poor quality loans, obtain favorable credit ratings for the resulting residential mortgage-backed securities (RMBS), and sell the RMBS securities to investors, putting billions of dollars of risky mortgages into the financial system. (All three mortgage lending firms filed for bankruptcy.) Second, the report states that Goldman Sachs magnified the impact of toxic mortgages by resecuritizing them in CDOs and then buying credit default swaps to profit from the failure of MBS and CDOs that failed. Third, the report asserted that the firm profited from its knowledge of how defective mortgage-backed securities were by taking short positions in the market in 2007 and profiting from these short positions. Fourth, the Senate subcommittee alleged that there was a conflict of interest between Goldman Sachs and its clients because, while its

sales force was selling securities to investors, the firm was looking out for itself in removing these toxic assets from its books, a
tactic the firm concealed from its clients. Fifth, the subcommittee specifically singled out the Abacus transaction for criticism.
In underwriting this CDO, Goldman Sachs did not disclose to
the Moody's analyst overseeing the rating the fact that a hedge
fund client of Goldman Sachs had taken a short position on the
CDO. Sixth, the subcommittee criticized Goldman for using
credit default swaps on assets it did not own to bet against the
mortgage market and realize profits while its investment clients
were losing money in this same market.[29]

In response to the charges set forth by the Senate subcommittee, Goldman Sachs issued the following statement:

> While we disagree with much of the report, we take seriously
> the issues explored by the Subcommittee. We recently
> issued the results of a comprehensive examination of our
> business standards and practices and committed to making
> significant changes that will strengthen relationships with
> clients, improve transparency and disclosure and enhance
> standards for the review, approval and suitability of complex
> instruments. An executive summary of those efforts can be
> found by (consulting this webpage): www2.goldmansachs.
> com/our-firm/business-standards-committee/executive-
> summary.html.[30]

Two months after the Senate report was issued Goldman's conduct and policies continued to be subject to analysis. Was the
report fair to Goldman; was it accurate? In a lengthy essay in
the *New York Times* financial writer Andrew Ross Sorkin wrote
an article analyzing how the report was researched, how Goldman documents were used by the Senate committee, and the
content of interviews with employees of the firm as well as staffers of the Senate committee. Ross Sorkin's conclusion was that
the report exaggerated the firm's profit from its short position
because the firm's profit from the short position used the

wrong figures for earnings, making the profit on the shorts appear to be a larger percentage of total earnings than was in fact the case. According to financial disclosure forms, Goldman's net profit in housing in 2007 was $500 million, not a significant percentage of the firm's total income of $45.98 billion. Because the report calculated the percentage of profit based on an erroneous net income total of $11.6 billion, and because the figure for the short position was inflated, made up of shorts on commercial as well as residential real estate instead of only RMBS, the report's statement of the firm's profit on short sales of RMBS was incorrect and presented the impression that Goldman Sachs had a big profit in this area. According to Ross Sorkin, this was simply not the case. Robert L. Roach, a counsel and chief investigator for the committee, admitted the error, calling it a typo.[31] Please note that this technical information, as well as the task of the Senate subcommittee, reveals a complex and multifaceted reality about which one should be cautious in drawing conclusions.

Shadow banking. During the subprime crisis a novel aspect of banking was ongoing. It was termed *shadow banking*. The shadow banking system consists of non-bank financial institutions that play a large role in banking by making short-term loans so that financial institutions will have the money they need to operate. For example, a pension fund, university endowment or hedge fund could lend money to an investment bank, charging a higher rate of interest than normal; the lender lends the money to make a profit and the investment bank pays a higher rate of interest than is generally the case in order to fund its operations. A lot of this borrowing and lending was done in short-term deals; in 2006 investment banks were rolling over 25 percent of their balance sheets every night.[32] Bear Stearns, Lehman Brothers, Merrill Lynch and other financial firms participated in the shadow banking system by borrowing money and using that money to finance purchases of investment products to sell to customers. Timothy Geithner, then President of the New York Federal Reserve Bank, said in early

2007 that lending through the shadow banking system exceeded lending by the traditional banking system.[33] Investment firms used money borrowed in the shadow banking system to purchase MBS-CDOs; when the market for these products imploded, the investment banks faced the possibility of bankruptcy. The counterparties from whom they borrowed demanded payment of the loans and refused to extend further credit. Since some assets of firms like Lehman Brothers had become toxic and impossible to value or sell, these firms were in jeopardy. They were over-leveraged and their dire straits affected the entire economy. It became obvious that there should have been regulations in place to prevent investment banks from such large borrowing and low capitalization, but there were no regulations and this lack of regulation was recognized as a significant cause of the economic crisis.

Hedge funds. Hedge funds are private investment companies whose employees handle financial assets of wealthy individual and institutional clients. Investment strategies include short selling and margin trades, as well as buying and selling stocks, bonds and mutual funds. In the years prior to the financial crisis, hedge funds also bought and sold MBS-CDOs and some hedge funds bought credit default swaps. The problems experienced by banks, AIG, Fannie Mae and Freddie Mac during and following the crisis had a direct impact on hedge funds in the form of more restrictive lending to hedge firms and higher borrowing costs. If hedge funds held MBS-CDOs or stock in companies that failed, such as Bear Stearns, Countrywide, IndyMac, Lehman Brothers, Wachovia and Washington Mutual,[34] these investments constituted losses.

While some hedge funds were passive participants in the financial crisis, losing money, other hedge funds made money and played a role in causing the crisis by short selling. Andrew Ross Sorkin makes this point by referring to the analysis of Tom Russo of Lehman Brothers who believed that the tactics of hedge fund managers contributed to the demise of Bear Stearns and the distress of Lehman Brothers:

A bunch of "hedgies," Wall Street's disparaging nickname for hedge fund managers, had systematically taken down Bear Stearns (in March 2008) by pulling their brokerage accounts, buying insurance against the bank – an instrument called a credit default swap, or CDS – and then shorting its stock.[35]

Failed investment banks. Bear Stearns was the first of the Wall Street investment banks to fail because of the crisis in the housing market. It was bought by JPMorgan Chase on March 16, 2008 at a fire sale price. In September 2008, plagued by the effects of the subprime crisis, Merrill Lynch was in jeopardy and it was taken over by Bank of America. In a more dramatic episode, Lehman Brothers, a 158-year-old firm, dangled on the edge of the precipice, trying to find a firm to take it over or to lend it enough money to stay in business. No buyers materialized and neither did the capital which the firm desperately needed. What caused Lehman Brothers to go bankrupt provides an overview of the interrelated factors that led to catastrophe.

Lehman's traders bought mortgage-backed securities without seeming to realize that these products were toxic; management did not direct the traders to stop buying MBS-CDOs. In September 2008 Lehman had billions of dollars worth of an unsellable asset on its books. Lehman also had a desk that issued credit default swaps; when swap holders demanded payments because *their* mortgage-backed securities had tanked, Lehman lacked the capital to make the payments. As Lehman's troubles became known, credit rating agencies lowered the firm's credit rating, requiring that Lehman post more capital to satisfy industry standards. Lehman sought to borrow money in the shadow banking system to meet this obligation, but, as its troubles intensified, no one would lend the firm money. Investment banks "are financed literally overnight by others on the assumption that they will be around the next morning."[36] Investors turned on Lehman Brothers and its

stock declined from $31.75 on March 17, 2008 to $3.71 a share
on September 11, 2008. The stock was also driven down by
short sellers at hedge funds who bet against Lehman's chances
for survival. Ultimately, there was not enough capital to keep
the firm afloat and the firm went bankrupt. When Lehman
declared bankruptcy on September 15, 2008 its stock was
worthless; no group of stockholders experienced more losses
than Lehman's employees whose retirement accounts were
made up of company stock.

Speaking before Congress on October 6, 2008, Richard Fuld,
the CEO of the failed firm, placed a major share of blame on
hedge funds that sold Lehman stock short in so-called *naked
short sales*:

> Short selling by itself can be employed as a legitimate
> hedge against risk. Naked short selling, on the other hand,
> is an invitation to market manipulation. Naked short sell-
> ing is the practice of selling shares short without first bor-
> rowing or arranging to borrow those shares in time to
> make delivery to the buyer within the settlement period –
> in essence, selling something you do not own and might
> not ultimately deliver to the buyer.
>
> Naked short selling, followed by false rumors, dealt a
> critical, if not fatal blow to Bear Stearns. Many knowledge-
> able participants in our financial markets are convinced
> that naked short sellers spread rumors and false informa-
> tion regarding the liquidity of Bear Stearns, and simultan-
> eously pulled business or encouraged others to pull
> business from Bear Stearns, creating an atmosphere of fear
> which then led to a self fulfilling prophecy of a run on the
> bank. The naked shorts and rumor mongers succeeded in
> bringing down Bear Stearns. And I believe that unsubstan-
> tiated rumors in the marketplace caused significant harm
> to Lehman Brothers. In our case, false rumors were so
> rampant for so long that major institutions issued public
> statements denying the rumors.[37]

Government regulation of banking. The regulatory failures that set the stage for huge losses in the banking industry were a proximate cause of the financial crisis. The report issued by a subcommittee of the U.S. Senate on April 13, 2011 entitled *Wall Street and the Financial Crisis: Anatomy of a Financial Collapse* explains how shortcomings by regulatory agencies contributed to the financial implosion. In regard to the failure of regulators to understand what they needed to do, the report states that neither the Office of Thrift Supervision (OTS) nor the Federal Deposit Insurance Corporation (FDIC) saw preventing Washington Mutual's sale of high risk mortgages into U.S. securitization markets as part of its regulatory responsibilities.[38] This resulted in a failure to take into account how Washington Mutual's multifaceted involvement in mortgage origination, purchase, sales and securitization could have deleterious consequences for the economy as a whole.

As a case study, the report addresses the role of the Office of Thrift Supervision and Washington Mutual Bank, the biggest bank to fail and be taken over by the FDIC. From 2004 to 2008 the OTS identified more than 500 serious deficiencies at Washington Mutual, but did not force the bank to improve its lending operations. Why did Washington Mutual executives continue to allow deficient practices while regulators objected to these practices? The Senate report contends that regulators approached the bank in a deferential manner, were reluctant to interfere in internal management functions, even when these functions imperiled the economic system, and were unwilling to force needed changes. Noting that the agency's officials viewed the institutions it regulated as "constituents," the report said that the OTS relied on bank executives to correct identified problems and the OTS was reluctant to interfere with "even unsound lending and securitization practices" at Washington Mutual. Additionally, the OTS pushed back against the FDIC, the secondary regulator of Wamu, when the FDIC became alarmed and advocated that enforcement actions be taken, thus allowing a bad situation to worsen.[39]

Government regulation and derivatives. Credit default swaps are derivatives. "Derivatives are contracts whose value is derived from stocks, bonds, loans, currencies and commodities, or linked to specific events."[40] Many kinds of derivatives are regulated by the Commodity Futures Trading Commission (the CFTC) in a manner similar to the way the Securities and Exchange Commission (SEC) regulates the stock market. However, credit default swaps were not regulated by the CFTC and, in view of the fact that volatility associated with these derivatives played a large part in the financial crisis of 2008, the lack of regulation was unquestionably short-sighted. The public should know how these products are priced and how many trade on a given day; protections should exist to prevent market manipulation through use of derivatives that could result in bankrupting financial firms and causing global panics. As already noted, billionaire financier Warren Buffett rightly characterized CDS as a "financial instrument of mass destruction";[41] the fact that the market in these instruments grew from a notional value of $95 trillion in 2000 to $672 trillion in June 2008 illustrates the problems they posed for the economy as a whole.[42] Had investors been aware of how the market in credit default swaps was growing and the amount of speculation that was going on in connection with MBS-CDOs, the fact that knowledgeable people were betting against the worth of these securities likely would have had a chilling effect on the market. Instead, because of a lack of transparency, the vast majority of investors were unaware of what was happening and the buying and selling of MBS and CDOs continued after insiders knew how deficient the products were and sought to make money by buying CDS.

General Motors and Chrysler. The automobile industry was not directly involved in the subprime mortgage debacle, but its economic survival was at stake during the fall of 2008 and the months following; the U.S. government had to decide to let General Motors and Chrysler cease to operate, or support these major U.S. industries through reorganizations. Whether or not to include a discussion of the issues faced by GM and Chrysler in the context of the financial crisis is debatable. Including the automakers in this book aligns with the argument that trying to save these automakers was economically and politically critical and that their problems should be considered part of the overall crisis.

The U.S. auto industry is a mainstay of the American economy. Three million jobs are tied to manufacturing and supplying auto parts, assembling cars in auto plants, selling vehicles and maintaining them. In 2008 and early 2009, General Motors and Chrysler, beleaguered by high operating costs, falling sales, large inventories, and blowback from the economic meltdown, were on the verge of bankruptcy. Auto sales suffered because of reduced consumer confidence and the lack of readily available credit for buying cars. High gasoline prices and plunging sales of sport utility vehicles had hurt auto manufacturers for a number of years. Had GM and Chrysler failed, the economic consequences would have been grave and far-reaching. As President Bush put it, "the immediate bankruptcy of the Big Three could cost more than a million jobs, decrease tax revenues by $150 billion, and set back America's GDP by hundreds of billions of dollars."[43] (Although President Bush said "Big Three," only two of the three were in jeopardy; Ford was not in danger of going bankrupt.)

At General Motors the situation was so dire in the summer of 2008 that its CEO Rick Wagoner tried to persuade Bill Ford, Executive Chairman of Ford Motors, to merge the two companies. Mr. Ford declined the offer from its desperate long-time rival. The story is detailed in a book written by Bill Vlasic, *Once Upon A Car*.

The federal government faced the choice of letting these companies fail, with the resultant unemployment and concomitant economic suffering, or intervening to stabilize them. Both the Bush and the Obama administrations chose to intervene. In exchange for more than $60 billion in government assistance, GM and Chrysler were required to overhaul their operations and auto unions had to relinquish benefits. Stockholders would get nothing and the status of debt holders was unclear. On June 1, 2009, GM underwent bankruptcy proceedings and emerged as a restructured company. Because of the money the United States lent to GM, the U.S. government retained ownership of 61 percent of GM stock. Chrysler underwent Chapter 11 bankruptcy reorganization on April 30, 2009, and emerged as a corporation owned by the United Auto Workers, the U.S. government and Fiat, an Italian automaker which took over control of the company. Both GM and Chrysler closed hundreds of auto dealerships and discontinued several brands. The revised business plans of these corporations call for building fuel-efficient vehicles and cars that run on alternate fuels so as to appeal to U.S. consumers and to build a significant market share. In so doing, they plan to compete directly with foreign car manufacturers and claim a larger percentage of the U.S. market.

It should be noted that GMAC Financial Services, at the time a subsidiary of GM and an issuer of auto loans, was an issuer of subprime residential mortgages. Because of its subprime home loan exposure, and also as a result of delinquencies in auto loans, GMAC was at risk in the fall of 2008 and was unable to assist GM in its operations. In addition, the demands GMAC put on GM added to the financial stress the automaker was facing.

Cultural factors. Cultural factors contributed to the economic crisis. In the United States people were accustomed to buying on credit and some people tended not to worry about the responsibility to pay their debts. Luxury goods were considered desirable and people wanted to accumulate them. On Wall Street there was an appetite for risk tolerance and gambling to make money seemed like a plausible strategy for securing profits. The assumption that smart people who make sophisticated financial projections based on obscure mathematical formulas know what they are doing was pervasive. Lack of financial acumen was the rule rather than the exception. These aspects of the culture set the stage for the crisis.

Alternative narrative. The interplay of the foregoing factors is generally cited as the reason that things went wrong
and the financial crisis happened. In the mix are too much
risk, too little capital, insufficient oversight, significant complexity, a panicked illiquid market in September 2008, and
human defects like deceit, imprudence, culpable ignorance
and greed. While this is the primary way of explaining the
causes of the crisis, an alternative narrative suggests that
accommodative U.S. monetary policy should be emphasized
as the precondition which set the stage for the implosion.
Low interest rates which were put in place by the Federal
Reserve in 2000 and kept low for several years led to a credit
bubble which encouraged borrowing and fueled the housing
boom. Because interest rates were so low for so many years,
foreign capital which traditionally invests in U.S. Treasury
bonds because they are considered a safe investment looked
for investment products that paid more interest. Over time,
investors increased their risk tolerance and purchased MBS-
CDOs because these securities provided more yield than
Treasury bonds. Thus, foreign (and domestic) money, searching for a higher return than that generated by traditional *safe*
investments, found its way to mortgage securitizers. To those
buying MBS-CDOs, the risks seemed small and the anticipated income worth the risk. Those who emphasize monetary
policy as the cause of the financial crisis argue that large capital inflows into the United States magnified appreciation in
housing costs and fed the bubble which resulted in the crisis.
If interest rates had been higher for borrowers, there would
not have been a surge in housing sales and the attendant
mortgage products would not have come into being; capital
seeking investment yield would not have had a surfeit of
MBS-CDOs to purchase in order to attain increased revenue;
and, absent the bubble, more rational investment strategies
would have been the norm.

While interest rates and investors seeking high rates of return
played a role in the financial crisis, the analysis in this book is

not derived from the alternative narrative just cited but, rather, proceeds along the same lines as that of the Financial Crisis Inquiry Commission and the U.S. Senate Subcommittee that issued the report *Wall Street and the Financial Crisis: Anatomy of a Financial Collapse.*

Conclusion. In 2008, a cluster of things went wrong simultaneously in the housing market, the mortgage market, the lives of borrowers, the bastions of finance, insurance and the auto industry to bring the U.S. economy to the brink of collapse. The fact that the economy was on the brink of collapse and that the possibility of a depression was openly discussed constituted what we have come to call the financial crisis. The economy is an abstract and technical reality but it affects real people in profound ways. In Chapter 2 we turn our attention to who was affected and how these effects were experienced.

Questions for Discussion

1   Describe how the issuance of subprime mortgages, the securitizing of mortgages into mortgage-backed securities and collateralized debt obligations, and the issuance of credit default swaps coalesced to cause the economic turbulence of 2008.

2   Comment on the roles played by mortgage lenders, banks, hedge funds and government-sponsored enterprises in the economic crisis.

3   In what ways did credit rating agencies contribute to the economic crisis?

4   Explain the role played by the shadow banking system in the financial crisis.

5   How did the U.S. government regulate credit default swaps?

6   Discuss the effectiveness of government regulators in overseeing financial institutions prior to the crisis.

7   What prompted the U.S. government to assist the auto industry in 2008 and 2009? Comment on whether or not this assistance was reasonable.

Chapters in this book are followed by case studies which require readers to consider alternatives and make decisions. These cases relate in one way or another to the financial crisis and each of them requires deciding what the right, or ethical, choice is. The cases in Chapters 1 to 3 are presented *prior* to the elaboration on ethics and readers may wonder why this is the case. There are at least two benefits. First, as a result of grappling with these conflicts, readers will discover the ideas, ideals and thinking that drive their personal analysis. And, second, after considering the ethical theory presented in Chapters 4 to 6, they will realize how much better prepared people are to deal with ethical conflicts when they proceed from a perspective informed by ethics.

Case Study: Financial Literacy – Is It Worth the Trouble?

Tim and Tara have been going out for three years. Their relationship is serious; sometimes they talk about "tying the knot" but this is a long range possibility. Recent graduates of a community college, they are employed at entry-level service jobs and their incomes are modest.

They receive postcards from the community college offering a free one-day workshop to alums; the topic of the workshop is financial literacy. Bullet points list the day's offerings: income, careers, budgets, credit, debt, mortgages, savings, checking accounts, online banking, investing, risk tolerance, insurance, retirement accounts and compound interest.

Tim tells Tara he does not know much about these subjects and he says that he thinks it would be a good idea for them to attend. Tara says she wants to think about it.

The next time the subject comes up Tara is negative about going. "We work all week. Why spend Saturday listening to people talk about boring stuff? We only make enough to pay our bills, so why should we care about finances? I don't think we'll ever be rich enough to save money or make investments. Do you?"

Tara's response leaves Tim feeling ambivalent. He knows he could go by himself, but, if Tara doesn't go, she will not learn what he learns and be able to talk things through with him about subjects like buying a house or establishing a rainy-day fund. Maybe she's right that they'll never make enough money to care about finances beyond paying their bills. And having a day off appeals to Tim, too.

1　Would attending the financial literacy workshop be a waste of time for Tara and Tim? Why or why not?

2　Should schools, community colleges and universities offer workshops or courses on financial literacy? Why or why not?

3　What problems could people avoid by being informed about financial matters?

4　Is it important for people who are in a relationship to understand finances and agree about money? Why or why not? What do they need to do to arrive at an agreement?

Case Study: The Burned Out Manager

Leslie Baron is a hedge fund manager at a New York City financial firm. She is an Ivy League graduate who takes her job seriously and works hard to manage her clients' money. Prior to the subprime disaster, Leslie purchased a security that lost $50 million in the CDO market, not an enormous amount, probably due to her conservative approach to investing. Although she considers her job secure, Leslie is experiencing feelings of burnout. Her job, which once commanded most of her energy and almost all of her enthusiasm, now wears her out. She has to push herself to get dressed and go to work.

Leslie is critical of the risk-takers who built the MBS-CDO market into a mammoth enterprise capable of undermining the entire economy. Leslie is angry that the Federal Reserve Bank did not utilize the authority it was given by Congress in 1994 under HOEPA (the Home Ownership and Equity Protection Act) to crack down on predatory lending practices. She hates the incompetence of the SEC which could have required that big banks have more capital but, instead, ignored the excessive leverage that led to the financial implosion. She also believes that regulators were asleep at the wheel when investment banks misrepresented the MBS they traded. She has no confidence that government is smart enough or tough enough to force necessary systemic changes. She wishes she had never purchased any CDOs to hold in her fund and, instead, had steered clear of them. Although she sometimes feels guilty for playing a small part in the financial crisis, she riles at being included in the category "Wall Street," the collection of bad guys that brought the nation to the verge of bankruptcy.

Leslie Baron has bills to pay and children to support but she does not want to continue to be a hedge fund manager. She vents to a friend who tells her that her negative mood will pass and that she owes it to herself, her clients and her children to keep toiling at what, for most people, would be a dream job.

1 What should Leslie Baron do, work out her issues with her job, or quit? Why?
2 What is more important: making money to support oneself and one's family or doing work that does not cause internal conflict? What should motivate a person to change fields?
3 Leslie Baron is angry with mortgage securitizers, high risk traders, the SEC and the government. As she goes about her job she feels powerless to counter the influence of these actors in the marketplace. She does not envision a brighter tomorrow. Is she overreacting to external forces or is she correct in feeling like a victim? What can she do to improve her frame of mind?
4 Leslie's friend advises her to ride out the difficult days. How would you advise her? Why?

Case Study: Make Money while the Market's Hot

Alfonzo Salazar Ramos is an investment banker who holds the position of Vice President at a leading investment bank. In this capacity Mr. Ramos is responsible for structuring and marketing mortgage-backed securities. He has successfully brought several issues to market, and is currently completing work on his latest securitization, a product known as Uranus 1. This process takes several weeks and, during that time, the market has softened because of concerns about long-term prospects of subprime mortgages.

In arranging this deal, Mr. Ramos relies on Residential Mortgage Backed Securities Analysis (RMBSA), a third-party management firm, to select close to half the mortgage-backed securities to be included in Uranus 1. Mr. Ramos also allows a hedge fund manager, Martin Meehan, to play a significant role in the portfolio selection process and Mr. Meehan chooses roughly half the mortgage-backed securities for inclusion. Mr. Meehan has done a lot of business with Mr. Ramos and both men have made money on these transactions.

Martin Meehan's interest this time around is in shorting Uranus 1 by purchasing credit default swaps. Therefore, the mortgages he selects for Uranus 1 are the worst subprime mortgages he can find. To profit from this deal, Meehan's firm will buy $1 billion worth of credit default swaps for $15 million. If Uranus 1 fails, the hedge fund will realize a profit of $1 billion, minus the $15 million cost of insurance. During an unguarded moment when they meet for drinks, Martin Meehan articulates his thinking and plan to short the deal.

Alfonzo Ramos feels uneasy about the low quality of the subprime mortgages Mr. Meehan is urging him to include in the issue. But Mr. Ramos thinks that he needs to market and sell Uranus 1 quickly in order to make money for his employer and strengthen his bonus prospects. He also wants to continue to have a good relationship with the hedge fund manager. The market may be softening, but there is still time to push another transaction through.

Knowing that buyers for Uranus 1 would be disinclined to purchase securities from this issue if they knew of Mr. Meehan's adverse interest and role in assembling the security, Mr. Ramos does not disclose this information in marketing materials or to his managers. Although required by industry standards to disclose the involvement of the hedge fund manager to the ratings agency, Mr. Ramos identifies only RMBSA so that the information the analyst uses in evaluating the product is incomplete. "She is just a rubber stamp, anyway," Mr. Ramos thinks.

Uranus 1 imploded during the subprime debacle; those who owned the MBS lost the money they invested; and Martin Meehan realized a profit of $1 billion, less the $15 million he paid for CDS.

1 Comment on what Mr. Ramos did. Considering the requirements of his job, what should he have done, or not done. Why?
2 Comment on the role of senior management of the investment bank. Did they fulfill their responsibilities to supervise Mr. Ramos? What should they have done?
3 Mr. Meehan wanted to make money and he did accomplish this goal for investors in his hedge fund. Should he have done what he did? Why or why not?
4 What steps could the analyst from the credit rating agency have taken to become properly informed about Uranus 1?

2

WHO IS AFFECTED?

Everyone needs water to live. If there were only one reservoir and each and every person on earth drank from that same reservoir, then whether or not the water in the reservoir were potable would be a crucial issue for everyone. Analogously, everyone, or almost everyone, participates in some way in the global economy so that tremors in the economy affect all of us. As a stone thrown into a pond causes rippling effects, so did the implosion of the subprime mortgage market and its aftermath cause repercussions that spread throughout the U.S. economy and around the globe. As we consider those affected by the meltdown we will begin to understand the human dimensions of the crisis.

Because everyone in the United States has an interest in the U.S. economy, each and every one is rightly considered a stakeholder in the economy. It is important to grasp the human dimensions of the financial crisis from the points of view of the various stakeholders who were impacted by the crisis. People who obtained subprime mortgages in 2005 and people who securitized these mortgages in 2006 could not have foreseen the scope, magnitude and pervasiveness of the crisis that was experienced by stakeholders in 2008 and the years to follow. Financial decisions that were made and ethical lapses that were tolerated during the boom years snowballed out of control, causing incalculable hardship. The goal of this chapter is to describe how people and institutions experienced this hardship.

The U.S. government. The U.S. government was affected by the crisis. The government needed to intervene and take action to quell panic and restore stability in the financial system. It allocated more than a trillion dollars in the process. In September 2008 the financial system was on the verge of freezing: the functions of lending and borrowing that are essential to economic activity were grinding to a halt; they needed to be restored. Public confidence was dangerously low and government leaders needed to communicate with citizens to alleviate their anxiety. Unless these goals could be accomplished the nation appeared to be on course for a severe depression. In order to bring about economic equilibrium, the government needed to undertake four critical tasks.

First, the government had to spend money to keep the economy going. Second, the government had to engage in problem solving and take immediate steps to stabilize markets. Third, the government had to face its own fiscal issues, particularly loss of tax revenues, a growing deficit and an expanding national debt. Fourth, the government had to deal with shortfalls in entitlement programs that were exacerbated by the negative economic climate. And the government had to address this unprecedented crisis without a script.

It was apparent that the systemic problems that contributed to the financial crisis had to be addressed. Government needed to get its arms around the big picture and come up with regulations to govern the granting of mortgages, the trading of complex financial products, and high risk financial practices so that there would not be a repeat of the economic implosion. The fact that, for the most part, regulatory authorities did not see what was coming and act in advance of the crisis to mitigate its effects was distressing to both citizens and government officials and prompted a sense of demoralization because people wondered if government were capable of fulfilling its mission of promoting the general welfare.

Governments exist on the local, state and federal levels. Governments employ millions of people and provide a vast array of services. Salaries and services are paid for with tax revenue and revenue from government borrowing. The so-called *Great Recession*, which followed the subprime debacle, affected state and local governments by decreasing the amounts they receive in taxes and forcing cutbacks in state and local services.

The recession affected the federal government in six ways: first, tax revenue was down because personal income declined due to unemployment and other factors; second, the money the government lent to commercial and investment banks, Fannie Mae, Freddie Mac, General Motors, Chrysler and AIG depleted its reserves; third, money provided directly to taxpayers in the form of stimulus payments added to the federal deficit; fourth, the $787 billion allocated for the American Recovery and Reinvestment Act of 2009 constituted enormous deficit spending; fifth, payments to the unemployed in the form of unemployment compensation also added to the deficit; and, sixth, the issuance of U.S. Treasury bonds to borrow money to finance the above increased the national debt.

One example of an effect of the recession on a program of the federal government is the shortfall in the Social Security trust fund. Working people pay FICA taxes (Federal Insurance Contributions Act) and these taxes are intended to cover what the program pays to retirees and provide additional funding for the future in which the number of workers is expected to decrease while the number of retirees increases. Trustees of the fund reported in August 2010 that for the first time ever Social Security was projected to pay out more than the $41 billion it was expected to generate in payroll taxes[1] and this shortfall was cause for concern as the Social Security, Medicare and Medicaid entitlement programs account for 42 percent of federal spending. Approximately fifty-three million Americans collect Social Security, which is projected to run out of money by 2037 unless Congress makes benefit cuts or raises revenue sources to restore the program to fiscal balance.[2] While most of today's Social Security recipients do not have to worry that the trust fund is going to run out of money and cease making payments to them because the fund will not be depleted for more than two decades, a bigger picture view requires acknowledging that government entitlement spending has been negatively impacted by the economic crisis and this situation needs to be addressed.

(Millions of workers saw their take-home pay rise during 2011 because the Tax Relief, Unemployment Insurance Reauthorization, and Job Creation Act of 2010 provided a two percentage point payroll tax cut for employees, reducing their Social Security tax withholding rate from 6.2 percent to 4.2 percent of wages paid.[3] This worked out to approximately $1,000 more in income for a person making $50,000 a year, a benefit designed for financial stimulus. However, the benefit was not without cost. Emily Brandon comments:

> The Social Security system's finances are not expected to be harmed because the trust fund will be reimbursed for the full amount of the tax break from the general fund of the Treasury. However, this change also means that the Social Security trust fund will no longer be completely funded directly by citizen contributions.[4]

Thus, the advantage to workers in 2011 was tempered by the fact that the manner of funding Social Security could be undermined, if the 2010 tax law sets a dangerous precedent.)

It is estimated that tax revenues to state governments were down 9 percent in 2010.[5] An example illustrates one effect of the recession on state government. State governments are required to provide legal counsel to indigent persons who are charged with a crime. In the best of times, lawyers who provide counsel are stressed by large caseloads but, in the recession following the economic crisis, defenders complained that they had so many cases to handle that it was impossible to do their job. States countered by stating that their revenues were down and that they did not have enough money to hire more lawyers. A case in point is Missouri which in 2010 faced $550 million less in general fund revenues than in 2009. The state's public defender office estimated that it needed an increase in its budget of $21 million, an amount the state said it simply could not afford. "Missouri's public defender system has reached a point where what it provides is often nothing more than the illusion of a lawyer," a report requested by the Missouri Bar concluded.[6]

Financial institutions. Investment banks, large commercial banks, the government-sponsored enterprises Fannie Mae and Freddie Mac, mortgage lenders, hedge funds, the insurance giant AIG, and some community banks were directly affected by the subprime mortgage debacle. These businesses lost enormous amounts of money and, as we have seen, in some cases, ceased to exist. In the fall of 2008, financial firms which weathered the storm saw their ability to buy and sell securities in order to make profits and ensure cash flow placed in serious jeopardy. Banks and lenders that were dependent on receiving mortgage payments to stay solvent were also in a precarious position. Counterparties throughout the world who lent money to firms that faced bankruptcy or who insured the debt of firms that faced bankruptcy were on the hook. Which counterparties and for how much? The situation was complicated and no one knew for sure.

Companies that were not making money could not pay their employees or their bills. If financial institutions could not borrow money, they could not purchase securities to sell, essentially paralyzing them. At the same time, the capital reserves of some financial institutions were stressed because, in the context of the crisis, depositors and debt holders demanded payment. Since the United States is an interconnected capitalist economy, the entire network of businesses that are engaged in financial activity was in danger of disintegrating. People began to realize that the financial system resembled a house of cards that was in danger of collapse as a consequence of bad loans in the housing sector and the securitization of these loans into mortgage-backed securities.

In March 2008, Bear Stearns, an investment bank that was imperiled as a consequence of exposure to subprime mortgages, was taken over by JPMorgan Chase for $10 a share, a price far below the one-year high for the firm of $159.36. Many employees of Bear Stearns lost their jobs in the takeover, and stockholders saw a big decline in their equity. Six months later the story at Lehman Brothers was much more grim; that investment bank declared bankruptcy, essentially wiping out investors and leaving employees jobless.

Large banks like Bank of America, which in 2008 acquired the troubled mortgage lender Countrywide as well as the brokerage firm Merrill Lynch, faced hard times as a result of exposure to subprime mortgages and related issues, such as foreclosure proceedings. Merrill Lynch was losing billions of dollars monthly when it was taken over by Bank of America and these losses became the bank's problem. Bank of America paid $4.1 billion to acquire Countrywide, a deal that proved disastrous for the bank. Write-downs and legal costs have pushed the estimated cost of that purchase to more than $30 billion.[7] The reputation of Bank of America has suffered and its stock price declined from $31.14 on September 1, 2008 to $5.90 on October 7, 2011. This decline reflects a lack of confidence on the part of investors in the bank's stability and outlook, and this is troubling because Bank of America is the largest bank holding company in the United States. Ken Lewis, who was CEO of Bank of America when it acquired Countrywide and Merrill Lynch, was criticized for these acquisitions and retired in 2009. Ken Lewis is not the only Bank of America employee to lose his job; 6,000 were laid off in 2011 before news of a contemplated restructuring that would eliminate 40,000 jobs was circulated.[8]

The government of the United States promotes home ownership; one of the ways it does this is through its sponsored enterprises, Fannie Mae and Freddie Mac, which buy mortgages from lenders, securitize these mortgages (known as "agency paper"), and sell these securities to investors. As explained in Chapter 3, Fannie Mae and Freddie Mac function as autonomous firms with independent management answerable to stockholders. These firms are required to adhere to guidelines issued by the U.S. government but they are not run by the government. Prior to the financial crisis, Fannie and Freddie had big lobbying budgets and contributed heavily to political candidates so that they could influence legislation and regulations. The autonomous nature of the enterprises, the ability of executives to carry out policies that would result in big paydays for themselves, and the practice of influencing legislators and regulators turned out to be a deadly combination. Intent on short-term profits, during the run up to the financial crisis Fannie Mae and Freddie Mac dug a deep hole by buying and holding large quantities of subprime mortgages. Exposure to subprime resulted in a cost to U.S. taxpayers of an estimated $269 billion,[9] but this figure is far from certain because it will take a long time to sort matters out. The question of how to provide mortgages so that people can buy homes is a daunting one; Fannie and Freddie seemed to be the answer, but that is no longer the case. What should happen next? Should the enterprises be privatized or eliminated? Should they be more stringently regulated? What should happen at present, when they are losing money but insuring 90 percent of the mortgages currently being issued? No one seems to know, adding to distress about the state of the economy.[10]

Many mortgage lenders were shuttered as a result of the subprime debacle. New Century Financial provides an apt example. On March 20, 2007 the corporation announced that it could no longer sell mortgage loans to Fannie Mae or act as the primary servicer of loans for the government-sponsored enterprise. On April 2, 2007 New Century filed for bankruptcy in Wilmington, Delaware. In its filing New Century listed liabilities of more than $100 million and announced the termination of 3,200 jobs.[11] Julie Creswell wrote in the *New York Times* that

it seemed to come as a shock to investors when, in February (2007), the company said it would have to restate its earnings for the first nine months of 2006 and record a loss for the final quarter because it had understated the damage caused by a growing number of soured loans.[12]

Two hedge funds owned by Bear Stearns lost all or almost all their capital and led to the demise of the investment bank. These funds were known as the Bear Stearns High-Grade Structured Credit Fund and the Bear Stearns High-Grade Structured Credit Enhanced Leveraged Fund. The latter fund lost 90 percent of its value; the former 100 percent.[13] On July 31, 2007 both funds filed for bankruptcy. The parent firm, Bear Stearns, would hang on for another seven months but would then implode as a consequence of the residual effects of the exposure of its hedge funds to the subprime market. Half of Bear Stearns' 14,000 employees lost their jobs when the firm merged with JPMorgan Chase.[14]

The stock price of AIG fell to $1.25 on September 16, 2008; buyers had paid $21.87 on August 31, 2008, and the one-year high was $70.13. Stockholders were not the only ones affected by the troubles at AIG. The government takeover of the insurance giant meant that top management lost their jobs (although they received their bonuses); profitable businesses run by AIG were put up for sale in order to repay government assistance; and confidence in the U.S. economy was shaken not only for AIG counterparties but for ordinary people all over the world. The number of employees declined from 106,000 in 2008[15] to 63,000 in 2010.[16]

Credit rating agencies. Credit rating agencies were affected by the financial crisis in several ways. As noted in Chapter 1, Standard & Poor's and Moody's gave inaccurate ratings to the financial products that became the toxic assets at the center of the financial crisis. In regard to debt obligations, the responsibility of a credit rating agency is to analyze the products and issue dependable reports regarding the likelihood that the debts will be repaid. Because Standard & Poor's and Moody's did not meet this responsibility, their reputations were badly damaged. Loss of reputation led to decline in stock prices;

Moody's traded at around $70 a share in January 2007 and "recovered" to just over $30 a share going into the fourth quarter of 2011. Distrust of rating agencies also led to demands that systemic changes be made in the way the agencies operate. Systemic changes have not been instituted in that rating agencies continue to be paid by the institutions that need a rating for their products, but the rating agencies are subject to much more scrutiny with respect to the process and specific rating which their research produces. The scrutiny comes from investors who have learned difficult lessons and also from the SEC which has become much more thorough in its regulation of the agencies in the aftermath of the crisis. The Securities and Exchange Commission regulates the credit rating agencies and currently issues annual reports on internal controls at the agencies, disclosure of performance statistics, and disclosure about third-party due diligence.[17] These disclosures began after the passage of Dodd–Frank in 2010. This scrutiny is a good effect of the crisis and requires much more rigorous analysis of investment products by rating agencies in order to meet new standards. (The Dodd–Frank Act will be discussed in Chapter 3.)

Investors. Some people buy stocks or bonds because they want to own part of a corporation that contributes particular goods or services to the economy. They believe in the overall soundness of the economy and expect growth and prosperity. Because they think a company will contribute to the economy and make a profit, they buy shares of its stock. For them, buying securities represents faith in a company and hope that the company will prosper and that they will share in its prosperity.

Most people buy securities to make money; they are speculators and are more interested in a company's stock price than in its plans or the contributions it makes to society. Speculators tend to trade frequently in order to realize profits. Individual investors speculate but so, too, do institutional traders like hedge funds and pension funds, which sometimes employ computer models to make trades. According to this scenario, an algorithm decides the pricing, quantity and timing of the trade and quantities tend to be large. Once the computer model is set up by the institutional investor, the trade is carried out without human intervention.

Retirement accounts such as 401Ks frequently contain stocks or mutual funds made up wholly or partly of stocks. Frequently, 401K accounts contain stock in an employee's company. All told, as of 2005, just over half of U.S. households, 56.9 million out of 113 million, owned stock directly or through mutual funds.[18] Put another way, in 2005 there were approximately ninety-one million Americans who owned stock. Long-term investors, people saving for retirement, and many speculators lost money. September 29, 2008 was an especially bad day in a dismal fall as the stock market lost 778 points and $1.2 trillion in market value. Although by early 2011 the stock market recovered most of what it lost in 2008 and the first half of 2009, many investors were not back to even. However, improvement did not continue during the third quarter of 2011, when the stock market declined 12 percent[19] and investors worried that the economy was in (or moving toward) another recession. That fear was tempered in early 2012 as the stock market improved; however, high gas prices and concerns about debt issues in Europe weighed on investors' confidence.

A fourth type of investor is a so-called *short seller*. Short selling is complicated. Speculative investors borrow stock from brokers and sell it. On a specified date, the borrower buys the same quantity of stock and returns it to the broker. The goal is to pay less for the stock the second time it is purchased. For example, an investor may borrow 100 shares of stock trading at $10 a share and sell it for that price, receiving $1,000 on that transaction. When the date arrives for the short seller to return the stock to the broker, she needs to buy 100 shares of the stock at the price at which it is then trading. If the price is $1 a share, the short seller will pay $100 for 100 shares. She will return the 100 shares to the broker and she will realize a profit of $900. Short sellers who bet against investment banks, mortgage lenders, troubled banks like Washington Mutual and Wachovia, businesses related to the housing market, and corporations such as AIG, realized profits when the financial system imploded.

Corporations. Corporations are a form of business that are organized to provide goods or services which are sold in order to make a profit. Corporations are owned by stockholders who appoint a Board of Directors to oversee the business. The Board hires a Chief Executive Officer who in turn hires executives who manage the business, hiring workers and carrying out necessary functions. If the business is profitable, the price of the stock goes up and the equity of stockholders increases. Stockholders in many profitable businesses share in the profits by receiving dividend payments. If a business is not profitable, the opposite occurs. If a market for a product or service provided by a corporation disappears, or if a business cannot pay its employees and meet obligations to lenders, it will be forced to declare bankruptcy, which would result in many unemployed people and stockholders losing their investment. Many financial corporations failed as a result of the implosion of the MBS-CDO market; included are Washington Mutual Bank, Countrywide Financial, IndyMac and Lehman Brothers. For employees of these corporations whose retirement accounts consisted wholly or largely in the stocks of these companies, the financial effects were devastating.

Nonfinancial corporations felt the effects of the recession; those involved in housing-related businesses were most affected. For example, Home Depot's sales were down 7 percent in 2009[20] and Toll Brothers, a company that builds housing, went from delivering nearly 8,600 homes in 2006 to fewer than 3,000 in 2009.[21] Many businesses that fare poorly in a recessionary climate laid off workers, did not replace workers who left, did not hire new workers, avoided outlays for advertising, research and product development, and production of goods that would likely sit, unsold, in warehouses. Their earnings declined, as did their stock prices. Newspapers were adversely affected by a loss of advertising revenue and two long-running daily papers shut down in 2009: the *Seattle Post-Intelligencer* and the *Rocky Mountain News*. In both instances people lost jobs and regions lost important conduits of information.

Just as an economy is not static, neither is the functioning of corporations which respond to the ebbs and flows of the overall economy. In time, productivity of remaining workers increases and, eventually, demand for products or services grows, bringing companies to a better place than they were in 2008. As a matter of fact, in the second quarter of 2010, "Capital expenditures among non-financial S&P companies increased an average of 11 percent from a year earlier to about $96 billion."[22] Companies were again able to make capital expenditures because they had an estimated $1.24 trillion in cash and short-term investments, money that could be spent for increased dividends, merger and acquisition activity and operational spending. These corporate expenditures contribute stimulus to the overall economy[23] but, by the fall of 2010, there was concern that the strength of the recovery was not sufficient to lead to a lowering of unemployment and a return to sufficient growth to restore a modest level of prosperity.

Auto industry. The auto industry was in poor shape before September 2008 but the economic implosion and subsequent recession made a bad situation worse so that the continued existence of General Motors and Chrysler was in question. With the severe tightening of the credit markets impacting people's ability to borrow, consumers reluctant to purchase major items, lack of cash flow and low capital reserves, General Motors and Chrysler were struggling to survive. As noted in Chapter 1, the U.S. government lent these automakers $61 billion with stipulations attached. Top management officials of these companies were forced to resign, labor unions had to renegotiate benefits, plants were closed, workers were laid off, and stockholders lost their equity. Eventually, if and when these automakers become profitable, those they employ will benefit from job security and the overall economy will benefit as a result of cars produced and wages earned and spent. At the time of the reorganizations, however, those who lost jobs or the money they invested in stock suffered economic loss. Union employees who continue to work for GM and Chrysler agreed to receive reduced pay, benefits and pensions going forward.

Small businesses. Small businesses are the backbone of the U.S. economy. Small businesses hire workers and provide goods and services; just over half of private sector employees work for small businesses with 500 or less employees. Small businesses account for 44 percent of the total U.S. payroll. Over the past fifteen years, small businesses have generated 64 percent of new jobs and created more than half the nonfarm gross domestic product (GDP).[24] In prosperous times the presence and contributions of small businesses are obvious. The absence of small business start-ups and the financial distress experienced by small businesses at times of economic decline play a significant role in the faltering of the economy. During hard times two issues plague small businesses: first is the unwillingness of consumers to engage in discretionary spending and provide revenue. And, second, is the difficulty experienced by small business owners in obtaining financing to begin or continue operations. In the aftermath of the financial collapse lenders became overly cautious about lending to small businesses and this resulted in a climate in which it was difficult for small businesses to operate. Failed small businesses and unemployed workers from these enterprises added to the bleak economic scene.

An agency of the federal government, the Small Business Association, enacted policies designed to help small business owners navigate through the hard times, but, at this writing, contributions to the overall economy from the small business community are insufficient to reduce unemployment and stimulate needed economic growth. Debate about tax strategies and other initiatives to improve the climate for small businesses and their performance is ongoing, with no consensus on action yet in place.

Homeowners. Many categories of homeowners were affected by the economic meltdown. People who owned their homes and did not have mortgages likely saw the value of their properties decline after the bursting of the bubble. People with mortgages also saw their homes decline in value. Depending on when they bought the home and the amount of the mortgage, homeowners might or might not have been underwater. Subprime borrowers who were unable to make mortgage payments faced foreclosure. Homeowners who lost their jobs and were unable to find comparable work could not make mortgage payments and faced the possibility of foreclosure if they did not have savings or family to help them through the difficult time.

Real estate and related industries. Among other things, real estate professionals list homes for sale and sell these properties. When the subprime mortgage meltdown resulted in the financial implosion, the selling and buying of homes was at a standstill. Buyers were few because they wanted to wait for prices to fall before buying, and/or because they could not secure financing. Sellers were many because their properties lingered on the market. There were more sellers than usual because some people were trying to sell in order to avoid defaulting on their mortgages. The result was that the real estate business was in turmoil and those who made their living listing and selling homes saw substantial decline in their incomes.

Home builders build houses for customers who engage them or they build on speculation, anticipating that once a property or a development is built people will buy the new homes. During boom years both contract work and speculation paid off for home builders and the industry was thriving. As the housing boom slowed down in 2006 and 2007 and imploded in 2008, individuals stopped building houses and there were few buyers for new units built on speculation. Not only did this result in a bleak situation for builders, it also caused abandonment of finished and unfinished developments and major losses for lenders. Although there was some improvement in 2009, 2010 and 2011, the housing sector remained weak, causing financial hardship to home builders.

Warren Peterson, a real estate broker and a builder of new homes in Bakersfield, California, was hit hard by the subprime crisis. From 2003 to 2005 Mr. Peterson built between twenty and thirty houses a year; since 2005 he has built one new home and he estimated in mid-2010 that there was a twelve-year inventory on the market in his area. Mr. Peterson offers no solution to the situation that affects him and others like him, but he does ask that the U.S. government listen to his input before the government formulates programs to deal with the issues of local communities.[25]

The building trades are made up of many types of subcontractors including architects, framers, carpenters, roofers, plumbers, electricians, sheet rockers, painters, decorators, landscapers and others. Constructing residential real estate requires materials provided by lots of different types of manufacturers which employ many people. All of these workers and suppliers were negatively impacted by the collapse of the housing market. Since their incomes decreased, they altered their spending practices, impacting a vast array of retail and service industries. For the unemployed, the fallout from the Great Recession was bleak indeed as they struggled to make due on unemployment compensation.

Media. The media plays a large role in society, informing people of what is happening and offering analysis as to the causes and implications of whatever is occurring. When the weather is terrible people turn to the media to learn if an approaching storm is a hurricane and if evacuation is necessary. As it turns out, meteorology is a lot more straightforward than economic analysis, yet, in September 2008, it was to the media that people turned to learn about what was going on and to find out how bad things were. One question raised at the time was why, with a twenty-four-hour news cycle and financial commentators in print, online and at the networks and cable outlets, the collapse of financial firms and ensuing economic turmoil came as a surprise. The answer was not simple because the financial system is not simple and because very few people possess the requisite level of financial acumen to understand what had been going on and to sound a warning.[26] One lesson the media learned was that its audience was in need of remedial education in finance as well as accurate information about how the economy functions. People needed to preserve their assets and they needed to have a sense of confidence to go on spending and keep the economy going, even when the housing and financial sectors were in disarray. Unfortunately, when the full story of the economic collapse is told, the probability is that there will be a consensus that the media lacked the information and skill to carry out this daunting responsibility. Such is the thinking of Danny Schechter who said in an interview that

> There was little or no examination into the new breed of exotic financial products that caused many of the problems, such as CDOs, and ... the media ignored the warnings from community housing organizations of the predatory lending practices in some of America's poorest communities. "This was a big media failure, we were not warned about it." Why did the media fail to fulfill its role? Newspapers, and the media in general, are supposed to be the fourth estate, a watchdog for citizens. Is it a lack of knowledge on the workings of high finance or has the media lost its way and become part of the problem?[27]

For our purposes, it is enough at this point in the narrative to note issues related to the media's role. Schechter wrote a book (*Plunder*) in which he questions whether the print media's dependence on income from real estate advertising influenced newspapers not to inform their readers about the possibility of the collapse of the residential housing market so as not to antagonize the industry and lose advertising revenue. Whether or not this contention can be substantiated, it remains a fact that media organs generally failed to warn of the coming collapse. The media's inability to do its job, when viewed alongside the government's failure to prevent the confluence of events that led to the crisis, added to the sense of demoralization felt by the citizenry.

Consumers. Consumers play the central role in a capitalist economy. Consumers include many categories of people. Children and teenagers are consumers, as are retired people.

Workers are also consumers. Consumers purchase goods and services and these purchases provide income to businesses. Consumer spending accounts for two-thirds of economic activity. If consumers stop discretionary spending on items such as automobiles, retail goods, restaurant meals, hotel accommodations, toys, concerts, newspapers and cleaning services, owners and workers associated with businesses that provide these see their income dry up and, in a worst-case scenario, they are forced into bankruptcy and unemployment. Since people without incomes do not have funds for discretionary spending, they drive demand down further, adding to economic woe. The situation would improve if consumers who had money to spend were to spend it, but being willing to spend on things that are optional requires a sense of confidence that conditions are going to improve within a reasonable period of time. The worst fear of consumers is a protracted depression during which economic activity grinds to a halt and their paychecks stop coming because they become unemployed and/or their savings become exhausted.

In the months following the events of September 2008 people tended to hold on to their money so that they would have enough in reserve to weather an economic storm; this kept them from spending so as to stimulate economic activity at a time when consumer spending was most needed. People who owed money on credit cards paid their balances instead of adding to them. A psychological change took hold in which demand for acquiring status symbols was replaced by a more frugal frame of mind. People began to save money. As time passed, consumer confidence remained negative and consumer spending for the most part did not resume at a level that provided economic stimulus. The fact that from mid-2007 to mid-2009 household net worth in the United States fell 25 percent, $17.5 trillion, exacerbated the general sense of negativity. Although advances in the stock market beginning in 2009 lessened the extent of these losses, gains were insufficient to change consumer attitudes.

Another factor that influences consumer behavior is that "consumers who used their skyrocketing home values to borrow ever larger sums of money to feed further spending are now paying off that debt, which hampers their spending."[28] The process of digging out from a pile of debt is slow and painful for indebted individuals and also traumatic for the overall economy which depends heavily on consumer spending.

Workers. There are between 150 and 160 million people in the U.S. workforce and they were impacted in many ways by the downturn in the economy. As we have seen, people in the real estate profession, the building trades, building supplies and production and sales of non-necessary items were negatively impacted. Many workers in the mortgage lending field and in financial services lost their jobs or had lowered earnings. Since taxes paid to federal, state and local governments pay the salaries of public employees, and, since tax revenues are down, in some cases public employees lost their jobs, and, in others, furloughs were enacted to reduce government spending. Physicians and hospitals saw their incomes decrease because some people canceled elective procedures; colleges and universities experienced shortfalls because students did not enroll or dropped out due to lack of money to pay for tuition. This resulted in layoffs at hospitals and colleges. Industries that depend on discretionary spending such as entertainment, travel, retail sales and restaurants experienced losses that resulted in worker layoffs. Just as consumer confidence is a driving force in a capitalist society, so is worker confidence. If those workers who remain employed feel insecure about their future, they will hesitate to make discretionary purchases, opting, instead, to save for a rainy day. Unemployed, underemployed and worried workers exert a negative impact on the economy. These categories of workers do not fulfill the role of consumer and their inability to do so is detrimental to the economy.

Denise Kimberlin's experience provides an example. Ms. Kimberlin has a steady job as a government contractor, but she knows many people who are out of work, and she finds herself

asking "What if that happened to me?" This question, and not
declining income, has caused Ms. Kimberlin and her husband
to cut at least $250 a week of spending on clothes, dinners out
and other purchases. When does she intend to resume her pre-
recession level of spending? She is looking for signals from the
same people whose experiences caused her to fasten her pock-
etbook in the first place. "When someone I know actually finds
a new job," she said. "I haven't seen that. I haven't seen that in
months. That would be a good sign."[29]

The unemployed. The U.S. economy is going well when the
unemployment rate is between 5 and 6 percent. Following the
events of fall 2008, the unemployment rate climbed to more than
10 percent; it remained at approximately 9 percent through 2011
and declined to 8.2 percent in the first quarter of 2012. The
unemployment rate is not expected to decline significantly for
the next few years. It is estimated that there are fifteen million
unemployed people. This figure is deceptive in that it does not
include many long-time unemployed who have given up looking
for work, or people who were formerly employed full-time and
are now making do with part-time work or working for considerably less money than before. The effects of the economic collapse
on the unemployed are manifold. It is psychologically difficult to
deal with the frustration of trying to find a job in a context in
which there are many more job seekers than job openings; dealing with no responses or rejections is very hard. It is painful to
have to rely on unemployment compensation to meet one's
financial needs, as this amounts to less than the income people
had earned. It is humiliating not to be able to provide for one's
family and it can be heartbreaking to face foreclosure. The
unemployed are people who used to have jobs and their strug-
gles are easier to comprehend than the complex financial instruments and transactions that precipitated the economic tsunami.

Alexandra Jarrin's story was told in a lengthy article in the *New
York Times*. After Ms. Jarrin was laid off from a $56,000 a year job
as director of client services at a small technology company, she
collected unemployment insurance for the ninety-nine-week

maximum. In spite of attempts to find another position, anything from minimum wage to something comparable to her previous job, she remained unemployed. Adding to her stress was the fact that she had overdrawn her credit cards and contracted $92,000 in student loans. Even though her car loan payments were overdue, Ms. Jarrin told the reporter that she expected to be sleeping in the car when her week in a motel was up; the waiting list for the shelter was long and she did not know when there would be an opening. Friends had given Ms. Jarrin money which she used for the motel and gas for her car, but she said that she had exhausted their generosity and she was anticipating having no money at all. We are indebted to people like Alexandra Jarrin who tell their stories and put a human face on the plight of the unemployed during the Great Recession.[30]

Retirees. Retirees are people who worked for many years and who retired from their jobs. They no longer depend on a paycheck to pay their living expenses and their bills. In the United States senior citizens who paid Social Security taxes when they were working collect monthly payments from Social Security after they reach retirement age. Some retirees also receive a pension from their former employer. During their working years many retirees put part of their pay into retirement accounts and they count on the amount they withdraw from these accounts to supplement Social Security and pension. The income these accounts generate allows retirees to enjoy a lifestyle for which they have planned and saved. Retirees with retirement accounts were negatively affected by the economic collapse if their money was invested in stocks that lost value or in securities or mutual funds that were made up in whole or in part of MBS-CDOs. For millions of senior citizens, starting in fall 2008, their retirement account statements brought bad news followed by more bad news and their desire to have enough money to take care of themselves for the rest of their lives was undermined by factors they did not anticipate. This effect of the subprime crisis was experienced in the homes of retirees in every city and hamlet in the United States. For some retirees it meant selling their home in order to raise money to pay living expenses. For others, it meant cutting out the discretionary spending they planned to enjoy during their retirement. For still others, it meant moving in with their children or going back to work in order to have enough income to pay their bills.

Students. Since 1996 parents and grandparents have had the option of opening accounts referred to by the numbers 5–2–9 as investment vehicles to provide money to be used for college tuition. Congress included provisions for these accounts in the Internal Revenue Code and there are tax advantages in using them to save for college. Attending a college or a university costs a substantial amount of money; 529 plans are designed as investment products which appreciate in value over time in order to produce revenue for tuition when children are ready for college. Prospective college students were negatively affected by the financial meltdown because, if their 529 accounts were tied to stocks and other investments that lost a significant amount of money, anticipated revenues were not forthcoming and this limited their options for higher education. High-school students whose parents lost jobs or lost income had to rethink their college plans. From research conducted by the College Board in 2009 about how the recession affected the choices students were likely to make about college, we learn:

> Over 40 percent of the students surveyed indicated that economic circumstances will change their college choice behavior. One fifth of this group said they'll consider a community college and one third indicated they'll look at colleges closer to home. Over 40 percent indicated that they'll look at public over private colleges; over half said they'd need a scholarship to attend college, and nearly 80 percent strongly agreed that they would need financial aid. But the very hopeful news in all these findings is that only a very small number reported that they would forgo college altogether: Only 3 percent strongly agreed that not attending college was an option.[31]

A second way in which students were affected is that the set of assumptions that young people tend to hold was undermined by the financial collapse. High-school students had tended to think that if they attended college and applied themselves they would secure a good job and be ready for a prosperous future. Actually, this is what Ms. Jarrin believed, which prompted her to go into debt to finance getting a degree. The imagined future, which would include home ownership and college for their children, is no longer considered a sure thing. As the U.S. economy unraveled in 2008, so did many facets of the American dream, contributing even more to the malaise that gripped the nation.

The poor. The poor do not thrive in the best of times, but their lot is worse in the worst of times. Donations to charities go down; donations to food banks fall off; shelters fill up; government programs are scaled back; Medicaid reimbursements are lowered; charity care in hospitals is harder to come by; scholarships are fewer; and entry-level service jobs dry up. The homes of poor people are crowded with unemployed and displaced family members who move in with relatives; social service providers are stretched thin. Whether the prevailing political sentiment is to provide for the poor through trickle-down economics in which they benefit from the prosperity of a robust economy, or to provide for them directly through targeted government spending, in the aftermath of the financial collapse there was less for the poor and their plight was bleaker than it had been.

On September 13, 2011 the U.S. Census Bureau announced that in 2010 the median household income declined to $49,445, a drop of 2.3 percent from 2009. The poverty rate increased from 14.3 percent in 2009 to 15.1 percent in 2010, with 46.2 million people living in poverty; this constitutes the fourth consecutive annual increase and the largest number in the fifty-two years for which poverty estimates have been published. The number of people without health insurance coverage rose from 49.0 million in 2009 to 49.9 million in 2010, while the percentage without coverage – 16.3 percent – was not statistically different from the rate in 2009.[32] The reason for the surge in poverty is because of high unemployment due to the recession. When there is full employment, which is calculated as 6 percent or less unemployed, there is upward pressure on wages for low paying jobs, making economic circumstances better for low wage earners.

These are alarming statistics and what may be even more alarming is the context in which they exist. The United States today is a nation in which people who are not poor are troubled by unemployment, declining assets and bleak prospects. These factors may well impede their desire to lend a hand to those less fortunate. And the government, beset by deficit, debt and gridlock, seems incapable of taking meaningful steps to reverse the situation.

Marian Wright Edelman, President of the Children's Defense Fund, challenges us to take the poor into serious consideration as the nation tries to recover from the economic crisis:

> Where is our anti-poverty movement at a time when one in 50 Americans ... has *no* cash income? "Almost six million Americans receiving Food Stamps report they have no income. They described themselves as unemployed and receiving no cash and no welfare, no unemployment insurance, and no pensions, child support or disability pay. About one in 50 Americans now lives in a household with a recorded income that consists of nothing but a Food Stamp card."[33]

Ms. Edelman says that extreme child poverty, hunger and homelessness in the United States have increased since the recession took hold and she warns that, if the nation does not provide for children who live in poverty, irreparable harm will be inflicted on them and on the nation.[34]

International impact. The housing bubble, fueled by subprime mortgages, was a U.S. phenomenon in that people bought houses in the United States and mortgages were issued in the United States that subprime borrowers were unable to repay. However, the crisis that began in the United States impacted investors and corporations internationally. Because of the global nature of the financial system, institutions all over the world transact business with U.S. financial firms. As a result of the subprime crisis, financial contagion impacted counterparties to U.S. financial firms in that counterparties that lent money to troubled U.S. firms faced the possibility of not being repaid and, in turn, of not being able to meet *their* financial commitments. All but the most isolated financial institutions were likely counterparties to U.S. financial institutions, some being owed little, some being owed a great deal. Those who were owed a lot faced a liquidity crisis.

Corporations that owned large amounts of mortgage-backed securities experienced significant financial losses. Of the £30 billion in subprime assets purchased by Royal Bank of Scotland traders in 2007, the bank posted £12 billion in losses in April 2008. The Bank suffered an additional £28 billion in losses in April 2009, putting it in a position in which it did not stand a chance of surviving without government assistance.[35] Dexia, the largest bank in Belgium, was nationalized by the government there on October 11, 2011. Dexia was facing severe liquidity issues as a result of exposure to the sovereign debt crisis in the European Union, and also because of the after-effects of Dexia's ownership of U.S. issued mortgage-backed securities. Liz Alderman writes:

It was the second bailout in three years for Dexia, a lender to European and American cities that got into trouble in 2008 after a huge portfolio of subprime loans it owned went sour. Dexia received billions of euros from France and Belgium, and was the biggest European recipient of loans from the Federal Reserve's discount window at the time.[36]

Mortgage-backed securities and collateralized debt obligations were bought by investors all over the world and these individuals and groups lost money. Narvik, a remote seaport in Norway, provides a distressing example. The municipality, far from Wall Street, invested part of its annual budget in the complex securities issued during the subprime era and stands to lose at least $64 million dollars because of the market implosion.[37] Narvik's chief administrator, Trond L. Hermansen, wanted the town to invest cash on hand to increase its balance but, instead, imperiled the municipality's ability to meet its financial obligations by buying toxic products that lost most of their value. Narvik learned an expensive lesson, a lesson with no winners.

The lack of confidence triggered by the U.S. subprime crisis affected markets around the world, leading to uncertainty, which is bad for markets. To the extent that foreign banks were uncertain that U.S. firms would pay their debts, these banks were reluctant to make loans and tended to scale back, laying off workers. Foreign manufacturers were also impacted in that the loss of purchasing power by American consumers resulted in less product sales for their companies.

Conclusion. Everyone is a stakeholder who was affected by the financial crisis and subsequent recession. With the exception of short sellers and people who took advantage of bargain prices in houses or consumer goods, millions of people suffered as a result of a stagnant housing market, high unemployment, falling stock prices, and business failures. Harder to document, but just as real, people experienced a sense of malaise that the nation's problems were too big to solve and that a brighter tomorrow is not a realistic expectation. Governments experienced diminished incomes and needed to meet more human needs than ever to keep the safety net from disintegrating. An even bigger challenge to government leaders is meeting the expectation that they can put strategies in place that will indeed promote the general welfare.

Questions for Discussion

1 How was the U.S. government affected by the financial crisis?

2 How was the financial industry affected by the financial crisis?

3 How were small businesses, real estate and related industries affected by the financial crisis?

4 How were consumers affected by the financial crisis?

5 How are unemployed individuals and their families affected by the financial crisis?

6 How are poor people affected by the financial crisis?

7 Cite one group not mentioned in 1 to 6 above and state how this group is affected by the financial crisis.

8 Relate a personal insight that you have about the effects of the financial crisis on an individual or a group.

Case Study: Student Loans and Unemployed Students

Martin Adams is twenty-five years old. He works part-time, earns $12 an hour, and sleeps on the couch in his father's living room. Martin's mother is deceased and he has one sibling, an older sister who is married and lives in a different part of the country.

Martin's father works as a painter; he belongs to a union and makes a modest living. Because Martin was an outstanding student in high school and because Martin wanted to go to college, Mr. Adams agreed with his son's inclination to go to a top-tier university and pursue a major that would result in a high paying job. Martin completed college in four years, majored in finance, and ranked in the top 5 percent of his class. He has sent out more than 1,000 résumés but has landed only a handful of interviews and has had no job offers. Martin attends night school classes, studying Japanese, so that he can improve his résumé and defer payments on his student loans. Martin's loans total more than $90,000 and, even though he has been able to defer making payments, interest continues to be added to the principal. He does not foresee any way of digging out from under his pile of debt.

Even though he is more fortunate than some of his peers because he has health insurance through his father's employer and a place to live, Martin is frustrated and angry. He decides to write a nasty letter to the admissions staff at the university and vent his feelings. How could they have advised him to borrow so much money and imply that he would be able to pay it back once he had a high paying job? How could they boast about the success of their graduates when he, and some of the alums he keeps in touch with, are in such dire straits? What are they going to do to help?

1   Is Martin justified in blaming his school for the amount of debt he accumulated while attending classes there? What responsibilities does the school have for his predicament?

2   There are many students in similar situations. What, if anything, should lenders and the government do to assist them?

3   Should Martin's father have encouraged his son to go to an expensive university or should he have steered Martin to the local community college? What factors prompt your answer?

4   Do you think that Martin's situation is a temporary one caused by the recession or do you think that his long-term prospects are bleak? What leads you to your conclusion?

5   Based on his struggle with a heavy burden of student debt, how do you think Martin will approach the task of buying a house and getting a mortgage loan in the future?

Case Study: Loan Modification

Stuart and Ginny Dobson are underwater on their house and two months behind in their mortgage payments. Ginny was laid off recently but Stuart's job is secure. He is a public works employee and works for the road department. The Dobsons have a traditional $400,000 thirty-year mortgage at 6 percent; they obtained it in 2006 and their monthly payments, before taxes and insurance, come to $2,398. When Mrs. Dobson was earning $52,000 a year they were able to make payments but, since she lost her job, their financial circumstances have deteriorated. Mr. Dobson makes $39,000 and they have not been able to keep up with payments on his salary alone. Ginny is pessimistic about her chances for landing another job any time soon. Stuart and Ginny consider their options.

They paid $450,000 for the house ($50,000 down payment, plus $400,000 mortgage). The current market value of the house is less than $350,000. Since they are underwater on the house, they discuss turning the keys over to the lender and walking away. Stuart makes enough for them to rent an apartment and they will not have the hassle of calls from the bank about delinquent payments. Their credit score will be adversely affected but that seems a minor issue compared to the sacrifices they will have to make to continue paying off their mortgage. Ginny is not willing to take minimum wage work and Stuart does not want to work a second job or do odd jobs to supplement his paycheck. Being homeowners, which a few years ago had appealed to them, now seems like more trouble than it's worth.

Ginny's parents, who never before interfered in their decisions, react strongly to the idea of walking away from the house. They plead with the couple to pursue a mortgage modification program. Ginny and Stuart could be eligible for such a program, and, if they are successful, they could end up with a new mortgage at a better rate. This would translate into lower monthly payments and, by being frugal and sticking to a budget, the parents insist that the couple could manage it. Ginny will have to take any job she can get, but she is an adult and this is what adults have to do. "You'll own your home in the end; your credit score will be good; you won't let your neighbors down; and you'll make us proud."

Ginny's parents' advice propels Stuart and Ginny in one direction, and the thought of being free of the demands of home ownership pulls them in the opposite direction. They feel the weight of their decision as they try to figure out how to proceed.

1   What responsibility do Ginny and Stuart have to make mortgage payments on a house that is underwater?
2   Ginny does not want to take a minimum wage job and Stuart does not want to take on extra work to make the money needed to pay the mortgage. Would they be justified in walking away from their house because trying to keep it is too much of a hassle? Why or why not?
3   Comment on the advice Ginny's parents give the couple. Are they asking too much? Why or why not?
4   What happens to communities with large numbers of foreclosures? What obligations do individual homeowners bear to the larger community?
5   If Stuart and Ginny decide to pursue mortgage modification, in what ways should the bank be willing to work with them? List reasons that the bank should be motivated to help struggling homeowners.

Case Study: Unemployed at Fifty

People in their fifties have been hit hard by the recession. They joke that their 401K retirement accounts have become 201Ks because these accounts lost 32 percent of their value from September 2007 to March 2009. As housing prices plummeted, the equity they had in their homes diminished or disappeared altogether, leaving many underwater. For those who lost their jobs, prospects for finding comparable work, or any work, are slim, with nearly 30 percent of unemployed people over fifty-five out of work for more than a year. A poll of older people taken in 2010 showed that more than three in five fear depleting their assets more than dying.

Marilyn Lane is a fifty-year-old single mother of twin sons who are seventeen years old. The twins are strong students who have always planned on going away to an elite (and expensive) liberal arts college. Until she lost her job and saw her home equity disappear, Ms. Lane enthusiastically supported her sons' plans. They are the center of her life and she wants the very best for them. But, given the radical nature of the changes in her circumstances, Marilyn Lane has to face the fact that the boys will not get to go to the college of their choice.

Ms. Lane's father is in the early stages of Alzheimer's. Her mother is deceased and she has always been close to her dad. Her intention had been to bring father to her house in a year or two when he was no longer able to live independently. She planned to hire an aide to stay with him during the day when she was at work. Now, without an income or prospects for employment, Marilyn Lane is distressed by the realization that she will likely need to assume the role of uncompensated caregiver. The prospect of being home 24/7 with her dad depresses her because she enjoys working and being active. But that prospect is in the future. Today she has to deal with paying her bills from her meager unemployment compensation and has to summon the energy to send out more résumés.

Ms. Lane is anxious, depressed and angry. She has trouble functioning and she thinks that her life will never be back to normal. Because she is discouraged and ashamed she has stopped networking by contacting friends and acquaintances. When the boys ask her what's wrong, she brushes off their questions by attributing her mood to a "bad hair day." She is glad that her father doesn't notice how stressed she is.

1   What advice, if any, would you offer to Marilyn Lane?
2   Marilyn Lane is in a bad financial situation. How important is this aspect of a person's life? She did not cause the economic crisis, but she needs to adapt so that she and her family can function. What steps can she take?

3   What kinds of community support are available to help Ms. Lane?

4   How could her sons contribute to their mother's mental health and to support of the family?

5   What kinds of preparations can Marilyn Lane put in place to address her father's progressive decline? Is it realistic for her to take on the role of caregiver? Why or why not?

6   What initiatives should Marilyn Lane take to deal with her depression?

7   Do certain groups, such as older unemployed people, suffer more from a recession than others? What groups are you aware of who suffer disproportionately and what steps would you recommend to assist members of these groups?

3

WHAT NEEDS TO BE DONE
TO SET THINGS RIGHT?

Rebuilding the U.S. economy is the task at hand and it is a major project. Some stakeholders have bigger roles to play and others lesser roles, yet everyone is invested in this project and everyone needs to contribute in order for progress to be made and financial stability to take hold. What needs to be done so that conditions improve, with stability replacing uncertainty and prosperity rising from the ashes of the Great Recession? In answering this question we will examine the interconnected roles of government, the financial industry, the housing sector and the public, among others, in moving forward.

Government actions. The U.S. government did not cause and will not resolve the financial crisis because those directly responsible for the economic implosion were not government officials. Borrowers, lenders, builders, bankers, investors, insurers and credit rating agencies bear most of the burden of responsibility. However, lack of government oversight and faulty regulations that allowed the subprime mortgage/MBS-CDO debacle to happen facilitated the crisis. As the events of September 2008 occurred, government intervened to sort matters out and put a rescue plan in place. Going forward there is broad consensus that effective government regulations and monitoring are necessary to avoid a repeat of the financial collapse. Let us consider three stages – before, during and since 2008 – so that we can understand government's role.

Alan Greenspan was Chairman of the Federal Reserve from 1987 until 2006. In this capacity Mr. Greenspan exerted significant influence and his economic ideas were very influential. Economics is a complex and evolving discipline and Chairman Greenspan set a steady and prosperous course in guiding the economic engine through the 1990s and into the new millennium. When things were going well there was no reason to question his economic approach. In retrospect, however, Federal Reserve policies of low interest rates for borrowers accompanied by a bias against government regulation of private industry are seen as contributing to the financial crisis. Questioned in October 2008 by Representative Henry Waxman (D, CA) about whether or not during his tenure at the Fed he was concerned about the direction in which the nation was heading, Greenspan said, "I made a mistake in presuming that the self-interests of organizations, specifically banks and others, were such as that they were best capable of protecting their own shareholders and their equity in the firms."[1] In so stating, Greenspan pointed out an implicit weakness in the economic theory of Ayn Rand and Rand's conviction that the free market would self-regulate with a minimum of external government control. Greenspan's admission that he had been wrong on such a fundamental matter pointed to a need for change in government's role vis-à-vis the financial sector from hands-off to oversight and, perhaps, greater regulation.

The executive branch of the U.S. government is headed by the president who proposes policies to Congress for legislative enactment. In hindsight it is apparent that policies implemented at the direction of at least three presidents contributed to the financial maelstrom. Fannie Mae was created by Congress in 1938 to function under the auspices of the U.S. government. In 1968 President Lyndon Johnson, in an attempt to reduce the national debt, made Fannie Mae a government-sponsored enterprise (GSE). Fannie Mae then began to function as a freestanding financial institution whose policies were set by its Board of Directors and implemented by its senior management. In retrospect, this decision was a mistake in that Fannie Mae and its counterpart GSE lender Freddie Mac made big investments in private label MBS-CDOs which led to financial calamity for both firms. The fact that these financial firms retained the identity of government-sponsored entities implied that the U.S. government would provide funds to insure that they regained solvency, at a huge cost to U.S. taxpayers. (Freddie Mac was established in 1970 in order to prevent Fannie Mae from having a monopoly on the secondary mortgage market.)

On September 6, 2008, the U.S. government took over these mortgage companies because of the special circumstances constituted by their relationship to the government. If the government had been in charge, many argue, management's decisions to invest in high risk mortgages and mortgage-backed securities to earn large profits for investors would have been rejected in favor of conservative investment strategies. The managements of Fannie and Freddie are also criticized for making decisions and authorizing transactions with a view to increasing their bonuses while disregarding the financial stability of the firms.[2]

In 1993 President Bill Clinton loosened housing rules by rewriting the Community Reinvestment Act (CRA), putting added pressure on banks to lend in low-income neighborhoods.[3] The change in the CRA required banks that were insured by the FDIC to increase the number of mortgages underwritten in historically underserved areas. As a result, over the next decade home ownership would grow from 63 percent of the population to 69 percent. During the first several years after amending the CRA, most new homeowners made their mortgage payments and the nation's prosperity increased. However, the years 2005 and 2006, the height of subprime issuance, saw a major change, in which borrowers became delinquent and defaults grew dramatically. While it is laudable to advocate in behalf of home ownership for low-income citizens, it is essential that people who buy homes make payments on time. Men and women who earn low wages should not be encouraged to secure mortgages they cannot pay off. The altering of the Community Reinvestment Act followed by the proliferation of subprime mortgages, contributed to the crisis in that reasonable standards were abandoned in order to accomplish two goals:

first, satisfy the terms of the CRA and issue mortgages in low-income neighborhoods; and, second, originate large numbers of subprime mortgages which were in demand by securitizers.

President George W. Bush took office in 2000 and his overall economic approach was one of deregulation. In spite of his philosophy, President Bush sought tighter controls of Fannie Mae and Freddie Mac that would require that the enterprises have more capital on hand and be restricted from involvement in high risk transactions. However, President Bush could not get Congress to go along with him and require stringent regulation of these government-sponsored enterprises. As a result, the GSEs were able to participate in the secondary subprime market in a big way, buying large quantities of subprime mortgages from 2004 to 2006 and packaging these mortgages into securities. If the mortgages did not meet their standards, Fannie and Freddie did not guarantee them; nevertheless, they bought and securitized them, providing a market for subprime originators and a conduit to investors. The large volume of subprime mortgages and toxic MBS-CDOs on their books in 2008 brought Fannie Mae and Freddie Mac to the verge of bankruptcy.

The Securities and Exchange Commission (SEC) is an agency of the executive branch of government which is empowered to oversee the transactions of investment banks and require that their practices not imperil the economy. During the administration of President George W. Bush, Christopher Cox was the Chairman of the SEC. In this position Mr. Cox did not assume an activist role and allowed troubling practices to occur. What could Chairman Cox have done? Analysts say that the SEC should have limited the massive leveraging that set up the financial crisis and that it should have required more disclosure and transparency from financial institutions that were undercapitalized and engaged in dangerous risk taking.[4]

Blame for the financial crisis also rests with Congress. The Senate Banking Committee is powerful in that it regulates how banks function. Senator Phil Gramm (R, TX) was Chairman of this committee from 1995 until 2000 and during his tenure a significant piece of legislation was repealed. In 1999 Congress repealed the Glass Steagall Act which separated commercial banks from Wall Street investment banks. With the repeal of Glass Steagall, large commercial banks such as Citigroup were allowed to underwrite and trade mortgage-backed securities. As we have seen, to the extent that commercial banks had MBS-CDOs on their books, they were in varying degrees of jeopardy when the market for these products ceased to exist. Gramm also inserted a key provision into the 2000 Commodity Futures Modernization Act that exempted over-the-counter derivatives like credit-default swaps from regulation by the Commodity Futures Trading Commission.[5] When credit-default swaps took AIG down, and the U.S. government had to lend the firm $182 billion to keep it from failing, the public realized what an enormous mistake it was to exempt CDS from regulation.

In 2001, a new accounting standard, SFAS 140, changed the way investment banks raise money in short-term loans. (This accounting rule was issued by the Financial Accounting Standards Board, an accounting industry organization that operates under the supervision of the Securities and Exchange Commission.) Investment banks secure short-term loans in a repurchase market, commonly referred to as a *repo* market. In order to borrow short-term money, banks need to put up collateral. SFAS 140 allowed banks to remove these assets, used as collateral, from their balance sheets. Removing these assets from the balance sheet allowed the banks to present financial statements that tended to be misleading. It also allowed them to further leverage their capital. Increased leverage means increased risk and accounting regulations need to control risk, not facilitate it. An example may help to clarify this. "According to Anton Valukas, the examiner appointed to investigate the collapse of Lehman Brothers by a New York bankruptcy court, the bank used Repo 105 to flatter its balance sheet, making its financial position look healthier than it was:"[6]

Removing $50.4 billion of assets from its reported balance sheet in 2008 reduced Lehman's leverage ratio – a key measurement of a bank's reported assets compared to its reported capital – from 13.9 to 12.1.

Against the backdrop of 2008, when fears were rising about the safety of certain banks, including Lehman, that reduction in the leverage ratio may have made a crucial difference in persuading investors that it was still safe to lend to the bank.[7]

The Financial Accounting Standards Board issued a second relevant rule, FASB 157, which went into effect on November 15, 2007. FASB 157 specified how assets should be valued on balance sheets. This regulation is commonly referred to as *mark to market*. At the height of the subprime crisis, MBS-CDOs became next to impossible to sell, their market value was unknown and their value on a firm's ledger generally turned out to be significantly less than the firm had paid for the products. Consequently, the condition of major financial institutions changed quickly from sound to unsound. Whether mark to market accounting was a contributing factor to the problems of financial firms or a regulation that brought these problems to light is debatable. In other words, if banks had more flexibility in valuing MBS-CDOs closer to the amount they paid for the products rather than estimating what they could sell the products for when the market was frozen, higher statements of values might have given the impression that firms were in better shape and improved the market. As it was, large write-downs added to trauma in the financial world and put many financial firms at risk of insolvency.

Government interventions beginning in 2008. Just as it is important to understand how government policies may have contributed to the financial crisis, it is likewise necessary to review how the U.S. government intervened during the crisis to prevent economic turmoil from morphing into a situation similar to the Great Depression which began in 1929 and lasted for approximately ten years. It was apparent in the winter of 2007–2008, toward the end of George W. Bush's second term, that the nation was edging toward a recession and, in an effort to generate consumer spending, the government decided to pump more than $150 billion into the economy to encourage consumer spending. Accordingly, stimulus checks were mailed to U.S. taxpayers or direct-deposited to their accounts. Amounts as high as $600 for individuals or $1,200 for married couples were provided to 130 million people. The theory behind this program was that consumers would spend this stimulus, generating economic activity that would prevent a recession from taking hold. Unfortunately, however, the goal was not realized by the stimulus program and the economy continued to falter.

The National Bureau of Economic Research (NBER) is the entity that says when a recession starts and when a recession ends. Because of inconsistent data and the time it takes to make a conclusive statement, there is a time lag between reporting and the actual occurrence of a recession. Accordingly, the NBER dated the start of a recession in December 2007 and, on September 20, 2010, concluded that the recession ended in June 2009, making the one-and-a-half year downturn the longest recession since the Great Depression.[8] The 2010 statement from the NBER ended speculation that the United States was in so-called *double dip* recession.

In the case of the Great Recession, the U.S. economy shrunk by 6.3%, the sharpest decline in 26 years. A year later, that negative number turned positive: GDP (Gross Domestic Product) in the fourth quarter of 2009 showed 5.6% growth – the best in 6 years. For a double dip to technically occur, GDP would have to once again turn negative. Overall, economists are predicting that the U.S. recovery will slow to around 3% growth (in 2010). Nevertheless, growth is growth.[9]

Because, following the NBER statement, growth in the second quarter of 2010 was only 1.6 percent and unemployment remained stubbornly high at 9.5 percent, economic commentators generally agreed that, if the nation was in recovery, the recovery was weak, and the combination of anemic growth in GDP and high unemployment might be leading to a second recession. This fear was largely allayed by third quarter 2010 growth of 2 percent, not sufficient to undergird a robust recovery, but sufficient to make economists think that a double dip recession was unlikely. Unfortunately, one year later in the third quarter of 2011, confusion about economic conditions once again prompted speculation about the possibility of a double dip recession. A survey performed between August 10 and August 29, 2011 of more than 1,300 CFOs, CEOs/presidents, controllers and other financial leaders concerning the third quarter of 2011 revealed pessimism about the U.S. economy and concern about the fact that the United States might be in, or headed toward, another recession.[10]

Please note that the recession began at the end of 2007, largely triggered by distress in the housing market and the inability of homeowners with subprime loans to keep up with mortgage payments. Although financial firms were in trouble, their difficulties were not yet evident and the fact that contagion from subprime mortgages would soon imperil the entire economy was yet to be acknowledged.

On March 16, 2008, JPMorgan Chase took over Bear Stearns; this event was a precursor to those that would occur the following September and signaled the beginning of the financial crisis. The Federal Reserve Bank supported the JPMorgan offer for Bear Stearns and facilitated the purchase by agreeing to fund $30 billion worth of Bear Stearns' assets which, at that time, could not be sold. The reason Bear Stearns, the fifth largest investment bank in the United States, failed and had to be taken over is because two hedge funds the firm owned suffered huge losses in mortgage-backed securities, bankrupting the parent company.

On September 6, 2008, the director of the Federal Housing Finance Agency (FHFA), James B. Lockhart III, announced his decision to place two government-sponsored enterprises, Fannie Mae and Freddie Mac, into conservatorship to be run by the FHFA.[11] This decision was not a voluntary choice made by government; it was a step that was dictated by the special relationship the two firms had to the U.S. government because of their status as GSEs. Had the FHFA not taken over Fannie and Freddie and had the firms gone bankrupt, there was general agreement that a worldwide financial panic would have ensued.

On September 15, 2008 Lehman Brothers, the fourth largest investment bank in the United States, declared bankruptcy. This time the Federal Reserve Bank did not prevent the collapse. In the days leading up to the bankruptcy filing, the Fed tried to persuade one of the other U.S. investment banks (Morgan Stanley or Goldman Sachs) to take over Lehman, to no avail. In addition, Fed officials hoped that a foreign bank might be willing to purchase Lehman, but of those which showed interest, none persisted to work out a deal. As a result, Lehman, a financial services company that had existed for 158 years, ceased to function. Depending on their point of view, some people say that the government acted correctly in letting market forces play out and Lehman fail. Others argue that by not stepping in and making arrangements for Lehman to continue to operate or to be taken over, as it did for Bear Stearns, the U.S. government contributed to the economic trauma that followed.

The collapse of Lehman Brothers was not the only news on September 15, 2008. The same day Bank of America announced that it was acquiring Merrill Lynch in a $50 billion deal. The reason Merrill Lynch agreed to be taken over by Bank of America was because Merrill Lynch faced billions of dollars in losses from its exposure to subprime mortgages and also feared a run by depositors. Merrill Lynch, like Bear Stearns and Lehman, was an investment bank; unlike Lehman, it did not go bankrupt. Unlike Bear Stearns, it was taken over by a stronger financial firm, but this takeover happened without support from the Federal Reserve.

In the aftermath of the collapse of Lehman, there was considerable stress on the remaining investment banks as well as large commercial banks with exposure to MBS-CDOs. Bank of America, Citigroup, Wachovia and Washington Mutual were in precarious positions. Government leaders did not have a book of instructions to follow detailing steps to take to address the crisis in banking. They had to formulate a plan and put it into effect right away. At the time three men played pivotal roles in dealing with economic peril: Treasury Secretary, Henry Paulson, Federal Reserve Chairman, Ben Bernanke, and President of the New York Federal Reserve Bank, Timothy Geithner. Each had been appointed by President George W. Bush, and they met several times to try to grasp the extent of the crisis and figure out what to do about it. In the days following the collapse of Lehman, steps were taken to shore up the American International Group (AIG); on September 16, 2008 a loan of $85 billion was made to AIG.

On September 19 Treasury Secretary Paulson suggested a plan to buy the toxic debt and bad mortgages that were threatening the viability of banks. On September 21 the U.S. Federal Reserve allowed Goldman Sachs and Morgan Stanley to become bank holding companies so that these firms could borrow money at a favorable rate from the Fed and stabilize their finances. On September 23 Secretary Paulson and Chairman Bernanke testified on Capitol Hill to explain the crisis to Congress. From September 24 to 27 President Bush held meetings with presidential candidates John McCain (Republican) and Barack Obama (Democrat) and legislative leaders in order to work out a proposal for rescue legislation that a majority in Congress could accept. President Bush knew that at least four things had to be done at once in order to overcome the uncertainty and fear that were gripping the nation: "Guarantee all money market deposits, launch a new lending vehicle to restart the commercial paper market, temporarily ban the short sale of leading financial stocks. And purchase hundreds of billions of dollars in mortgage backed securities."[12]

As negotiations were being conducted at the highest levels, trauma continued: on September 26 Washington Mutual, a large thrift association, failed and its banking operations were taken over by JPMorgan Chase. The failure of Washington Mutual was the largest bank failure in U.S. history. On September 29, 2008, it was announced that Wachovia Bank, in danger of failing, would be taken over by Citigroup. The same day a proposed financial rescue plan was defeated in the House of Representatives because members of Congress thought it lacked sufficient detail, and the Dow Jones Industrial Average fell 777 points. On October 6, 2008, a much more detailed piece of legislation, the Troubled Asset Recovery Program (TARP), a $700 billion bill to provide the government with money to stabilize faltering banks, AIG and others, was passed.[13]

As it happened, Citigroup did not take over Wachovia; that deal was canceled and Wells Fargo Bank agreed to acquire Wachovia on October 3, 2008.

Strategizing continued.

On October 14, 2008 the U.S. government announced a series of initiatives to strengthen market stability, improve the strength of financial institutions, and enhance market liquidity. Treasury announced a voluntary Capital Purchase Program to encourage U.S. financial institutions to build capital to increase the flow of financing to U.S. businesses and consumers and to support the U.S. economy. Under the program, Treasury will purchase up to $250 billion of senior preferred shares on standardized terms.[14]

The proposal to purchase troubled assets by the government morphed into a program which was designed both to recapitalize banks so that they could continue to operate and to take toxic assets off their books. The intention was to restart the capitalistic engine so that it would resume generating economic activity. When Treasury Secretary Paulson originally came up with the idea he wanted troubled banks to sell their assets to TARP but it turned out that pricing these assets, which were MBS-CDOs, was not possible given that the market for them had all but evaporated. Instead of proceeding with this plan, the Treasury Department changed its approach and invested $115 billion in banks by purchasing preferred stock. The goal was for banks to regain fiscal equilibrium and, when that happened, the banks would buy back the preferred stock held by the government. President Bush explained the reasoning behind the change in TARP strategy:

> Designing a system to buy mortgage backed securities would consume time that we didn't have to spare. Buying shares in banks was faster and more efficient. Purchasing equity would inject capital ... directly into the under-capitalized banking system. That would reduce the risk of sudden failure and free up more money for banks to lend.[15]

In October 2010 the Treasury Department announced that more than three-quarters of the money banks owed the government had been repaid with interest.[16] TARP funds were not used by the Federal Reserve Bank to buy MBS-CDOs from Fannie Mae and Freddie Mac; the Treasury Department rescued Fannie and Freddie prior to the institution of TARP.

What happened to the remainder of the TARP funds? Eric Dash explains that $22 billion went to the Public-Private Investment Program:

> The Obama administration made the so-called Public-Private Investment Program a centerpiece of its plan to help unlock the frozen credit markets in the spring of 2009, when a lack of buyers for complex mortgage securities threatened the health of the nation's banks and put a

drag on lending. Under the program, the government provided matching funds and ultra cheap loans to investment
firms like Alliance Bernstein and Oaktree Capital that
agreed to buy mortgage securities from banks and other
financial institutions.[17]

These investment firms then sold the MBS-CDOs to investors
and, after restarting the market, actually reported a profit in
August 2010. It is estimated that $1.8 trillion worth of distressed
mortgage-related securities remain on the books of many Wall
Street investment firms, banks and insurers. In addition, the
Federal Reserve has about $69 billion of these securities in its
portfolio.[18]

The steps that were taken by the government in the fall of
2008 were reactive: a crisis was unfolding and efforts were made
to stop the bleeding. It was apparent that ad hoc measures
needed to be supplemented by new policies so that the systemic
problems that triggered the crisis would not be repeated. The
question the nation faced was: what does government need to
do going forward to promote economic stability?

Need for a process to deal with failing investment banks.
One of the main causes of the Great Depression was lack of
confidence by U.S. citizens in the solvency of the banks in
which they deposited their money. Following the stock market
crash of 1929 there was a run on banks and worried depositors
tried to withdraw their savings. In the late 1920s and early 1930s
many undercapitalized banks failed, leaving depositors with
losses. Congressional leaders realized that bank failures were
destabilizing and they sought to calm the public and strengthen
the banking system by enacting a law in 1933 which set up the
Federal Deposit Insurance Corporation (FDIC). The FDIC
established procedures for orderly closure of member banks
that it governs and it insured deposits up to $100,000; the
amount is currently $250,000.[19] The law requires supervision of
banks by the FDIC and demands that banks have enough
money on hand to meet the likely needs of borrowers in a

worst-case scenario. If it becomes apparent to banking supervisors that this is not the case, the FDIC shuts the bank down and transfers its assets and depositors to another bank. This usually happens over the course of a weekend. It is an orderly process and depositors do not lose money up to the guaranteed amount of $250,000.

At the beginning of 2008, the four largest investment banks in the United States were: Goldman Sachs, Morgan Stanley, Lehman Brothers and Bear Stearns. As noted in Chapter 1, the functions of investment banks are different from those of commercial or savings banks and these banks are not regulated by the FDIC. When Bear Stearns was in freefall in March 2008 and Lehman Brothers was on the verge of bankruptcy the following September, there was no mechanism in place to provide for an orderly closing of either of these large, complex financial institutions and no process for valuing their assets or dealing with their liabilities. This fact underscored the need for Congress to enact legislation to regulate investment banks and establish procedures for the orderly closure of systemically important failing financial institutions.

The Dodd–Frank Wall Street Reform and Consumer Protection Act. On July 21, 2010 President Barack Obama signed the Dodd–Frank Wall Street Reform and Consumer Protection Act into law. This law is more than 2,300 pages long, and it is a detailed and complex piece of legislation. The law deals with regulating the banking industry but does not address needed reforms at Fannie Mae and Freddie Mac. One aspect of the new law establishes procedures to close failing financial companies in an orderly way, without providing government loans to these companies. A motivating factor in formulating the legislation is that going forward taxpayer money may not be used to bail out failing financial firms. A major goal of the legislation is to insure, as far as possible, that there will not be a repeat of the events of September 2008.

In regard to regulation of investment banks and other financial firms, the new law sets up a financial early warning system.

A Financial Services Oversight Council (FSOC) will look for signs of trouble in the financial markets and intervene to set things right. As a last resort the Council could require big companies that are in trouble to sell off assets. The Council may require Federal Reserve oversight for large financial firms whose failure could imperil the U.S. economy. Members of the Council include the Secretary of the Treasury, the Chairman of the Federal Reserve Board and others who are capable of recognizing and correcting problems before they snowball. The U.S. regulatory structure that was in place before and during the financial crisis proved to be fragmented and ineffective; the goal of the new law is to establish effective oversight.

In order to stabilize financial markets, Dodd–Frank gives federal regulators authority to break up financial firms whose collapse would severely affect other firms. This authority will be implemented by the Federal Deposit Insurance Corporation, thus expanding the FDIC's jurisdiction beyond banks within its network.

Financial firms are now required to have so-called *Living Wills.* Citizens are encouraged to write instructions as to how they want to be medically treated if and when they are under a doctor's care or in a hospital or nursing home and not able to communicate with caregivers. By formulating a living will an individual lays out written directions to health care providers about what possible treatments are wanted or not wanted and many vexing issues are resolved because doctors know patients' wishes. In the aftermath of the financial meltdown, it became obvious that financial firms should plan for reversals and should have plans in place so that if and when a major crisis threatens the firm's existence an orderly structure for dissolving the firm is in place. In regard to the new law, financial living wills are to function as follows:

> The law requires systemic nonbank financial companies and large bank holding companies (those with at least $50 billion in assets) to submit to the FDIC, Federal Reserve,

and Financial Stability Oversight Council a plan for their rapid and orderly resolution in the event of severe financial distress or failure – otherwise known as a "Living Will." Jointly with the Federal Reserve Board, the FDIC will issue regulations on the development of "living wills" for the systemic nonbank financial companies and large bank holding companies, review the plans when submitted, and decide whether the plans are adequate. If they are not, then the FDIC and Federal Reserve Board can require changes, impose more stringent requirements or restrictions, and ultimately require the firms to sell operations or assets to reduce the risks they pose to the system.[20]

Systemically important institutions will be closely monitored by the FSOC to prevent their activities from threatening the stability of the overall economy. In order to qualify as a systemically important institution, a firm must have at least $50 billion in assets. In 2010, between thirty and forty financial firms operating in the United States had assets of $50 billion or more and were subject to supervision in the interest of economic stability.

The new law also set up a Consumer Finance Protection Bureau. The rationale for establishing this Bureau is because many consumers do not understand mortgages and this makes them vulnerable to exploitation. In addition, people are frequently confused about the fine print associated with obtaining, using and paying off credit cards, foreclosure procedures, student loans and predatory lending practices like payday loans. The mission of this new Bureau is to oversee providers of these kinds of financial services and intervene to stop practices that are not in the best interests of consumers. The Bureau has broad regulatory powers to write and enforce regulations that will prevent a repeat of the subprime mortgage debacle and it is required to address other consumer credit issues as well. The Bureau is located within the Federal Reserve System and funded by the Federal Reserve. On September 17, 2010, Dr. Elizabeth Warren, a Harvard professor, was named to head the Bureau on an interim basis. Dr. Warren was given the title, Assistant to the President, a designation that is held by senior White House advisers. She was also a special adviser to the Treasury secretary, and would report jointly to him and to the president.[21] Dr. Warren was given independent authority to make rules, hire and fire Bureau employees, determine and manage Bureau funding, give congressional testimony and make recommendations, conduct examinations and take enforcement actions.[22] Many Republican members of Congress objected to the authority given to Dr. Warren and, when it became clear that she would not be confirmed by the Senate, she resigned. In January 2012 President Obama named Richard Cordray, former Attorney General of Ohio, to head the bureau.

In regard to mortgages, the new law stipulates that in the future lenders must assure a borrower's ability to repay. Except for the first three years of a fixed rate mortgage[23] prepayment penalties can no longer be written into mortgage agreements.[24] Mortgage brokers and lenders who violate the new standards face significant penalties. On adjustable rate mortgages consumers will be told from the outset what their future payments could be. An Office of Housing Counseling will be established within the Department of Housing and Urban Development to counsel low-income citizens on home ownership and rental housing.[25]

For the most part, more than a year after its passage specific regulations emanating from the Dodd–Frank Act have not been formulated. What the Act does is identify issues, agencies, goals and exceptions and direct appropriate authorities to meet particular objectives. In reading the Act it is apparent that a regulatory structure is being built to counter the lack of regulations and oversight that allowed the subprime crisis to occur. It will be a few years before the requirements of Dodd–Frank are met by government agencies and many years before the effectiveness of the Act can be evaluated. It should be noted that the Act was passed in July 2010 when Democrats held the majority of seats in both the House of Representative and the Senate.

Elections were held in November 2010 in which Republicans gained the majority in the House of Representatives, with Democrats maintaining a smaller majority in the Senate. How does this changed situation affect Dodd–Frank? It means that citizens can expect disputes about appropriation of funding for personnel to staff agencies and write regulations and, if Republicans decide to block such appropriations, Democrats will be hard pressed to follow through on carrying out the provisions contained in Dodd–Frank.

Stress tests. In the immediate aftermath of the financial crisis a pressing issue was determining the financial solvency of the nation's banks. To address this issue representatives of the Treasury Department, the FDIC and the Federal Reserve designed and implemented stress tests for the nation's nineteen largest bank holding companies. The stress test is designed to determine whether banks have enough capital reserves to withstand an unlikely but plausible scenario which could threaten their viability, and to recommend changes, if appropriate. A stress test examines the amount of risk a bank takes on and determines whether or not the risk is excessive in the context of a fiscal worst case scenario. On May 9, 2009, detailed results of the first stress tests were released along with the reassurance that the banks which were examined had enough capital to stay in business even if possible, but unlikely, economic traumas affected them.[26] Prior to the economic crisis, neither the SEC nor the Federal Reserve had the authority to enforce capital standards; the new stress test procedures are designed to establish the needed mechanism to keep banks suitably capitalized.

Moral hazard. Moral hazard refers to the idea that people take bigger risks than warranted if they think that they will be rescued if their risks put them in jeopardy. An argument was made against the government's lending billions of dollars to banks, automakers and AIG on the grounds that these loans would encourage corporations in the future to engage in moral hazard. The argument in support of direct government intervention was that these were necessary steps to take to prevent a depression that would be as bad as or worse than the one that gripped the nation in the 1930s. A principal reason for the Dodd–Frank Act is to prevent financial institutions in the future from engaging in moral hazard. In this regard, Sheila Bair, Chairwoman of the FDIC said:

> What this (new) law will do is help limit the incentive and ability for financial institutions to take risks that put our economy at risk, it will bring market discipline back to investing, and it will give regulators the tools to contain the fallout from financial failures so that we will never have to resort to a taxpayer bailout again.[27]

Leverage and risk taking. Financial institutions are owned by stockholders and conduct business in order to make enough money to cover their expenses and pay dividends to stockholders. These companies need sufficient cash flow to pay their expenses; profits enable them to expand, attract investors, and pay bonuses to employees. Financial firms also want to improve their capital reserves, engage in research and development, and they may want to expand their product lines and grow bigger. Conservative practices are likely to result in sufficient income to meet the goals just mentioned; risky practices might result in more lucrative earnings. The amount of leverage and risk taking are major issues to be decided by the management of financial institutions. Leverage means borrowing to finance investments; leverage becomes a problem if a financial institution borrows more than it can pay back when it is losing money and its loans come due. The underlying question is, "Is it worth the risk to borrow a large amount in view of a big profit, if the deal could sour and wipe out the firm?" The Dodd–Frank Act deals with over-leveraging and risk taking by imposing tough new capital and leverage requirements that make it undesirable to get too big[28] or attempt to gain big profits by engaging in transactions that could lead to a firm's eventual liquidation. A lesson learned during the financial crisis was that banks did not manage risk, they created it. The remedy is to require banks to have a large enough capital buffer to absorb losses which may result from their transactions

Proprietary trading. Proprietary trading is done by investment banks which use their own capital to buy securities; a large amount of proprietary trading constitutes a big risk. Paul Volcker was Chairman of the Federal Reserve Bank from 1979 until 1987. Chairman Volcker's analysis of the financial crisis led him to think that one of the main causes of the collapse was the fact that banks gambled with their own money, engaging in proprietary trading. Congress took Volcker's input into consideration as it formulated the new regulations and it incorporated the so-called *Volcker Rule* into the Dodd–Frank Act. The Volcker Rule requires that

> regulators implement regulations for banks, their affiliates and holding companies, to prohibit proprietary trading, investment in and sponsorship of hedge funds and private equity funds, and to limit relationships with hedge funds and private equity funds. Nonbank financial institutions supervised by the Fed also have restrictions on proprietary trading and hedge fund and private equity investments.[29]

With the Volcker rule, not only are banks limited in regard to proprietary trading, they are no longer allowed to set up subsidiary companies to carry out trading that might create peril for the parent institution. As regulators work to formulate specific directions for financial institutions in regard to proprietary trading, Jesse Eisinger predicts that it will be difficult to draw clear lines delineating what constitutes proprietary trading and what constitutes making markets. "Defining proprietary trading is extremely difficult because it's almost impossible to distinguish from making markets.... Regulators are struggling to define this, and investment banks are pouring their lobbying muscle into educating them." (A "market maker" is a firm that stands ready to buy and sell a particular stock on a regular and continuous basis at a publicly quoted price.[30] Making markets is one of the functions investment banks perform; the legitimacy of this function is not disputed.[31])

Regulation of derivatives. Credit default swaps (CDS) are a kind of derivative; AIG was brought to the brink of bankruptcy because of the large amount of insurance the firm issued in the form of credit default swaps. Synthetic CDOs are another type of derivative in which speculators make bets on products they do not own. As noted above, in 1999 Congress specifically exempted derivatives from supervision by the CFTC, the Commodity Futures Trading Commission. This exemption proved to be a major mistake because trillions of dollars worth of these products were being traded without government oversight. (The FCIC puts the amount at $673 trillion.[32]) In the absence of oversight and transparency, no one knew who bought credit default swaps, how many were sold, who was on the line to pay off CDS, how many firms were in jeopardy and how much wealth could disappear. The lack of this critically important information led to fear and uncertainty in financial markets, driving stock prices down, and leading to paralysis, conditions that contributed to the financial crisis.

To compound a bad situation, in 2004 a number of large investment banks went to the Securities and Exchange Commission and received permission to exclude derivatives when computing their minimum net capital requirements. Net capital requirements limit the leverage available to a brokerage firm, and removing derivatives from this computation made it appear as though the firms were in a stronger financial position than was, in fact, the case. In order to set things right, the Dodd–Frank Act requires substantial reform of the derivatives market and elimination of the exemption to exclude CDS and synthethic CDOs from balance sheets. In the future derivatives will have to be cleared through a clearinghouse and traded on an exchange. The derivatives dealers who are members of a clearinghouse put capital at risk to guarantee clearinghouse obligations.[33] Members take an active role in managing the clearinghouse's risk and, based on the capital they pledge, clearinghouse members reduce or remove the threat of counterparty default. Dodd–Frank requires major derivatives dealers and major derivatives participants to register with the appropriate Commission, either the Securities and Exchange Commission or the Commodity Futures Trading Commission (SEC or CFTC). Dealers and major participants must comply with prudential standards (capital and margin requirements) and business conduct standards (anti-fraud and anti-manipulation requirements). The law further imposes additional reporting requirements to give regulators greater information about covered derivatives.[34] Whether or not this new framework will lead to transparency and prevent high risk practices that result in bankruptcy remains to be seen. In a lengthy article Louise Story questions the so-called *reforms* that are being put in place and contends that "Key committees at the clearinghouses are dominated by people from the banks that control the market. Other institutions have been blocked from entering the market, and trading information is still not freely available."[35]

Credit rating agencies. The agencies that rated MBS-CDOs as AAA did an incalculable disservice to investors and the public at large. There is no question that ratings agencies need to reach their evaluations with integrity and that the way they conducted business during the subprime era needs to be revised. The Dodd–Frank Act includes new regulations for ratings agencies but whether or not these regulations will stop future problems remains to be seen. The following provides a helpful overview:

> The Securities and Exchange Commission would inspect the biggest agencies annually and report its findings publicly. The SEC could fine agencies for failing to comply with financial regulations and deregister agencies that pile up a bad record over time. And agencies would have to disclose how they assign ratings and abide by more conflict-of-interest rules. The legislation also would make

it easier for investors to sue ratings agencies for failing to adequately investigate debt issuers. The bill would eliminate many federal requirements that banks and other investors rely on the agencies' ratings. Congress rejected a proposal to require the SEC to set up a board to randomly pick which agencies rate securities. Instead, it ordered the SEC to come up with a way to eliminate ratings-shopping.[36]

Government enforcement actions against wrongdoers. The U.S. government did not prevent the economic implosion and a primary focus of government going forward will be to address systemic weaknesses and close loopholes so that there will not be another crisis and another bailout.

In the aftermath of the crisis, it became obvious that financial firms violated some existing laws and government agencies penalized those firms which acted in contravention of regulations. The following list of government enforcement actions provides an overview of enforcement actions taken to punish misconduct:

Federal efforts. The Department of Justice (DOJ) and the Securities and Exchange Commission (SEC) are pursuing a range of financial fraud cases. The DOJ has brought 500 mortgage fraud cases and has 2,700 investigations pending.[37]

The SEC has brought 664 enforcement actions and ordered wrongdoers to disgorge $2.09 billion. Some of these cases are against the major financial institutions, including Citigroup, JPMorgan Chase, Bank of America, Countrywide, Merrill Lynch, UBS and others.[38]

In June 2009, the SEC charged Angelo Mozilo, the former CEO of Countrywide Financial, and two other former executives with fraud for allegedly misleading investors about the significant credit risks in the company. (On October 15, 2010, Angelo Mozilo agreed to pay $67.5 million to settle with the SEC; his co-defendants, David Sambol and Eric Sieracki, paid penalties of $5.2 million and $100,000, respectively.)[39]

The SEC entered into a series of landmark settlements with six large broker-dealer firms for allegedly misrepresenting to their customers the risks associated with auction rate securities (ARS).[40]

In November 2009, the Financial Fraud Enforcement Task Force was created to bring together numerous federal agencies to investigate financial fraud.[41]

The SEC brought a case against Goldman Sachs for misleading investors in a subprime mortgage product (Abacus) just as the U.S. housing market was starting to collapse. In order to settle the suit Goldman Sachs agreed to pay a $550 million penalty and reform its business practices.[42] Goldman Sachs did not affirm or deny the allegation.

On November 1, 2010, the SEC opened an investigation of JPMorgan Chase's involvement in a CDO called *Squared*. A hedge fund, Magnetar Capital, was involved in the selection of some of the underlying assets for the $1.1 billion CDO, and the hedge fund's role might have been to bet against the housing market. If this in fact is the case, the SEC may prosecute JPMorgan Chase for not disclosing Magnetar's involvement.[43]

On February 11, 2011, the SEC accused three former top IndyMac executives (the CEO and two chief financial officers) of filing false and misleading documents with regulators. These filings led shareholders to believe that the bank could rebound from months of hefty losses. As it turned out, the bank did not rebound and was forced to shut down in July 2008, causing the second-largest bank failure to date. Investors were deceived and wiped out.[44]

On April 13, 2011, the United States Senate issued a report entitled *Wall Street and the Financial Crisis: Anatomy of a Financial Collapse* in which the actions of Goldman Sachs in assembling specific CDOs were referred to both the Justice Department and the SEC for scrutiny. The report questioned whether or not four CDOs, Abacus, Timberwolf, Anderson and Hudson, which were assembled by Goldman Sachs, violated securities law based on the possibility that Goldman Sachs misled clients about the worth of these securities. The Senate panel lay much of the blame for the financial crisis on Wall Street banks which, the panel asserted, enticed clients to buy risky bond deals. At this writing, the matter is pending, although, as noted above, Goldman Sachs settled with the SEC in respect to Abacus without affirming or denying the allegation.

Writing in the *New York Times* on March 17, 2011, Eric Dash describes an as yet undecided case brought by the FDIC against executives at Washington Mutual:

> The Federal Deposit Insurance Corporation sued the former chief executive of Washington Mutual and two of his top lieutenants, accusing them of reckless lending before the 2008 collapse of what was the nation's largest savings bank.
>
> The civil lawsuit, seeking to recover $900 million, is the first against a major bank chief executive by the regulator and follows escalating public pressure to hold bankers accountable for actions leading up to the financial crisis.
>
> Kerry K. Killinger, Washington Mutual's longtime chief executive, led the bank on a "lending spree" knowing that the housing market was in a bubble and failed to put in place the proper risk management systems and internal controls, according to a complaint filed on Thursday in federal court in Seattle.
>
> David C. Schneider, WaMu's president of home lending, and Stephen J. Rotella, its chief operation officer, were also accused of negligence for their roles in developing and leading the bank's aggressive growth strategy.
>
> "They focused on short-term gains to increase their own compensation, with reckless disregard for WaMu's long-term safety and soundness," the agency said in the sixty-three-page complaint. "The F.D.I.C. brings this complaint to hold these highly paid senior executives, who were chiefly responsible for WaMu's higher-risk home lending program, accountable for the resulting losses."[45]

On April 5, 2011, Wells Fargo & Company agreed to pay $11 million to settle SEC claims that Wachovia Corporation units pumped up the prices of mortgage-backed collateralized debt obligations, even as the housing market began to collapse. The background to this case is that equity tranches in two CDOs, Grand Avenue and Longshore 3, were valued by Wachovia at 52.7 cents on the dollar, having lost worth as the market imploded in 2007. Wachovia overvalued these securities by more than 70 percent when they sold them to the Zuni Indian tribe and an individual investor. "Wachovia caused significant losses to the Zuni Indians and other investors by violating basic investor protection rules – don't charge secret excessive markups, and don't use stale prices when telling buyers that assets are priced at fair market value," SEC Enforcement Division Director Robert Khuzami said.[46]

On April 19, 2011, the former Chairman of one of the largest mortgage firms that collapsed in the U.S. housing market crash, Lee Farkas of Taylor, Bean & Whitaker Mortgage Corporation, was found guilty of fraud in federal court in Alexandria, Virginia. A jury deliberated for two days before returning the verdict in a case in which the fraud resulted in $1.9 billion in losses as well as the implosion of Colonial Bank. This verdict represents one of the few instances in which individuals responsible for the financial collapse were convicted for criminal actions.[47]

On July 20, 2011, the Federal Reserve Bank announced the largest fine it ever imposed, $85 million, to be paid by Wells Fargo & Company to settle civil charges that it falsified loan documents and pushed borrowers toward subprime mortgages with higher interest rates than the lower rates for which those borrowers qualified. Between 3,700 and 10,000 bank customers could be compensated under the settlement.[48]

On July 20, 2011 the Federal Trade Commission announced a settlement of $108 million to be paid by Countrywide Financial to more than 450,000 borrowers who were overcharged for default-related services such as home maintenance on foreclosed properties. "Some troubled borrowers were charged $300 by Countrywide to mow their lawns, for example."[49] Other borrowers incurred added fees and escrow charges without notice, or were given incorrect figures about how much they owed on their mortgages.

State efforts. The various state attorney generals have initiated numerous enforcement actions. Some examples, cited at hearings of the Financial Crisis Inquiry Commission, include:

The Illinois Attorney General sued Wells Fargo for discriminatory and deceptive mortgage lending practices alleging that the lender steered African-American and Latino homeowners into high-cost subprime mortgage loans.

The Colorado Attorney General obtained criminal convictions against the ringleader of a multimillion dollar mortgage fraud operation involving nearly three dozen real estate transactions. The ringleader and others fraudulently obtained $10.9 million in mortgages to buy thirty-four properties in Denver and surrounding counties.

The Iowa Attorney General took the lead in a global settlement with Countrywide in behalf of 400,000 borrowers.

The Massachusetts Attorney General and Goldman Sachs reached a settlement regarding subprime lending issues. Goldman agreed to provide approximately $50 million in relief to homeowners and pay an additional $10 million to the state.

The California Attorney General announced a landmark $1.4 billion settlement with three Wells Fargo affiliates to pay back investors, charities and small businesses that purchased auction-rate securities based on misleading advice.

The New Jersey Attorney General announced that they obtained $148 million in recoveries and judgments in behalf of the state in 2009 through debt recovery, consumer fraud, environmental and other litigation.

The Pennsylvania Attorney General announced the filing of a consumer protection lawsuit against nine individuals who allegedly were involved in a wide-reaching mortgage and investment "ponzi" scheme that collapsed in the fall of 2007, resulting in nearly $40 million in losses for more than 700 consumers throughout south central and eastern Pennsylvania.

The Ohio Attorney General sued national rating agencies for false and misleading ratings. The lawsuit against Standard & Poor's, Moody's and Fitch, three national agencies that are responsible for providing accurate credit ratings of investments, charged the rating agencies with wreaking havoc on U.S. financial markets by providing unjustified and inflated ratings of mortgage-backed securities in exchange for lucrative fees from securities issuers.

The Missouri Attorney General went after mortgage fraud targeting those facing foreclosure or other financial woes. Operation Stealing Home targets individuals and businesses that defrauded consumers through refinancing, advance fee and foreclosure consulting scams.

The North Carolina Attorney General stopped a foreclosure rescue operation from collecting any money from consumers for foreclosure assistance or loan modifications. Scammers would entice struggling homeowners with false promises of lower mortgage payments and then do little or nothing to help them.

The Alabama Attorney General announced $4.9 million in refunds to 8,907 Alabama consumers from Ameriquest Mortgage Company and its related companies, as part of a $325 million national settlement of a predatory lending lawsuit against the company.[50]

The attorney generals of all fifty states announced on October 13, 2010 that they were joining to probe mortgage loan servicers who are accused of submitting false affidavits;[51] false affidavits nullify foreclosure proceedings and add to traumas in the housing and banking sectors.

On December 21, 2010, Attorney General Andrew M. Cuomo filed a lawsuit against Ernst & Young LLP, charging the accounting firm with helping Lehman Brothers engage in an accounting fraud involving the surreptitious removal of tens of billions of dollars of fixed income securities from Lehman's balance sheet in order to deceive the public about Lehman's true liquidity condition. The Attorney General's lawsuit claimed that for more than seven years leading up to Lehman's bankruptcy filing in

September 2008, Lehman had engaged in Repo 105 transactions, explicitly approved by the accounting firm. The transaction's purpose was to temporarily park highly liquid, fixed-income securities with European banks for the sole purpose of reducing Lehman's financial statement leverage, an important financial metric for investors, stock analysts, lenders and others interested in Lehman. A major goal of the lawsuit is to recover the fees collected by Ernst & Young when it engaged in actions that the Attorney General concluded violated the law.[52]

The Supreme Judicial Court of Massachusetts ruled on January 7, 2011 that U.S. Bancorp and Wells Fargo erred when they seized two properties in 2007. The Court voided the foreclosures and returned the properties to the homeowners who had been foreclosed upon. Because foreclosures are supposed to occur only when lenders can prove they own the mortgage underlying the property, and because the banks did not do this in their foreclosure filings, the foreclosures were reversed.[53]

Since its creation in September 2007, Miami-Dade County Mayor Alvarez's Mortgage Fraud Task Force has made more than 150 arrests. The task force is made up of local, state and federal law enforcement officials, prosecutors, business leaders, elected officials and other public servants in a comprehensive approach to fight mortgage crime in South Florida.[54]

In addition to the government enforcement actions cited above, investors filed 392 prospective securities class-action lawsuits in 2008 and 2009 for $1.4 trillion in damages. Financial companies were targeted in half of the cases.[55]

Actions of the Federal Reserve Bank. The Federal Reserve Bank of the United States was founded by Congress in 1913 and functions as the nation's central bank. In this capacity its responsibilities include:

1   conducting the nation's monetary policy by influencing the monetary and credit conditions in the economy in pursuit of maximum employment, stable prices, and moderate long-term interest rates;

2   supervising and regulating banking institutions to ensure
    the safety and soundness of the nation's banking and
    financial system and to protect the credit rights of con-
    sumers;
3   maintaining the stability of the financial system and con-
    taining systemic risk that may arise in financial markets;
4   providing financial services to depository institutions, the
    U.S. government, and foreign official institutions, includ-
    ing playing a major role in operating the nation's pay-
    ments system.[56]

The twelfth postwar recession started in December 2007; it was a
deeper recession than those that came before it, distinguished by
threats of deflation and persistent high unemployment. Initially,
in trying to steer the economy out of recession and subsequently
responding to the financial crisis, the Federal Reserve lowered
interest rates as far as they could go to encourage borrowing and
stimulate spending. Subsequently, the Fed became the lender of
last resort in order to prevent the recession from morphing into
a depression. In 2007 the Fed held approximately $900 billion
worth of assets consisting almost entirely of U.S. government
debt. By the summer of 2009, the Fed's balance sheet was approximately $2.3 trillion, the overwhelming majority of which con-
sisted of assets accumulated during the crisis. Many assets were of
poor quality, particularly those derived from home mortgages,
credit card debt and auto loans.[57] Ben Bernanke, the Chairman
of the Federal Reserve, is a scholar of the depression of the 1930s
and his concern was to prevent a repeat of that economic disaster. Accordingly, Bernanke directed monetary policy with the
goal of avoiding deflation because in deflationary situations both
assets and dollars lose value, there is lack of growth and unemployment rises. In order to recover, the U.S. economy needs to
produce growth and employment; modest inflation of 1.7 to
2 percent is desirable.

   In implementing its strategy to counter deflationary trends
and encourage growth, the Federal Reserve employed three

tactics: it acted as lender of last resort, providing liquidity to financial institutions and corporations; it created special facilities to purchase short-term debt; and it became the investor of last resort by buying various types of asset-backed securities and taking these off the balance sheets of troubled firms.[58]

Beginning in March of 2008 the Federal Reserve acquired toxic assets from Bear Stearns and assisted JPMorgan in acquiring the firm; the following September the Fed bought CDS from AIG. Beginning in March 2008 the Fed allowed banks to obtain loans from its discount window for up to ninety days by establishing the Term Auction Facility (TAF) which targeted depository institutions and provided access to cash to them for longer than overnight. In the following months the Fed established the Primary Dealer Credit Facility (PDCF) to make overnight loans to primary dealers in exchange for illiquid securities. (As of May 31, 2011, there were twenty primary dealer banks; primary dealers are very important to the economy because these banks work with the Fed to carry our monetary policy and, in order to fulfill these function, they need to be solvent.[59])

Next came the Term Asset-backed Securities Loan Facility (TALF) in which the Fed committed $1 trillion to private securitization of credit card debt and auto loans; the Term Auction Fund (TAF); the Commercial Paper Funding Facility (CPFF); the Money Market Investor Funding Facility (MMIFF); the Term Securities Lending Facility (TSLF) and the Asset-Backed Commercial Paper Money Market Mutual Fund Liquidity Facility (AMLF). These various programs enabled financial firms to borrow from the Fed or to swap illiquid assets for government debt. At no time did the Fed accept junk bonds in exchange for loans or government bonds and economists generally agree that the actions of the Fed resulted in short-term liquidity in the financial market by the end of 2008. (Having fulfilled their missions, these temporary programs have been closed. Detailed synopses of the purpose, scope and dynamics of each program are available at www.ny.frb.org/markets/funding_archive/index.html.)

The Fed receives payments on the assets it acquired through its various initiatives; what to do with these payments was an issue for the Federal Open Market Committee at its meeting on August 10, 2010. The Fed, seeking to maintain stability and liquidity in the financial markets, announced a policy of "reinvesting principal payments from agency debt and agency mortgage-backed securities in longer-term Treasury securities. The Committee will continue to roll over the Federal Reserve's holdings of Treasury securities as they mature."[60] (The term "agency" refers to the GSEs, Fannie and Freddie.) By keeping the Fed's portfolio of troubled assets at a stable amount, the central bank was attempting to keep as much money as possible in circulation in the hope of stimulating the economy. In addition, by keeping interest rates at record lows, the Fed is trying to make it less attractive to save and cheaper to borrow so that businesses will borrow and spend money to produce growth, thus stimulating the economy.

Beginning in late 2008 and continuing until 2010 the Fed initiated two programs of Quantitative Easing (QE1 and QE2) in which the central bank intervened in markets for long-term debt in the same way that it did for short-term debt, buying hundreds of billions of dollars worth of government debt and injecting massive amounts of liquidity into the market. This tactic was adopted in order to drive the price of bonds up so that yields would go down. The Fed did this so that banks would put their money to work making loans rather than merely profiting from the interest on the bonds they held. If Treasury bonds did not bring much return, the thinking went, banks would lend money to small businesses, home buyers and other investors and this would generate economic activity and growth. The borrower's role in this scenario is to use the cash in ways that stimulate the economy. Explaining the rationale for the program, the Fed's Vice Chairwoman Janet Yellen said:

It will not be a panacea, but I believe it will be effective in fostering maximum employment and price stability. In

November (2010), the Fed started buying $75 billion a month in Treasury securities. The goal is to lower long-term interest rates and therefore ease borrowing by businesses and households, lift stock prices and stimulate exports by making the dollar somewhat cheaper relative to foreign currencies. The Fed is also trying to forestall deflation and the threat of a double-dip recession.[61]

In the months following the 2008 economic tsunami and its aftermath, officials of the Federal Reserve worked closely with the Treasury Department and the SEC to resolve the crisis. None of the people involved in working through these dark days was satisfied with the actions that were taken to avert a catastrophe and all of them agree that fundamental systemic changes are needed to set things right. U.S. citizens criticized the government for enabling moral hazard by bailing out financial institutions instead of allowing them to fail and for adding to the national debt by the outlays of government spending, TARP funding, the stimulus initiatives and the conservatorships of Fannie and Freddie. Citizens were confused about how a web of events that ensnared Wall Street came to strangle Main Street. Government officials, thinking themselves caught between bailing out the banks and watching the world sink, chose the former, sadly aware of how repugnant their actions were.[62] Financial institutions survived because they were able to privatize profits while socializing losses, a reality that the U.S. electorate resented and would be slow to forget.[63]

Going forward the Fed is faced with an enormous challenge. It needs to take steps that will improve consumer confidence and spending, reduce unemployment, lead to improvement in the housing sector and retail sales, while keeping inflation between 1.7 and 2 percent. Simultaneously, the Fed needs to monitor the federal deficit and promote fiscal discipline and lower deficits. During the financial crisis of 2008 the Fed served as the lender of last resort in order to stabilize the banking system; it pumped a massive dose of liquidity into the system.

Two years later the hoped-for recovery has not happened and the United States is dealing with a challenging economy in which sluggish growth and high unemployment generate unease. The interplay of economic conditions and actions is complex; cause and effect are not simple to predict. In this context, the Fed has decided to keep interest rates at historic lows for the foreseeable future. It also needs to determine what to do with the more than $1.25 trillion in mortgages and mortgage-backed securities that it holds. Is further stimulus needed and, if so, what role should the Fed play in providing this stimulus? The answers to these questions are obscure. Getting them right will play a large part in determining whether the U.S. economy recovers or continues to flounder.

Chairman Bernanke spoke at a symposium, sponsored by the Federal Reserve Bank of Kansas City, in Jackson Hole, Wyoming on August 27, 2010 about the state of the economy and how he interpreted the economic climate. Bernanke admitted that there were mixed signals and he noted that the pace of recovery in output and employment had slowed, in part because of slower than expected growth in consumer spending, as well as continued weakness in residential and nonresidential construction, but Bernanke cautioned that these occurrences did not necessarily suggest a double dip recession or deflation. On a positive note, the Chairman said that banks were beginning to pick up the pace of lending to small businesses and that "Stronger household finances, rising incomes, and some easing of credit conditions will provide the basis for more-rapid growth in household spending" in 2011.[64] When he spoke at Jackson Hole in 2011 Bernanke said that it was clear that recovery from the crisis was much less robust than the Fed had wanted and that officials were concerned about how to deal with high unemployment. He said that his hopes for long-term growth lay at the feet of the president and Congress,[65] a troubling idea in view of the partisanship and gridlock that gripped the nation's capital. Bernanke did pledge to continue to work with others at the Federal Reserve to come up with tactics to address the faltering economy and try to move the nation in the right direction.

Chairman Bernanke is a highly respected economist who was a professor at Princeton University and author of economic textbooks before entering government service. As an economist Chairman Bernanke fits the profile of a scholar who equivocates by saying "On the one hand..." and countering that position by contending, "On the other hand..." Therefore, it is important to bear in mind that, even though the Chairman of the Federal Reserve Bank is an exceptional scholar as well as an insider in the formulation of economic policy, he is not capable of predicting if or when a sustained recovery will take hold, nor is he able to design a plan that will accomplish the goal of economic prosperity.

Fannie Mae and Freddie Mac. These corporations are government-sponsored enterprises that faced bankruptcy in September 2008. Because of their connection to the government, the United States assumed 79.9 percent control of the two companies. Together, Fannie Mae and Freddie Mac own or guarantee roughly half of the nation's $11 trillion home mortgage market. In 2009, after the government takeover, "more than 9 in 10 new mortgages carried a government guarantee."[66] "The new overhaul of financial regulation (Dodd–Frank) did nothing to address the companies, even though they played a central role in inflating the housing bubble."[67] The Obama administration held a conference on the future of housing on August 17, 2010 to seek advice about reforming the rules governing mortgage finance. The goal was to deliver a proposal to Congress by January 2011[68] but that date has passed without action being taken. It is not possible to overstate the importance of resolving the issues attendant to Fannie Mae and Freddie Mac in the aftermath of the mortgage meltdown.

Gretchen Morgenson states that attaining remedies for the housing system is a difficult task that should entail an honest dialogue about the role the federal government should play in housing. Does promoting home ownership through tax policy and other federal efforts remain a good idea, given the economic disaster that occurred? The fact that management of Fannie and Freddie were relentless in pursuit of profits during the subprime boom years underscores how agents of a government-backed operation contributed significantly to the mess the government ultimately had to clean up using tax dollars.[69] This systemic flaw needs to be addressed and fixed but the fact that it was not even taken up by the Dodd–Frank Act suggests how politically sensitive this matter is.

In August 2010 both Fannie and Freddie disclosed that they had operating losses during the second quarter of 2010 and asked the federal government for additional money: "Fannie Mae requested $1.5 billion after posting a loss of $3.13 billion"; "Freddie Mac said it lost $6 billion ... in the quarter," and requested $1.8 billion in additional federal aid.[70]

William Poole, a past president of the Federal Reserve Bank of St. Louis, described how their backing by the government paved the way for Fannie and Freddie to take risks without concern about the ultimate consequences of their actions:

> Fannie and Freddie had a license to print money. They could borrow at an interest rate only a bit over the Treasury rate and then accumulate large portfolios of mortgages and mortgage-backed securities earning the market rate. What a deal – borrow at the low rate, invest at a higher one, hold little capital and let the federal government bear the risk! Investors enjoyed high returns, and management enjoyed high salaries. Incidentally, politicians also got a steady flow of campaign contributions from the companies' executives.
>
> Fannie and Freddie's risky policies led to their near collapse; in September 2008, the federal government brought them under federal conservatorship. Fannie and Freddie have cost taxpayers about $150 billion so far.[71]

Assuming that these GSEs continue in existence, going forward government policy needs to set strict capital requirements for

Fannie Mae and Freddie Mac and needs to require more vigilance in lending requirements. It is good for working Americans to buy homes, but prospective homeowners need to be able to make mortgage payments. It is good for corporations to make money, but not by engaging in risks that threaten their very existence. Figures central to the mortgage market like Fannie and Freddie cannot be allowed to act in contravention of these basic principles.

Auto industry. In the summer of 2010 General Motors was a different company than it had been before its rescue by the government and GM was preparing to start paying back its loan so that it could regain its footing as General Motors instead of operating under the disparaging moniker by which it had become known, Government Motors. With this goal in mind, GM prepared for an initial public offering, hoping to sell shares in the reorganized company and to raise sufficient cash from the sale to repay its debt to the U.S. government. The IPO occurred on November 18, 2010, at which time $23.1 billion was raised by selling equity shares in the new GM and raising sufficient capital to partially repay the debt to the government, reducing the U.S. share in General Motors from 61 percent to 26 percent.[72]

Part of GM's strategy to increase its market share and appeal to investors was to buy AmeriCredit, a subprime lender. The company's argument in favor of this purchase was that AmeriCredit would make loans to cash-strapped car buyers and then business would pick up, increasing GM sales and making the company profitable. Does it make sense for an automaker to make high risk car loans in order to improve its market share and profits? Those who answered in the negative said that GM should concentrate on making money from manufacturing and selling automobiles and should not count on profits coming from credit markets, given the risks involved.[73] There were also objections to the government spending $50 billion of taxpayer money to shore up a company and allowing that company to resume the kinds of credit practices that led to the economic crisis.[74]

The U.S. government lent Chrysler $12.5 billion to help the automaker avoid collapse. As the automaker reorganized and became solvent, it repaid most of the government bailout money. In 2009 Fiat, an Italian auto company, took over Chrysler's operations and continued to produce vehicles in the United States, thus preventing the loss of significant numbers of jobs. Since the bailout, $11.2 billion has been repaid and the Treasury Department announced on July 21, 2011 that the remaining $1.3 billion likely would not be recovered. The reason the government's loan to Chrysler was settled in July 2011 was because the government decided to sell its remaining stake in Chrysler to Fiat for $500 million rather than holding out to see if the stake could garner a better price at a later date. Commenting on the loan and repayment, Tim Massad, Treasury assistant secretary for financial stability, said: "The fact that the company has done so well – that they were able to go out and raise private capital to repay us the loan so quickly, is really the big story."[75] Chrysler employs 56,000 people and has added 9,000 jobs since the bailout,[76] an accomplishment that adds to the viability of the auto sector in the United States.

Government spending/stimulus. There are many economic theories. One influential theory is that government spending provides a means for bringing a nation out of a recession and restoring prosperity. This theory was developed by John Maynard Keynes and is central to Keynesian economics. In brief, the thinking is that a government should pump money into an economy in recession and let citizens spend the money, creating demand for goods and jobs, and this demand will keep growing and eventually turn things around. It is not an exact science; there are no formulas for how much government money is needed to stimulate the various sectors of the economy and get them moving at a desirable pace. There is no timeline that answers the question, "How long will it take to turn things around?" Uncertainties notwithstanding, the Keynesian approach to working through a recession is a popular one and it was adopted in 2008 by the Bush administration and continued in the succeeding year by the Obama administration. Accordingly, two government stimulus programs were carried out.

As mentioned above, on February 13, 2008, President Bush signed the Economic Stimulus Act into law. There were indications that the country was in the early stages of a recession and the intention was to generate sufficient economic activity to spur a recovery. To this end $152 billion dollars were sent by the Internal Revenue Service to taxpayers in the hope that citizens would spend their stimulus checks and this spending would generate demand for goods and services. Regrettably, the desired outcome was not realized and the economy continued to decline.

On February 17, 2009 President Obama signed a second stimulus plan, the American Recovery and Reinvestment Act (ARRA), into law. This Act had two goals: to create jobs and save existing jobs and to spur economic activity. The federal government provided $787 billion to achieve these results. A major emphasis of the spending was on infrastructure projects that were wholly or partially funded by the federal government and carried out under the auspices of state and local governments. Tax relief for low and middle class workers was also included in the legislation. For 2009 and 2010, ARRA created the Making Work Pay credit of up to $800 for joint filers and $400 for other filers. The credit does not apply to joint filers with adjusted gross incomes exceeding $150,000 or for individual filers with adjusted gross incomes exceeding $75,000. Unlike the 2008 recovery rebate, which was distributed via checks mailed to taxpayers, the new credit took effect through a reduction in income tax withholding. The act also provided a one-time payment of $250 to many people on fixed incomes, such as Social Security recipients and disabled veterans. Similarly, it provided a one-time refundable tax credit of $250 to certain government retirees who were not eligible for Social Security benefits.[77] Details of ARRA spending are available at recovery.gov.

Both these stimulus programs provided benefits to the economy; however, economists were troubled by the fragile nature of the recovery and agreed that ARRA did not achieve the desired effects. The program added to the national debt and constituted deficit spending. Proponents of the Keynesian approach to ending a recession oppose economists who argue against deficit spending and question the rationality of adding to the deficit and the debt to implement programs with unpredictable outcomes. In view of the fact that neither of the stimulus programs resulted in the desired turnaround, detractors suggest that it does not make sense to try more of the same. There are arguments over whether or not to institute another government stimulus program to get the economy moving. In the fall of 2011 President Obama proposed to Congress that it enact a $447 billion plan called the American Jobs Act.[78] Among other things, this plan aimed to put people to work on infrastructure projects, in updating public schools, and in rebuilding communities. The president proposed that the plan be funded by a tax increase on the wealthiest Americans, those earning in excess of $1 million a year. Although the pace of recovery was slow and government stimulus was one of the options to pick up the pace, a third stimulus was not enacted because of the deep political divide in the country and a sense that the new idea would not be more beneficial than the American Recovery and Reinvestment Act of 2009. As reported in the *Washington Post*:

> Obama's plan died at the hands of Senate Republicans on Tuesday, (October 11, 2011) even though the president had been campaigning for it across the country for weeks. The $447 billion plan died on a 50–49 tally in the 100-member Senate, falling well short of the 60 votes needed to crack a filibuster by Republicans opposed to its stimulus-style spending and tax surcharge for the very wealthy.[79]

Two government programs designed to stimulate the economy produced temporary beneficial results. The first was aimed at encouraging sales of houses and it ran from January 1, 2009 to April 30, 2010. First-time home buyers, defined as people who had not owned a home in three years, received an $8,000 tax credit if they purchased a home. This program was successful in that it resulted in 1.8 million home sales. The second program was known as *Cash for Clunkers.* People who owned old, gas-guzzling cars received a tax credit for turning these cars in to dealers and buying new, fuel-efficient vehicles. The number of people who took advantage of this program was approximately 677,000 and their tax credit per vehicle ranged from $3,500 to $4,500. The program ran from July 24, 2009 until August 24, 2009. The downside of these two programs was that demand for housing and new cars dropped after the programs ended, thus slowing the pace of the weak recovery.

On December 17, 2010 President Obama signed into law a compromise bill (H.R. 4835 Tax Bill) which extended the tax cuts put in place by President Bush and Congress in 2001. While this bill was primarily a two-year extension of the Bush tax cuts, it included two features that were seen as providing stimulus. The first feature was a 2 percent decrease in the pay-roll tax paid by workers to fund Social Security. For a person whose salary is $50,000 a year, this constitutes $1,000 in addi-tional take-home pay and the hope was that this *extra* money would be spent to stimulate the economy. According to Jim Kuhnhenn, the bill "represents the most money that President Obama was likely to have been able to dedicate over the next year to the slowly recovering economy."[80] The second stimulus incorporated into the tax bill was an extension of benefits to the unemployed for an additional thirteen months. At a cost of $858 billion over two years, the tax bill added to the federal def-icit and, for this reason, generated criticism. On the other hand, those who favored passage of the bill argued that the gov-ernment needed to continue to take measures to improve the economy and that, once unemployment decreases and eco-nomic growth increases, the emphasis can shift to reducing the deficit.

Government assistance to unemployed. More than eight million jobs were lost during the recession. In the first nine months of 2008 unemployment became a concern as the unemployment rate grew from 5 percent to 6.2 percent. Following the financial crisis of September 2008, the number grew to 7.4 percent in December 2008, and continued to rise throughout 2009, hitting a high of 10.1 percent in October 2009.[81] In the following months unemployment declined slightly from this high but still remained close to 9 percent. This figure is deceptive in that it does not include long-term unemployed people who have stopped looking for work and workers who want full-time employment but have settled for part-time positions. The problems faced by unemployed people are serious and troubling. In the summer of 2010 it was estimated that there were five people looking for work for each job opening.[82] The way the government helps the unemployed is by job creation programs and providing unemployment compensation. By action of Congress in November 2009, unemployment benefits were extended to ninety-nine weeks, but in 2010 many people had been unemployed longer than ninety-nine weeks and their benefits had run out. As noted above, on December 17, 2010, unemployment benefits were extended for thirteen months in the hope that a sustained economic turnaround would occur in 2011.

The ultimate answer to the needs of the unemployed is for the economy to create 300,000 jobs a month to replace those that were lost during the economic crisis and to provide work for those entering the workforce. It turns out that accomplishing this objective is far from easy. In order for the private sector to generate new jobs, the gross national product needs to grow between 3 percent and 4 percent. In the second quarter of 2010, the increase was 1.6 percent; in the third quarter of 2010, the increase was 2 percent. These figures fall below the output needed to stimulate sufficient job creation. In January 2011, Federal Reserve Chairman Ben Bernanke expressed optimism that the economy would strengthen, but warned that it would take up to five years for unemployment, then at 9.4 percent, to drop to a historically normal level of around 6 percent.[83] Mr. Bernanke was much less sanguine when he spoke about unemployment in September 2011:

> "This unemployment situation we have, the jobs situation, is really a national crisis," he said. "We've had now close to 10 percent unemployment for a number of years. Of the people who are unemployed, about 45 percent have been unemployed for six months or more."
>
> "This is unheard of," he said. "This has never happened in the post-war period in the United States. Those folks who have been out of work for six months or a year or two years – obviously they are losing the skills they had, their connections, their attachment to the labor force. Policies that could help them find work, train for work and retain their skills and to contribute to a productive society ... that's another area where other parts of the government could contribute to help the economy recover."[84]

Financial institutions. Because of new financial regulations, some of the ways investment banks have made large profits such as by trading, establishing hedge funds and dealing in equity markets must be overhauled.[85] Market conditions, including declining revenue from arranging mergers, initial public offerings and bond deals, are negatively impacting the bottom line of investment banks. Highly paid personnel whose skill sets focus on these areas must now function in different ways, and financial firms need to undergo reorganization in order to employ these workers in a manner consistent with the new regulations and the new economic climate.

In the aftermath of the financial crisis the securitizing of mortgages and marketing of MBS-CDOs by investment banks stopped. Nevertheless, it remains possible for the market in mortgage-backed securities to restart at some future time. If this market starts up again, what regulations should government put in place to keep investment banks from repeating the mistakes of the past? New rules have been proposed by the Securities and Exchange Commission and, responding to these proposed rules, investment banks argue that they should not be required to evaluate the credit quality of the mortgages they package and sell. They reason that they lack the expertise to do this. Pointing out that during the heyday of mortgage-backed securities, "institutional investors were in search for higher yielding securities and took the AAA ratings as a reason not to study the security carefully,"[86] bankers suggested that responsibility for evaluating investment products should rest with the customer and the credit rating agency rather than the assembler or the seller. There is an obvious divergence between the caveat emptor stance of investment bankers and the thinking of regulators who are intent on designing a system in which future underwriting and securitization of mortgages do not lead to another financial crisis. How this tension will be resolved remains to be seen and there is no question that financial firms will play a major role in determining procedures.

In order to comply with new government regulations contained in the Dodd–Frank Act, Wall Street financial institutions will face limits on proprietary trading. Going forward, investment and commercial banks will need to determine who in their management structure is responsible for oversight and enforcement on limits on proprietary trading; this area will be subject to regulatory limits as well as in-house risk management. The strategy of borrowing money to make risky investments will be restricted; banks will have to pursue less risky ways to gain profits. Financial institutions will need to meet higher capital requirements, meaning that as they conduct business they will have to have more money on reserve. The reason for this is so that they can absorb future losses with their own funds. Referring to this requirement, Treasury Secretary Geithner said:

> In contrast to the rules prevailing today, which allow a wide range of other forms of capital, the requirements will

be set in terms of real common equity, tightly defined to mean capital that will truly absorb first losses when firms get into trouble.[87]

The new law means that government will exert more oversight of financial firms than in the past, but it is these firms that will need to restructure to comply with both new regulations and new societal expectations.

Lack of accurate information contributed to the financial crisis. Going forward, reporting by financial firms needs to disclose more detailed information so that regulators, investors and the public will have factual information on which to base decisions. One example of implementing thorough disclosure is contained in a new policy adopted by Goldman Sachs: "The most noticeable and important change is the creation of a segment called investing and lending. The new category, among other things, sheds more light on the firm's hedge fund, private equity and real estate operations, analysts say."[88] In the wake of the financial crisis a great deal of criticism was directed at the amount of executive pay. Top performers at investment banks were paid big bonuses for buying and selling MBS during the housing bubble. After financial institutions returned to profitability there was a consensus in society that executive compensation was out of line with what well-paid personnel in other industries were making. In order to deal with issues related to executive pay, the Dodd–Frank Act states that shareholders shall have a non-binding vote on executive pay and the SEC will have legal authority to let shareholders nominate candidates for seats on corporate boards. Only directors who are independent of the company shall be allowed to sit on compensation committees. While these moves do not foreclose the possibility of overpaying executives in the financial industry, they do improve the situation and should contribute to more reasonable compensation structures in the future.

Mortgage companies, banks, real estate professionals and appraisers. These players in the economy have been hit hard by the collapse of the housing market and they need to play an important part in the recovery. Mortgage lenders can extend assistance to people who are struggling to make mortgage payments by renegotiating the terms of mortgages so that people can remain in their homes. Lenders can forgive late fees, extend the terms of mortgages, reset the rates and make changes in terms, so that, for example, only interest is due for a period of time. Lenders can also reduce the principal of the loan, a step they are loathe to take both because they expect to be repaid what they are owed and because they do not want to create an atmosphere tolerant of moral hazard.

However, making reasonable accommodations for borrowers who are delinquent would likely benefit both homeowners and lenders. Banks would gain by not becoming owners of foreclosed properties that would probably be worth less than amounts remaining on mortgages and might take years to sell. According to a spokesperson for Fannie Mae, the average sale of a foreclosed home in the third quarter of 2010 recouped only 57 percent of the money left unpaid by the original borrower.[89]

Real estate agents are dealing with a vastly different market today than the market that existed a few years ago, meaning far fewer sales and much less income. Nevertheless, they can assist in the recovery by making their expertise available to home buyers and sellers and taking the time to work with people in this troubled market. Assisting in the purchase of foreclosed homes is a complicated task for prospective buyers, but, if real estate professionals provide assistance, it can result in sales and habitation of properties rather than the properties lingering on the market and being open to the possibility of vandalism, and it will be a meaningful aspect of the recovery.

Mortgage lenders can be open to so-called *short sales*. In short sales, lenders agree to let borrowers satisfy their mortgage commitments by selling properties for less than the amount owed on the mortgages. This benefits borrowers because their credit scores will not be as badly impacted as by

) alone, 92,858
ogram, HAMP
ch pays lenders
merican Recov-
al: either banks
ent or less of
a property sale
10, HAMP had
lifications. The
by the time the
y 700,000 fore-
million to four
ent anticipated

oated by 2012.[91]
) only $500,000
have not rene-
who are delin-
prime loans do
anything, their
ere worse than
operty. Lenders
oid foreclosure
o is once again

dherence to an
onditions need
. Even getting
r borrowers as
ny hands in the
to track down
instrument. A
was created the
hind on their
ey had recently
, these people

losed upon. Short sales
ions result in the sale of
ies that accompany fore-
ime consuming and it is
of providing subprime
but this is what the new
iation of Realtors estab-
source (SFR) certification
fully complete this pro-
navigate the confusing,
ng an owner to get out of
r to purchase a home for
.

ole in the mortgage pro-
erties and issuing a state-
ific unit. Lenders depend
ch a property is worth and
order to render an accur-
independent and honest;
the property and its loca-
e appraiser should not be
or a lender to adjust an
f these parties. During the
e issued in large numbers
appraisers accommodated
ated their estimates of the
its were able to get better
ers were able to convince
ges for their clients. In the
ir independence and hon-
ate market on a rational

losure scene? In July 2010,
w, there were more than
g default notices, auction
cording to RealtyTrac, a

marketer of foreclosed properties. In July 201
homes were repossessed. The government ̩
(Home Affordable Modification Program), wh
to modify loans, began in 2009 as a part of the ̩
ery and Reinvestment Act. HAMP had a clear g̩
would reduce mortgage payments to 31 pe̩
homeowners' monthly gross income or facilitat
before foreclosure occurred. As of December 2
processed almost 520,000 permanent loan m̩
Congressional Oversight Panel estimated that
program is finished, it will have prevented on
closures all over – quite a contrast to the three
million modifications that the Treasury Departi
when it rolled out its plan.

Up to thirteen million foreclosures are antici
Of the $30 billion allotted to HAMP, by mid-201
million was spent. The main reason that lender
gotiated terms with the millions of borrowers
quent is that most borrowers who obtained su̩
not have the means to make payments and, i̩
circumstances after the program's start in 2009
they were in 2005 or 2006 when they bought p̩
do not want to renegotiate a mortgage and a̩
only to face the same borrower at a later date w
delinquent and facing foreclosure.

A second issue with HAMP is that it requires ̩
extremely demanding process in which a lot of
to be met and a lot of paperwork complete
started with the program can be perplexing f
their mortgages may have passed through so m̩
securitization process that they may not be abl
and contact the firm that currently services th̩
third flaw with HAMP is that when the program
thinking was that many people who were b
mortgages were not making payments because t̩
lost their jobs. When they started working aga̩

would be able to make payments. They needed temporary assistance. As it has turned out, however, the reality for many unemployed people is that they have not been able to find new jobs and their financial circumstances have become grimmer and grimmer. Thus, they are unable to avail themselves of the assistance HAMP offers.

It is possible for borrowers to deal directly with lenders and bypass the government program but, if borrowers do not have a dependable source of sufficient income to make modified payments, lenders will likely refuse to rework the terms of their loans. Banks such as JPMorgan Chase, however, are likely to work with underwater homeowners in order to keep them from abandoning their properties. Roger Lowenstein explains:

> One area where JPMorgan Chase sees an opportunity to assist people is among homeowners who are current on payments, but might be tempted to walk because their mortgage debt is significantly higher than their property is worth. At the Monday meeting I attended, Ravi Shankar, a senior executive in Chase's mortgage business, described a new program to modify a batch of particularly bad loans that Chase inherited from Washington Mutual. The WaMu loans were due to "reset" to roughly twice their current interest rate, at which point many of the borrowers would probably default. Shankar's unit had reduced the principal on billions of dollars of these mortgages by about a sixth, bringing them in line with market value and avoiding foreclosure.[92]

Because so many people face foreclosure procedures, scams exist that purport to assist homeowners to keep their homes. These generally require that people pay fees in the range of $1,500 to $2,000 and up to engage a lawyer who will arrange a loan modification. What should people watch out for so as not to be scammed? Lynnley Browning explains:

According to PreventLoan-Scams.org, a new online site operated by the nonprofit Lawyers' Committee for Civil Rights Under Law, homeowners should be cautious about: any guarantees that a loan will be modified, since not all can be; requests for an upfront fee or that the property title be signed over to a third party; and offers to redirect the monthly mortgage payments to a third party who will forward them to the lender or mortgage servicer.

"My best advice is, be wary of the too-good-to-be-true remedies," Mr. Mackin said.

(William Mackin is a bankruptcy lawyer in Woodbury, NJ)[93]

Foreclosed properties quickly become blight to a community and, if lenders do not or cannot work with delinquent borrowers, it would be helpful if lenders set realistic prices so that people could buy these properties and occupy them. Sales of foreclosed properties, at so-called *realistic prices*, have a downside in that neighbors who are struggling to make mortgage payments or who are underwater may decide to abandon their properties rather than continue to make payments on homes that are worth much less than other houses in their communities. Should this happen, lenders will see their inventory of foreclosed properties grow, which will not be an advantage for anyone. Homeowners who walk away from underwater mortgages will suffer a blow to their credit scores, but the lenders who issued their mortgage loans will likely not have claims against the borrowers. This is because most mortgage loans are so-called *no recourse*; this means that after seizing the house the lender cannot come after the borrower for money owed.

In October 2010 foreclosures became page one news as a result of legal challenges to foreclosure practices of leading U.S. banks. In the United States, foreclosing on a property is a multifaceted legal process that is governed by the laws of the fifty states. After a borrower is in arrears more than 30–60 days on mortgage payments, the lender can begin foreclosure proceedings to evict the borrower from the premises and take control of the property. It usually takes three to six months for a lender to move to foreclosure; during this time lenders may be willing to talk with borrowers and assist with loan modifications.

When the decision to foreclose is made, one of three processes is generally undertaken. The first is known as *judicial foreclosure*. The lender files suit with the judicial system and the borrower receives a note in the mail demanding payment. If the borrower does not make the payment in thirty days, the lender forecloses and sells the property at auction to the highest bidder. The auction is carried out by a local court or sheriff's office. *Power of sale* is the second kind of foreclosure. It is allowed by many states if the mortgage includes a power of sale clause. After a homeowner has defaulted on mortgage payments, the lender sends out notices demanding payments. Once an established waiting period has passed, the mortgage company, rather than a local court or sheriff's office, carries out a public auction. Non-judicial foreclosure auctions are more expedient, though they may be subject to judicial review to ensure the legality of the proceedings. The third type of foreclosure is known as a *strict foreclosure*. A small number of states allow this type of foreclosure. In strict foreclosure proceedings, the lender files a lawsuit on the homeowner that has defaulted. If the borrower cannot pay the mortgage within a specific time ordered by the court, the property goes directly back to the mortgage holder. Generally, strict foreclosures take place only when the debt amount is greater than the value of the property.[94]

Putting together documentation related to foreclosures is a necessary task for the bank, other lender or servicer that carries out this process and it was because of laxity in this regard that foreclosures became a major issue in 2010. The media discovered, and major lenders concurred, that some foreclosure filings were invalidated by sloppy paperwork and others by robo signers. In cases of sloppy paperwork, the documentation

required to foreclose was incomplete or inaccurate, some documents were not properly notarized, and/or verification procedures were incomplete, making the filing invalid. In the case of
robo signers, it was learned that some individuals who worked
for lenders signed hundreds of documents a day, thousands a
week, without reading the documents or verifying the loan history. Such filings do not meet the standards required by the
courts. As issues related to foreclosures dominated headlines in
late 2010, a shift occurred in which judges became less inclined
to rubber-stamp the filings of banks that sought to foreclose.
Instead, judges began to scrutinize filings more carefully and
began requiring that banks prove that they had the legal standing to foreclose, either by producing documents that showed
that they were holders of a mortgage loan or acting as agents
for a mortgage holder.[95]

Since people lose their homes to foreclosure, and since it is
estimated that more than three million homes received foreclosure notices in 2010 alone, the system needs to operate
according to the law. The people affected by the foreclosure
process are entitled to due process, which is one of the basic
rights of U.S. citizens. It should be noted that, in the worst case
of improper foreclosure action by a lender, an individual's
property is seized, the locks are changed, and a foreclosure
notice is posted in error. The individual is a homeowner, without a mortgage or with a mortgage on which payments are current, and the lender makes a major mistake in seizing the
property. Cases of this kind have come to light and underscore
how badly flawed the foreclosure process can be.[96] One case is
illustrative:

> Angela Iannelli was up to date on her payments when she
> arrived home in October 2009 to find that Bank of Amer-
> ica had ransacked her belongings, cut off her utilities,
> poured antifreeze down her drains, padlocked her doors
> and confiscated Luke, her parrot of ten years. It took her
> six weeks to get the bank to clean up the house.[97]

If lenders submit faulty documentation, courts allow a foreclosure to proceed, and an individual buys the foreclosed property, a new set of problems is introduced. Those who buy the property and the company that insures the title run the risk of being sued by the people who were improperly evicted. Should this happen, the parties in the middle (the purchasers of the foreclosed property and their title insurance company) will turn to the lender who foreclosed to recoup their losses. Given the number of homes in the United States that have been foreclosed or are about to be, the way lenders handled foreclosures from 2007 forward may well cause additional trauma to financial institutions, residential real estate and the larger economy.

One idea being suggested for aiding homeowners facing foreclosure and stabilizing the housing market is to have the homeowner relinquish all claims to the property and assist the mortgage holder in establishing title. Then the mortgage holder becomes the uncontested owner. Once this happens, the bank or other owner rents the property back to the people who live there at a rent they can afford for a fixed lease term. Should a program such as this take hold, homeless people, vacant homes and lost revenues would be replaced with a more stable situation. According to David E. Kapell:

> Here's how it would work. The borrower would lose ownership of his home, but be allowed to remain as a tenant paying fair rent for a reasonable period after foreclosure, with the requirement that he cooperate in the foreclosure. He'd pay fair market rents as published by the federal government, ensuring a clear, national standard. If the borrower couldn't afford to pay market rent, existing federal rent-subsidy programs could be extended to help tide him over.[98]

Dr. Kenneth T. Rosen, a professor at the University of California at Berkeley, offers a different suggestion about how the U.S. government could act to assist the millions of people who face the loss of their homes, especially those whose homes are underwater and those who are unemployed. Dr. Rosen's suggestions provide ideas that could be explored and amended, eventually leading to practical efforts to restore stability to the housing sector:

> The "underwater" mortgage problem must be addressed through a loan modification plan that reduces the mortgage amount. A shared appreciation second mortgage that allocates part of the future appreciation of the home to the government and to the private lender involved in arranging the loan modification would reward taxpayers and private lenders with a portion of the appreciation of the value of the homes when housing markets recover, while reducing the incentive for borrowers to take unwarranted advantage of the loan modification program.
>
> With eight million people already losing their jobs in the "Great Recession," the government's foreclosure relief program needs to address the issue of how to deal with newly unemployed households who lack the income to qualify for a loan modification. The government should consider an "unemployment bridge loan" for up to half the mortgage payments due for a two-year period or until the person is re-employed. This bridge loan would be secured with a second mortgage against the house and could be administered through the unemployment compensation system.[99]

The economic costs of foreclosure are one thing, and the personal costs are another. Research into foreclosures reveals that for every 100 foreclosures there is a 12 percent increase in anxiety related emergency-room visits and hospitalizations; a 2008 survey of 250 people in the Philadelphia area who were undergoing foreclosure showed that 32 percent of them had missed doctors' appointments and 48 percent had let prescriptions go unfilled. People living in hard-hit neighborhoods in the sand states were more likely to be hospitalized for conditions like diabetes, high blood pressure and heart failure.[100] In light of this information it is obvious that there is a public health dimension to the foreclosure crisis which our nation needs to confront.

Putbacks. A related effect of the foreclosure mess is that investors are charging that shoddy loan originations, securitization and servicing have increased their losses. These investors are trying to force banks to buy back or repurchase loans that were packaged and sold as investments, a process known as a putback. Investors, such as the New York City pension fund, are also calling for independent audits of banks in order to determine the amount and extent of the problem. As it stands,

> the amounts that the nation's four largest banks have reserved for possible mortgage repurchases, about $10 billion as of the third quarter of 2010, is microscopic when compared with the more than $5 trillion in mortgage securities issued from 2005–2007.[101]

Should this movement gain traction, banks are certain to suffer a setback in their recovery and the second phase of the financial crisis that peaked in 2008 could begin.[102] The principal basis on which investors in MBS-CDOs could bring lawsuits against mortgage originators and securitizers is the probability that the mortgages or securities they purchased were misrepresented in the offering documents or did not conform to underwriting standards. If transactions contained assurance that individual mortgages met all required legal standards, and, if in fact this was not the case, investors could have grounds to allege that fraud was committed and sue for damages. Inadequate due diligence at the origination or securitization stage could come back to haunt banks and imperil their solvency. Thus, the sloppy paperwork uncovered in conjunction with the foreclosure mess could have a second, unintended detrimental consequence. A report compiled by the Congressional Research

Service and released in November 2010 stated that, if investors succeed in forcing banks to buy back bad loans, $425 billion in losses could be shifted from investors to banks, undercapitalizing some banks and causing further trauma to the financial system and more bank failures.[103] The survival of MBIA, the Municipal Bond Insurance Association, a company that insures municipal bonds and that underwrote insurance for MBS, depends on its winning a lawsuit against banks whose securities it insured: "MBIA claims that the banks defrauded it because many of the loans did not meet the stated underwriting criteria."[104] If MBIA wins the suit, the insurance firm will recoup enough in damages to reestablish solvency; if it does not prevail, a probable bankruptcy awaits it.

In an effort to resolve the putback issue and allow banks to move past costly litigation and the problems that go with uncertainty, the U.S. Justice Department and Attorney General of Iowa tried to broker an agreement whereby banks would pay approximately $25 billion to settle putback claims and the Obama administration would use the money to assist homeowners avoid eviction. Banks engaged in the negotiations maintained that they would only agree to the deal if a waiver was issued that stated no further charges would be brought against them related to foreclosure issues. Some homeowner groups, thinking the settlement would not constitute a sufficient penalty for banks or enough compensation for people facing foreclosure, balked at the settlement terms. Kamala D. Harris, the Attorney General of California, aware of this dissatisfaction, withdrew from the negotiations, effectively derailing the effort to resolve the issue.[105] Harris' objections were satisfied and the deal was finalized in February 2012.

Investors. People buy securities in the hope of making more money on their investments than they would make from bank accounts, U.S. Treasury bonds or other so-called *safe* investments. Interest paid by banks and interest paid on Treasury bonds is modest and investors question whether the interest paid will keep pace with inflation. Seeking to make more from their money, investors buy stocks and other securities. A lesson learned in 2008 was that there are no sure things in the stock market and that bonds and mutual funds can lose value in troubled times. As a result, investors are now likely to approach investing with more realistic expectations about profits. They have also learned the hard way how important it is to be informed about what they are investing in and the need to study and understand the securities they buy. Credit rating agencies and securities sales personnel let investors down; now there are revised expectations regarding transparency and accountability and more awareness that investors need to hold their advisers to high standards.

The wariness of investors can contribute to an economic recovery in that their caution is likely to propel them to put their money in sound investments with strong prospects. Since the private sector holds the greatest potential for creating wealth and jobs, investors, by standing with sound U.S. corporations, hold a key to restarting the economic engine.

One of the consequences of the crisis was that people became aware of the earnings of Wall Street executives and began to see how oversized these earnings are in comparison to the average person's income. Some of the financial firms that received loans from the government in rescue programs resumed paying their executives millions of dollars and awarding bonuses. (Resumption happened after repayment of borrowed money; the firms were restricted in respect to executive pay until they repaid the government.) The backlash from citizens continues, however; citizens argue that those responsible for the financial crisis should not benefit while ordinary people on Main Street suffer the effects. Exerting influence on corporate directors to rein in compensation for executives in the financial services industry is something stockholders can do to change the overall climate in a positive way.

Citizens. People all over the United States are feeling the effects of the economic crisis and subsequent recession. Prior to the events that triggered the crisis, most people did not know about the major underlying problems with subprime mortgages and highly leveraged investment banks. As a result, the crisis took them by surprise, perhaps reducing their wealth and shrinking the equity in their homes. If they had seen what was coming, could citizens have taken steps to alter the course of history? We do not know the answer to this hypothetical question, but what we do know is that in the future citizens will need to insist on government regulation of financial firms, monitoring of financial practices and granting of loans. This will require a degree of sophistication and dedication but the cost is more than commensurate with the result of financial stability.

Consumers. Consumers learned two lessons from the crisis: first, that their spending is necessary to reinvigorate the economy; and, second, that they need to live within their means. However, consumers seem reluctant to prime the pump; they are saving more and spending less, thus contributing to a sluggish recovery. As consumers pay down their debts and build up their savings they will eventually strengthen the economy, which is a good thing. But it is also problematic in that sluggish demand for goods and services, if it is long lived, may lead to deflation, a situation in which the price of goods and services falls instead of rising. In deflationary circumstances there is little or no economic growth, new jobs are not created and economic suffering intensifies. Consumers will need to find a balance between spending, saving and debt reduction and there is no way to predict how long this will take.

The second lesson consumers learned is that they need to live within their means. Those who borrowed more than they could pay back played a significant role in causing the housing crisis, and people with large credit card bills and insufficient income to make payments know how hard it is to dig themselves out of a hole. Going forward, consumers should be wiser and less inclined to spend money they do not have in the mistaken belief that there is a magic way to pay the bills when they come due.

Just as consumers are older and wiser, so, too, they need to take proactive steps to end the recession. The economy will turn around when people engage in a substantial amount of discretionary spending. Buying a new car, a new appliance, a new coat, a restaurant meal and a vacation package impact the economy. If people with financial resources were to spend money in the interest of providing stimulus, this would improve the economy and be of benefit to the whole society. How to achieve this goal remains a major unanswered question. At the end of 2010 economic commentators made cautiously optimistic assessments about consumer attitudes and behavior based on good retail sales during the Christmas season, suggesting that these purchases were improving the chances for recovery to take hold.[106] In the months that followed, however, anemic growth became the pattern and the hope that consumer spending would lead to recovery waned.

Job creation. The United States needs large corporations and small businesses to hire workers. How many jobs are needed? As of October 7, 2011, following the announcement of meager Non-Farm Payroll expectations, this number rose to an all-time high of 261,200. This means that unless that number of jobs is created each month for the next five years, the United States will have a higher unemployment rate in October 2016 than it did in December 2007 when the Great Recession began.[107]

If people are working, they will have discretionary income which they can spend, creating demand. This demand will lead to the creation of more jobs, leading to more people with money to spend, further increasing demand and building prosperity. Without jobs, people working at those jobs and earning wages, there can be no recovery. According to Moody's Investor Services, U.S. nonfinancial companies sat on $1.2 trillion in cash and short-term liquid investments at the end of 2010. That's up 11 percent from the $1.1 trillion at the end of 2009. These cash levels are probably only going to increase. Moody's review ended at December 31, 2010, at which Apple Inc.'s cash and short-term investments balance totaled $60 billion. When it reported quarterly earnings in September 2011, that balance had climbed to $78 billion.[108] The naïve response to this report is that companies which are doing well should hire workers to ease the unemployment problem. But this is a capitalistic economy and companies do not hire workers to do a good deed; they hire workers if they need those workers to produce goods or services which they can sell to consumers. Until consumers start demanding products, big companies will not start hiring. This is reality and the way beyond this reality to employment growth and economic well-being is proving elusive.

Most job creation in the United States is done by small businesses, firms employing less than 500 people. There are several reasons why small businesses are not hiring and unemployment remains stubbornly high. Owners of small businesses are reluctant to invest money given the economic uncertainties surrounding us. They know that the chances for a small business to be successful are slim, while the likelihood of failure is significant. For those without capital, it is not easy to borrow enough to get a business off the ground. And, there are probably big ideas that will prompt a lot of start-ups to take shape and spur hiring but, at this point, no one knows what the next big idea is or when the breakthrough will happen. Finally, entrepreneurs are leery of the dictum, "if you build it, they will come," fearing the opposite may be the new normal. In the current context, it would be foolish to assume that there will be demand for a product or service once that becomes available in the marketplace.

Media. The media plays a large role in educating people who no longer attend school, that is, most people. The media also plays a role in the education of students who are in school. Since the media finds its way into the lives of Americans through the morning paper, the car radio, television and online sources, the media is close at hand and influential. The media can argue that it is not its job to explain complex economic ideas to people or to describe the interconnected aspects of the ordeal they have lived through. But, if the media will not assume this role, who will? And, if the media were to take on this task, how could it accomplish the job in an unbiased way?

As with so many of the ideas we are considering, the answer to this question is not simple. Credible authorities with different viewpoints will need to appear side by side and be allowed enough time to present their analyses and answer thoughtful questions. Sound bites will not suffice. Media managers will need to reject partisan advocates for one position or another who refuse to be questioned about points with which their opponents disagree. Civility will need to replace stridency and the goal will have to shift from entertaining the audience to informing the listener. Pessimism about the possibility of the media's functioning in this capacity will need to be rejected.

Conclusion. What needs to be done to set things right? The Financial Crisis Inquiry Commission concluded that

> this crisis was avoidable. It found widespread failures in financial regulation; dramatic breakdowns in corporate governance; excessive borrowing and risk-taking by households and Wall Street; policy makers who were ill prepared for the crisis; and systemic breaches in accountability and ethics at all levels.[109]

The economic crisis was a big mess, with many actors and practices contributing to a devastating implosion. Many of the same players who, by action or omission, caused the meltdown are the ones who need to step up and institute measures to bring about a sustained recovery. The government, with the Dodd–Frank Act, has taken a major step, but it remains only a first step. The financial industry, credit rating agencies, mortgage lenders, real estate professionals, investors, consumers, businesses and the media need to accept their appropriate roles in fixing what is broken and supporting a healthy status quo going forward. We are currently in the litigation stage of the financial debacle of 2008;[110] this is a time for education, legal action to recoup losses, and attempts to shore up the financial infrastructure so as to strengthen it against future storms.

Questions for Discussion

1 In view of the fact that the economic collapse of 2008 was systemic in nature, describe the role the U.S. government needs to play in setting things right.

2 Tolerance of moral hazard, highly leveraged trading and proprietary trading undermined the financial viability of financial firms, setting the stage for the economic crisis. Describe the structural changes financial firms need to put in place to prevent a repeat of the crisis.

3 What steps do credit rating agencies need to take in order to restore their damaged credibility?

4 How can the real estate and building sectors contribute to economic recovery?

5 Millions of people face foreclosure. Describe what people whose homes are in foreclosure, their lenders, government agencies and others can do to resolve the foreclosure crisis.

6 Describe how investors and consumers can participate in improving economic conditions.

7 Unemployment has reached a crisis stage. Why don't companies hire people and alleviate the crisis?

8 When the nation faces a major economic issue such as a recession, how can the media help the public to understand causes, context and possible solutions?

Case Study: Act Now on Securitization

Marilyn Matthews is the manager in charge of processing mortgages for securitization. She gets an email from a senior vice president who tells her there is a tricky situation and the bank needs her department to step up right away because the bank has a lot of mortgages and market for these securities is going south.

Ms. Matthews calls a meeting of her department. She tells the workers she supervises to hurry up and get the mortgages in the bank's inventory bundled right away. "Push the folks who are writing the prospectuses; push the guys at the rating agencies, push anyone who is part of the process. I need to have MBS in hand, and I need them yesterday. There are still buyers for them, but we don't know for how long. If we don't get them bundled, the bank will end up owning them. That won't be good for you and it won't be good for me."

Ms. Matthews asks, "Any questions?"

One of the employees says, "Are you sure that the real estate market and the market for MBS/CDOs is in decline? I read business news and the opinions seem to be split."

Another employee asks, "If these securities are not sound, should we be selling them?"

Ms. Matthews answers that when she asked if there were questions she meant technical questions about assembling the securities or pulling the relevant information together. "I'm not a market analyst or the Chief Ethics Officer," she explains. "I just work here; I don't make policy or determine the big picture; in my role as a manager I don't consider myself very important. Our team's job is to assemble a product and pass it along the chain; we just need to get the pieces and put them into place."

Not everyone on Marilyn Matthews' team is satisfied with her answer but all of them return to their cubicles. They feel pressured and know that they will be working overtime until they complete their task.

1 Marilyn Matthews says she just works for the bank and carries out the orders she receives. Do you have any problem with her attitude?

2 One of the team members asks if the bank should be selling unsound securities. Is it right to sell problematic investments in order to benefit the bank?

3 Another team member says that the state of the real estate market is not clear. If this is in fact the case, should

people involved in assembling mortgage-backed securities go ahead with what they are doing?

4 Those responsible for setting policy and determining the details of the big picture want to move mortgages off the bank's books before the market declines further. Comment on whether this decision is worthy of praise or blame.

Case Study: Member of Board of Directors

Aaron Bolton is the retired president emeritus of a large Midwestern university. Dr. Bolton currently serves as a member of the board of directors of a manufacturer of industrial equipment. In this capacity he attends six meetings a year and participates in weekly conference calls. His compensation is $85,000 a year.

Dr. Bolton is contacted by the chairman of the board of a bank holding company and invited to become a member of that board. The compensation would be $125,000 a year and the amount of participation roughly the same as the board position he currently holds. Dr. Bolton is hesitant to accept: he mentions the responsibility for overseeing complicated financial transactions and expresses concern about the consequences he might experience if he were to fail to raise an alarm about destabilizing transactions that could imperil the bank as well as the economy.

The board chairman tells Dr. Bolton not to worry. Public outrage over the subprime fiasco was directed at CEOs; members of boards were largely unnoticed. There is enough leeway in the new law to allow us to carry out our responsibilities and we don't need to worry that there is a regulation the bank might be violating. In any event, directors have insurance so that, if anyone were to bring a case against us, we would not have to dig into our own pockets to pay damages.

Aaron Bolton asks for a few days to reach a decision. He feels conflicted because the compensation would be nice and he would enjoy the prestige that accompanies membership on the corporate board. At the same time, he thinks that the chairman is too glib about the downside of membership and he wonders whether the chairman and the other board members are seriously committed to meeting their obligations. Finally, he questions his own competence to oversee complex financial proposals because, given his background in higher education, he lacks sophistication in this area.

1 Should Aaron Bolton accept the offer and become a member of the board of directors? Why or why not?
2 What considerations should Dr. Bolton take into account as he weighs his decision?
3 What responsibility do members of boards of directors bear for financial institutions?
4 What standards should members of boards of directors abide by in their work on corporate boards?
5 How should the balance of power in financial corporations play out, with the CEO holding the upper hand, or the board? What factors lead you to your conclusion?

Case Study: Approving a Mortgage

Theresa is delighted with the news from her mortgage broker: she and Jim have been approved for a $300,000 mortgage. They have 10 percent to put down on a house, and, with this mortgage commitment, they will be able to go ahead and buy the lovely colonial home that is for sale in their neighborhood. Theresa and Jim have been renting a one-bedroom apartment ever since they married four years ago; with a toddler sleeping in the living room and a new baby on the way, this move could not come at a better time.

Theresa's first call is to Jim's cell; he puts on an act to sound pleased and enthusiastic. Actually, learning about the mortgage commitment is disconcerting to him. Jim was laid off just a few days ago and, since he cannot bear to share this news with Theresa, he has been leaving each morning as though going to work and walking the streets trying to figure how to get another job.

Mark, the mortgage broker, is pleased that he will be earning a commission. Business has been so slow for so long that he is way behind on his bills. When Mark's manager reviewed Theresa and Jim's file he did not even ask Mark if he had double-checked everything so Mark did not have to fib and say that he had not actually verified Jim's employment data. Jim had produced four pay stubs for the past two months and that, in Mark's opinion, was proof enough that the client had sufficient income to make payments.

Jim decides not to let Theresa know about his work status. He hopes to find another job before long. In the meantime, he is counting on three months of severance pay to tide them over. Beyond that, there will be a new baby and, he hopes, new employment.

1 Identify the people in this case who fail to act correctly in regard to Theresa and Jim's mortgage application and state the ways their conduct is deficient.

2 How would you counsel Theresa, a pregnant woman who is living in a space that is not big enough for her growing family?

3 Should Jim tell Theresa that he lost his job or should he wait until he has a new job before he tells her about his setback? What factors influence your answer?

4 Is it unrealistic to expect Mark, the mortgage broker, to dot every "i" and cross every "t" before submitting a mortgage application to his manager for approval?

5 How much checking should the manager do before approving an employee's work?

6 What issues can Theresa, Jim and their lender expect to face in the coming months? How should these issues be resolved?

4

ETHICS AND RECOVERY

When we understand how the U.S. economy arrived at the brink of disaster it comes as no surprise that the economic forces at play in the financial sector are complicated and not easily grasped, even by insiders. Common generalizations about the ethical aspects of the crisis do not explain how it happened. These imprecise statements take into account human weakness, but not the grave systemic flaws that permitted the meltdown. Oversimplified explanations include the ethical dimension and tell part of the story, but these explanations leave a lot out. Consider the following examples: consumers are ignorant, or greedy, or exploitable, or irresponsible and make poor decisions; CEOs do not understand the ramifications of the sales, marketing, trading and investment practices of their subordinates, and unwittingly allow highly risky practices that undermine the firm; or, management understands what is going on, but, focused on making money, turns a blind eye to destabilizing practices; people who work in the financial industry and investors are greedy – they only care about Number One; government regulators are inept, clueless, complicit or active collaborators in engineering financial catastrophe; the credit rating agencies lack integrity and inflate ratings to keep clients happy; mortgage brokers care only about their commissions and don't worry about home buyers or the big picture; lenders do not scrutinize the arrangements made by brokers because they intend to sell mortgages to securitizers – they, like the others, are focused solely on how deals affect them.

However people tend to generalize about the underlying attitudes and choices that led to the crisis, there is no question that these generalizations are so sweeping, so black and white, that they obscure the fact that society manifested a sense of complacency about the multitude of practices that led to the economic crisis and that the society, as well as business and government leaders, played a role in causing economic turmoil. An apt comment by Rowan Williams, Archbishop of Canterbury, makes this point: focusing on the greed of bankers makes people lose sight of the fact that

> governments committed to deregulation and to the encouragement of speculation and high personal borrowing were elected repeatedly in Britain and the United States for a crucial couple of decades.... Add to that the fact of warnings of some of the risks of poor (or no) regulation, and we are left with the question of what it was that skewed the judgment of a whole society as well as of financial professionals.[1]

This and the following chapters will take into account the complexity of financial systems as well as the complicated motives of individuals and groups as we try to understand the role ethics should play in the recovery.

The value of considering the ethical dimension. Can we improve upon the conditions in which financial transactions take place and commit ourselves to better behavior so as to participate in orderly, profitable markets that benefit everyone? Are there ethical lessons to be learned from what happened? If so, what are these lessons? If, going forward, individuals and institutions resolve to abide by ethical standards, will systemic change lead to an improved economy? Is it worth our time to ponder these questions, or should we accept the ideas that financial markets are motivated by greed and fear and that the term *business ethics* is an oxymoron? Can ethics make a difference in the real world, or is ethics a waste of time?

The cynical answer, of course, is that ethics is a waste of time: plug up one set of loopholes and someone will find another way to game the system. Government regulations will make it harder but, where there's a will, there's a way. Regulations bring new bureaucracies and bureaucrats; they are just another way to spend taxpayer money. Lobbyists have too much of a role to play in formulating regulations so that rules are written to the advantage of a lobbyist's clients and the disadvantage of the public. The way forward is to stress the importance of caveat emptor (buyer beware!) and be smart enough to protect ourselves and our loved ones. It would be stupid to depend on Big Brother to watch out for us.

The cynic's argument is appealing in its simplicity and disheartening in its pessimism. An optimist would counter by saying that government, the financial industry and consumers should work together to create a system without loopholes in which everyone functions rationally and fairness is achieved. The marketplace is self-regulating and it tends to reward ethical behavior and punish unethical behavior, so laissez-faire (non-interference in the free market) is the way to go. There is no need to devote time to refuting this utopian position. After what we witnessed in the lead up to the financial crisis and suffered in the recession, this Pollyannaish response lacks credibility.

Fortunately, there is a middle way between unfounded optimism and cynical pessimism that respects the role ethics can play in bringing about change. According to this way of thinking, judicious regulations and fair enforcement will not eliminate immoral financial behavior but these strategies will bring about systemic improvement and the economy will be stronger as a result. According to the middle way, the fix that is needed is more than technical and involves more than regulations and enforcement provisions. New regulations need to be based on ethical values and complemented by a commitment to ethical conduct. Fine print and enforcement mechanisms alone will not get the job done; society's values and practices need to change, too.

Ethical lessons from U.S. history. In the United States there are pertinent lessons that we can learn from our own history. When civil rights legislation was enacted in the 1960s this legislation did not eliminate prejudice but it improved the overall climate and created a better society. Today people of all races participate in business, government and the media; they decide where they want to live and what school or college they want to attend. Skin color is not a relevant consideration in choosing the CEO of a corporation or electing the president of the United States. The United States is better than it used to be because the ethical norm that all persons are created equal and endowed with certain inalienable rights is being upheld in law and in practice.

In the 1980s and early 1990s there was a crisis in the savings and loan industry (S&L) and the resolution of this crisis provides us with another example. The S&L crisis was similar to the financial crisis of 2008 in that it involved banks; the issues were different but the problems, though on a smaller scale, were similar. Savings and loan associations bankrupted themselves by contracting to pay higher rates of interest to depositors than were being collected from borrowers. Congress assisted the S&Ls in undermining their solvency by passing laws that allowed S&Ls to engage in unsound practices in their attempts to increase revenue through growing their lending businesses. Before Congress passed enabling legislation, S&Ls only lent to individuals who were buying homes and the amount of interest they could collect on the loans was limited. After the law was changed, S&Ls could lend to borrowers other than those who were seeking residential mortgages and charge high rates of interest. This change in the law allowed the S&Ls to get into trouble. S&Ls lent large amounts of money to developers of commercial properties, such as shopping centers, at high rates of interest, increasing, for a time, their revenues. These increased revenues allowed S&Ls to pay more to depositors than they traditionally had paid; this caused the depositor base to grow. When many shopping centers defaulted, however, the

S&Ls had to deal with large losses, undermining their ability to keep up with payments to depositors. Accounting gimmicks by bank management and, in some cases, outright fraud, caused S&Ls to get into a situation in which they did not have sufficient cash flow to meet depositor demands and pay their operating costs. Between 1980 and 1995 more than 5,000 S&Ls, commercial banks and thrift associations failed. To deal with this crisis the Financial Institutions Reform, Recovery and Enforcement Act was signed into law in 1989. This law changed the ways S&Ls were regulated and outlawed the practices that resulted in bank failures. The Act also created the Resolution Trust Corporation to resolve insolvent S&Ls. The cost to American taxpayers was more that $190 billion. The positive outcome that followed was that the nation moved from economic crisis to recovery. An expensive lesson was learned; its pertinence for us is the knowledge that it is possible to work through a financial mess and come out, on the other side, in a better place.

In regard to the question of how the banking system could falter again and create economic chaos less than twenty years later, the answer is that the MBS-CDO debacle involved different kinds of financial institutions and different practices. Millions of subprime residential mortgages issued during the peak years of the real estate market were the first link in the weak chain. The financial crisis that began in 2008 is different from the S&L crisis because the nation was brought to its knees by financial practices that were not part of the playbook three decades ago and the scope of the contagion is much larger.

The underpinnings of economic recovery from the crisis of 2008 depend on meeting four conditions: first, limiting the amount of risk banks can engage in; this will prevent large, complex financial institutions from practices that could put them in jeopardy. Second, requiring that banks be adequately capitalized so that they have sufficient funds to meet their obligations even in a situation that could be classified as a worst-case scenario. Third, regulating practices relating to consumer credit; this will keep borrowers from being seduced by lenders to overcome rationality and take on more debt than they can repay. And, fourth, requiring government to act in behalf of the common good; government is the only institution capable of exercising this role, and it must do so. These conditions need to be coupled with the notion that reason and restraint are possible and that ethical people are capable of acting with both reason and restraint.

What is ethics? Ethics is the sound standards that govern the conduct of a person, guiding the person's choices. In regard to major personal and professional decisions, there is no question that these decisions are significant and making the right decision contributes to a person's character. To act in such ways as to be an ethical person is very important. By consistently choosing to do the right thing we distinguish ourselves as ethical. By habitually acting in virtuous ways, we develop integrity. When faced with daunting dilemmas ethical people can be counted on to thoughtfully consider what is at stake and come to appropriate decisions. The sum total of our ethical choices, reasonable attitudes and good habits constitutes the basis for self-esteem and enables us to cultivate a good reputation.

People who work in finance and related fields know that developing ethical competency is a professional responsibility which enhances the status of an employee as well as the reputation of a firm. Ethics capacity is an element which business leaders are expected to demonstrate. This is done when business leaders clearly communicate that ethical conduct is required of all members of the firm, and when these leaders act as models by making ethically appropriate decisions and rewarding subordinates who do the same. Ethics capacity is demonstrated by corporations that put corporate policies in place to facilitate and support ethical conduct.[2]

Just as it is important for individuals to be good, or ethical, people, so it is important for government to be ethical, for business to be ethical and for society to embrace ethical standards. Expectations of how government, business and society should act and interact comprise a large part of the subject matter of ethics. There are objective principles that should be honored in resolving issues of social ethics in a morally sound manner. These principles are broad in nature and rules governing human conduct are logically derived from them.

> These principles remind us that the origins of a society existing in history are found in the interconnectedness of the freedoms of all the persons who interact within it, contributing by means of their choices either to build society up or to impoverish it.[3]

Thus, the rational choice of financial firms to act in behalf of the common good and to uphold principles such as justice, truth, accountability and transparency is a core requirement of social ethics. Government officials should choose to focus on the common good of the nation and its citizens; their interactions with the financial industry should be conducted in light of their responsibilities to the common good. There is no place in an ethical system for returning favors to campaign contributors that imperil the common good.

Jim Wallis makes these points well when he says:

> I would say this is a moment, a teachable moment to talk about habits, practices, and assumptions about greed that we've lost conversation about for a long time. I think government should encourage innovation, but it must limit greed. Self-interest and success is one thing. Losing sight of what is best for the common good is another thing. So capitalism run amok here is really what's happening, and so restoring a sense of what's good for all of us is, in fact, the best business model.[4]

Wallis is correct in that ethics deals with individual and social matters as well as the role of government. But the reach of ethics is broader still in that it includes specific fields such as organizational ethics, professional ethics, industry ethics, economic ethics and political ethics. Each of these specialized fields represents a development of business ethics. Business ethics dates from the 1970s when the term first came into use and colleges and universities began to offer courses in the subject. Prior to the 1970s ethical reflection was done under the aegis of philosophy, and it is to the various philosophical approaches to ethics that we now turn our attention.

Ethical methodology. Moral questions are intuitively understood as having a special kind of importance. It doesn't make much difference whether a borrower makes a mortgage payment by check or credit card, but it does make a difference whether or not people pay their bills. The bonds of trust and community are strengthened if people meet their obligations; these bonds can be weakened or rent asunder if they do not. Meeting personal financial responsibilities is ethically significant.

Moral discourse involves using terms such as good and bad, right and wrong, should and should not, ought and ought not. In moral discourse, people are also apt to disclose what their values are, the beliefs they hold, and what principles influence their decisions. Their values have been interiorized as part of the process of searching for truth. Those who have clarified their values and who seek to live by them tend to be clear in their thinking as well as capable of making sound decisions.

Ethical people can be counted on to argue in favor of doing what they consider to be the right thing and against what they consider to be the wrong thing. This is because of the special kind of importance that moral matters possess. Ethical people recognize this importance and experience a hard time letting go of moral issues which they believe require attention. Journalists, lawyers, government regulators and lenders who insist that foreclosure processes be carried out with scrupulous attention to ethical and legal standards are admired for advocating the morally right course of action.

Regrettably, it does not always happen that ethical people work through issues and arrive at a political consensus. In the summer of 2011 the U.S. government faced a crisis in connection with the debt limit. The executive branch, headed by President Obama, a Democrat, urged Congress, the legislative branch, to pass a bill raising the debt ceiling so that the United States would continue to pay interest to bondholders and meet its other obligations, such as paying members of the military, government employees and social security recipients. If the debt limit were not raised, the United States would be in default, and cause major economic instability. The House of Representatives (with a Republican majority) refused to agree to raise the debt limit unless the president agreed to cut government spending. The president said that he would agree to cut government spending, but only if the House of Representatives would agree to a tax increase to raise needed additional revenues. A majority in the House refused to vote for a tax increase, thus triggering a stalemate. Negotiations played out over a few weeks and, during this time, tension built and the ideal of reasonable people working together for the common good was not in evidence. With the deadline looming, on August 1, 2011, a debt ceiling bill was passed and the following day the president signed the bill. Because the process was so fractious and the division between the executive and legislative branches so pronounced, in view of the political dysfunction in the U.S. government and the nation's deficit and debt, on August 5, 2011 Moody's lowered the U.S. credit rating from AAA to AA. The question the debt limit stalemate raised is whether or not the idea that rational people can come together and work for the common good is a valid one or wishful thinking. If it is wishful thinking, then the theoretical basis for democracy is an illusion. The lesson of this episode is the need to redouble efforts to reason and work together so that the system can function.

There can be disagreements about how to go about deciding if an action or policy is right or wrong. In other words, in pluralistic U.S. society, as in most of the Western world, we lack consensus as to which moral methodology is soundest and most coherent. In addition to the fact that the methodological issue is unresolved, the actual process of engaging in moral reasoning within any particular system is complex. While the existence of disagreement may be disconcerting, it is important not to become pessimistic about morality because, in the absence of ethics, the marketplace will lose its compass and the rights of people will not be protected.

There are frequently disagreements about moral judgments involving financial transactions because this area is complicated and it is not easy to understand the components and ramifications of various courses of action. For example, in the fall of 2008 after the collapse of Lehman Brothers and the government rescue of AIG, an atmosphere of panic enveloped the financial markets. There was tremendous volatility in the stock market and the risk of the economy's grinding to a halt and triggering a worldwide depression was real. In this context, the Securities and Exchange Commission banned short selling of financial stocks from September 19 to October 9.[5] The ban on short selling was a temporary action taken by a regulatory authority in order to promote stability in the markets. There was disagreement with this government intervention, with the duration of the ban, and with the fact that it applied only to short selling financial stocks. However, thoughtful people can be counted on to agree with the basic ethical premise that government agencies are morally required to enact policies that promote the common good. And there is no question that a stable marketplace constitutes a benefit for society.

Sometimes moral questions are so difficult that people cannot even decide into which category to put them. While most people would classify theft as an evil deed, a moral wrong and a crime because deciding about taking something that does not belong to you is fairly straightforward, other questions strike us as much more perplexing. For example, people tend to be confused about evaluating the moral value of government stimulus programs because these programs have good and bad consequences. They result in employment and consumer spending, which are economically beneficial. However, they add to the deficit in the year they are enacted, and to the nation's long-term debt, which are economically troubling consequences. The fact that some issues are extremely difficult to resolve should prompt thoughtful people to call for rigorous examination of these issues and serious dialogue about them.

In addition to disagreements about which moral judgments are correct, there are also disagreements about who is competent to make these judgments. Some say individuals should decide for themselves; others contend that authorities such as judges, legislators, regulators, business leaders or philosophers are the ones who are equipped to decide what is right or wrong. The decisive element in deciding what is right or wrong is likely the rationale on which the argument is based, not the status or title of the person who articulates the position.

In order to engage in moral reasoning, one needs to analyze decisions, motives and consequences. There are various approaches to moral analysis and each has its limits. Nevertheless, one needs to consider the moral issue under discussion along with the strength of each approach in order to arrive at the most ethically satisfactory decision. A critical assessment of contemporary culture will also be required. This task will be difficult because it is hard to achieve the necessary distance from one's culture in order to determine how it influences values, behaviors and goals, as well as how it might distort judgment.

Some methods of moral reasoning. There are many ways to reason morally and varying answers to the question, "How can the morally correct choice or course of action be determined?" Philosophers generally situate ethical theories within one of four categories: teleological theories, deontological theories, virtue-based theories and moral sense theories. Answers to ethical dilemmas may differ depending upon which theory is used. Each theory has some attractive features and each has limitations; familiarity with them can be helpful in analyzing how ethics should contribute to financial recovery.

Teleological ethical theories. The word *teleological* has its root in two Greek words: *telos* which means goal and *logos* which means word; the suffix *ology* (derived from logos) is generally understood as *the study of.* According to teleological ethics the morally good act is determined based on the consequences of human behavior rather than the content of the behavior. The issue to be resolved is whether or not a particular action or course of action achieves the desired goal.

Hedonism. Hedonism is a teleological ethical system based on the fact that the goal of the hedonist is pleasure. Hedonism dates to the Greeks and the philosopher Epicurus (341–270 BC) is credited with its formulation. To the extent that actions bring pleasure they are good actions; to the extent that actions cause pain, they are bad actions. Hedonism is not as simple as it sounds because pleasure and pain can be sensory or intellectual, thus adding a layer of complication to the system. A borrower who negotiates a liar loan mortgage might evaluate obtaining the mortgage as ethically good based on the pleasures associated with home ownership. Another buyer might think obtaining the same kind of mortgage ethically bad if she experiences stress related symptoms because of her inability to make payments.

Hedonism is further complicated by the fact that pleasure can be sought for oneself, in which case it is egoistic, or the drive to achieve pleasure can be altruistic, with a goal of having other people experience pleasure. The economic theory of the Invisible Hand seems to be compatible with the concept of egoistic hedonism. The assumption that the marketplace tends to reward ethical behavior and punish unethical behavior is a corollary to the concept of the Invisible Hand. The economic markets are considered to be self-regulating in that self-interest, competition and supply and demand constitute a mechanism, an Invisible Hand, that work together to efficiently allocate resources in society. According to this theory, the self-interested goal of financial executives of achieving financial rewards will result in a functional, profitable marketplace. The notion of the

Invisible Hand is attributed to Adam Smith (1723–1790); Smith's seminal work, *The Wealth of Nations*, made him the father of modern economics. Past Chairman of the Federal Reserve, Alan Greenspan, blamed himself for being too taken with Adam Smith's belief that free market capitalism could be counted on to be self-regulating:

> As I wrote last March (2008), those of us who have looked to the self-interest of lending institutions to protect shareholder's equity (myself especially) are in a state of shocked disbelief. Such counterparty surveillance is a central pillar of our financial markets' state of balance. If it fails, as occurred this year, market stability is undermined.[6]

The Golden Rule, "Do unto others as you would have them do unto you," is an apt example of altruistic hedonism. When financial firms cooperate with one another based on mutual self-interest they are engaging in free market capitalism and are dealing with each other in such a way as to secure their own advantage as well as market stability. Both realize that what is good for the other is also beneficial for the firm they represent. One could argue that there is no altruism involved; that individuals carry out transactions for the benefit of their firm and not the well-being of the other or the overall stability of the market. In September 2008 when Lehman Brothers was in crisis the market certainly did not restrain itself in the interests of Lehman Brothers or that of market stability. Short sellers drove the stock price down and lenders refused credit, or demanded payments, or required the posting of additional collateral on outstanding loans. The result was financial catastrophe.

In summary, an egoist who reasons as a hedonist thinks that moral decisions should be based on how his personal pleasure or happiness is affected by the choice; an altruistic hedonist thinks that ethical decisions should also take into account how others are affected.

Utilitarianism. Utilitarianism is also a teleological approach to ethics. Adam Smith, mentioned above, was a utilitarian. Utilitarianism is an approach to ethics which seeks to avoid the arbitrariness of subjective approaches as well as the nonnegotiability of rule-centered approaches. Accordingly, utilitarianism seeks to establish a method for arriving at ethical conclusions through means of mathematical calculation. The action or policy which is deemed ethically correct accomplishes the goal of bringing about the greatest good for the greatest number. The action or policy which is considered morally wrong might benefit a small percentage but would not be beneficial for the majority. Utilitarianism appeals to business leaders and corporations. It also appeals to politicians because it suggests a rationale that may lead to a political consensus.

Ethical theoreticians associated with utilitarianism are Jeremy Bentham (1748–1832) and John Stuart Mill (1806–1873). Bentham maintained that actions produce units of pleasure and that the task of ethics is to help people discern which actions will produce the greatest amount of pleasure for the individual and the community. Mill differed with Bentham in that he challenged the idea of always being able to measure pleasure and he placed more emphasis on the social character of happiness.

As a methodology for resolving ethical issues, utilitarianism has both strengths and weaknesses. Among its strengths is the attractiveness of equating ethically good acts or policies with those which bring pleasure or happiness to people because, on the surface, it seems a commendable goal. In addition, striving to bring about good for the greatest number seems reasonable to citizens in democracies wherein it is customary to follow the will of the majority. Utilitarianism also manages to bypass intractable disagreements over conflicting principles by foregoing debate and simply acting to bring about the greatest good. Utilitarians consider it immoral to act for narrow personal goals such as to secure a bonus or a promotion to the detriment of a larger number, such as other members of the firm. Making a decision requires developing a cost–benefit calculus and applying this to all parties who would be affected by the decision. This is not easy because it is hard to figure out what will happen before a policy or plan is actually put in place.

Utilitarian concepts are understandable to business people and are compatible with business interests and, therefore, utilitarianism is the method frequently adopted to arrive at ethical decisions involving finance. This method justifies pursuit of maximum profits and takes into account the many stakeholders whose interests are affected by business decisions. It also encourages productivity because productivity results in economic prosperity, which is advantageous to everyone in society. Two drawbacks with utilitarianism are, first, that it is next to impossible to quantify all future consequences of financial decisions and, second, that individual and minority rights can be neglected while actions are being taken based on the best interests of the majority.

It was utilitarian thinking that drove the decision by the U.S. government to enact the TARP program. This legislation was initially designed so that the government would buy and hold toxic mortgages in order to relieve banks of the weight of these bad assets on their balance sheets. As it turned out, however, the government did not purchase subprime mortgages from banks but, instead, lent money to banks to recapitalize them. This allowed the banks to continue to function and get back to viability. Many argue that the TARP program did not bring about the greatest good for the greatest number and point to the fact that TARP did little for millions of homeowners who faced foreclosure and nothing for underwater homeowners. They said that government funds should have gone to people who were behind on their mortgages as well as to banks that were short on capital.

It may well have been utilitarian thinking that prompted Wells Fargo Bank to contract with the robo signing mill America's Servicing Company to deal with delinquent mortgages.[7] Processing large numbers of mortgages that are in arrears for a small fee per mortgage could appear to be a strategy that would contain costs and serve bank stakeholders by allowing for maximization of profits. However, the interests of the group that was placed at a disadvantage by the robo signers, homeowners whose properties were being foreclosed, were denied the protection of the law when documents were signed by agents of America's Servicing Company who frequently had no knowledge of the facts of the cases on which they were signing off. After government regulators and the public became aware of the tactics of foreclosure mills legal actions were taken against banks that employed these firms. When these cases are settled banks who employed robo signers will end up paying fines in the tens of billions of dollars.

Many philosophers reject teleological approaches to ethics and argue that moral goodness has nothing to do with generating pleasure or with consequences. Most of these philosophers argue for deontological theories.

Deontological theories. Deontological theories are by definition duty-based. The word *deontological* has its roots in two Greek words: *deon*, which means that which is binding, or duty, and the suffix *ology* (derived from logos) which is generally understood as *the study of*. Morality, according to deontologists, consists in the fulfillment of moral obligations, or duties. Duties require that people obey moral rules. Rightness and wrongness are determined without taking into account whether carrying out duties or obeying rules bring pleasure or pain. Many ethical rules have been codified into laws, and people are penalized if they disobey laws. An example of laws that are derived from ethical rules are laws against fraud. Ethics requires that people carry out fair and truthful transactions. Doing so is an obligation for all parties involved in a transaction. Laws against fraud presuppose the ethical obligation of actors in the marketplace to be fair and truthful. Accordingly, lawsuits have been filed against securitizers of mortgage-backed securities based on the fact that adequate disclosure was not made about defective subprime mortgages in bundled securities and the fact that, in some instances, the securitizer was influenced by a short seller in the selection of mortgages for the issue.

There are several manifestations of deontology: natural law, Kantian theory, the theory of justice, moral rights theory and divine command theory.

Natural law. Natural law is a system for doing ethics which dates to the ancient Greeks. The philosopher Aristotle (384–322 BC) was its chief proponent. According to natural law, sane, mature individuals discover a reasoning process within themselves which is an accurate tool for determining which actions or courses of action are morally appropriate or inappropriate.

A key to understanding natural law lies in understanding the concept of substantial form. By substantial form is meant that each specific category of being has a particular nature and can be counted on to act according to its nature. Thus, we expect dogs to bark, horses to gallop and apples to grow on apple trees. This is because dogs, horses and apple trees act in accordance with their natures or, in other words, conform to their substantial forms.

The substantial form of the human person differs radically from those of plants and animals. Plants follow the natures inscribed in them and animals act in accordance with their instincts. Humans are different. According to natural law, in their essence humans possess reason which will allow them to act in conformity with their nature or go against their nature. Thus, humans can respond to the possibility of a big payday by entering into a highly risky transaction or they can reject a windfall and abide by sensible risk tolerance guidelines. Humans can satisfy a desire to acquire a splendid residence by taking on more debt than they can reasonably handle, or they can choose to live modestly within their means. A primary focus of natural law ethics is to explain how human intellect and volition interact in ethical decision-making.

The theory of natural law starts with the premise that the person has a goal: to become happy, or complete, or good.

With this goal in mind the person acts in such ways as to bring about the desired result. It is morally right actions which will bring contentment or satisfaction or the happiness for which the person hopes. Individuals do not decide which actions are morally right or morally wrong; it is in the nature of the action itself that moral rightness or wrongness is located and individuals (and society) are obligated to do the right thing and follow the right rules. This is why natural law is considered a deontological system of ethics.

The natural law approach to ethics is theoretically capable of yielding objective standards because it is based on the assumption that people will agree that what promotes human dignity and the well-being of society is morally good and what retards dignity or the social order is morally objectionable. These standards are expressed as rules. It is further held that by processes of both individual and group reflection fair-minded people will affirm the inherent soundness of this fact. Natural law assumes that the consciences of the individual and the society will validate the premise that certain actions facilitate human development and are morally good and other actions retard development and are morally evil. Principles function within natural law as the fundamental truths or motivating forces from which norms, or rules of conduct, are derived.

It is fairly simple to demonstrate that general rules derived from natural law are evident in the marketplace. Some examples are: financial firms should have sufficient capital on hand to be able to pay their debts even if a worst-case scenario should impact the firm; government regulators should monitor the capital positions of financial firms as well as the risks these firms take; credit rating agencies should render the service they claim to provide and accurately state the merits or deficiencies of securities they evaluate. These are general rules about which rational people do not argue because they are straightforward. Why, then, is it far from simple to formulate and enforce financial rules? When we move from general statements about ethical conduct to formulating rules to be applied in specific contexts we inevitably encounter complexity and difference of opinion. There will be disagreements about the amount of money that constitutes sufficient capital, the specific steps regulators should take in monitoring financial firms, and the precise words credit rating agencies need to use in evaluating mortgage-backed securities. Proponents of natural law contend that these disagreements do not detract from the merit of the theory but, rather, indicate that deriving financial rules is a complicated undertaking.

How useful is natural law to people in general and to those who seek guidance in regard to financial conduct? It is a system that has been in existence for 2,500 years which presents a concept of authentic human development and argues for objective ethical standards based on reason. A reservation about the utility of natural law as a system for doing ethics comes from those who see it as a system which pays too little attention to how human emotions impact ethical choices. The answer to this objection may be that many questions require definite answers, and this is especially true in regard to financial conduct. The fact that financial conduct is transactional, that is, conducted between parties such as individuals, firms and regulators, underscores the need for clear ethical guidelines.

In the process of moral deliberation, natural law relies heavily on act analysis. Human acts are those considered actions which disclose an individual's beliefs and values and which are of ethical import. Compensation committees need to grapple with moral concerns as they try to decide on appropriate pay and benefits packages of upper level management. Decisions about bailing out firms that are too big to fail are difficult for government officials and their resolution incorporates ethical considerations.

In analyzing human acts, natural law proponents suggest that the four aspects of the act be examined and that the act be considered morally acceptable only if it can be justified in its entirety. The aspects are:

Object: that which is done. This is a description of what transpires without any elaboration in terms of values or appropriateness. For example, short selling of financial stocks is halted.

Intention: the reason a particular course of action is chosen. According to natural law, good intentions are necessary in order for an action to be good. If the SEC halts short selling of financial stocks for a specified period of time with the intention of stabilizing the market, then this action would be good and the agency could credit itself with ethical conduct. If, however, the SEC halts short selling in order to settle scores with political enemies who prosper by short selling, this would not be an ethically good action. (It should be noted that even if, in the second case, the halt on short selling benefitted the market, the SEC's hypothetical action would not be considered good because it would have been done with a bad, or deficient, intention.)

Circumstances: these are the unique features of time and place under which an act takes place. The SEC regulates markets; a ban on short selling of financial stocks is an extraordinary step to take. In evaluating whether or not a ban by the SEC is an ethically appropriate action, the circumstances under which this course is taken need to be considered.

Effects or consequences: these are the foreseeable results of actions or omissions. The effect of banning short selling is undertaken to stop manipulation and result in stabilization of the financial markets. The ban on short selling constitutes interference in the free market and a judgment needs to be made as to whether or not such interference is justified by the effect (market stabilization) which prompts the action. Is the tradeoff worth it?

It sometimes happens that in carrying out human acts there are two effects, one good and the other evil. Consider the case of the U.S. government in assuming a majority share in AIG. This would save AIG but it would also contribute to a sense of moral hazard. What should the government do? What should the Board of AIG agree to? According to the natural law principle of double effect, as long as the intention for government involvement is to prevent a worldwide depression, and under the circumstances there are no other possible ways to stop the panic, the bailout may occur and the Board should welcome it. Thus, an action which includes a bad effect can be tolerated based on the fact that less than ideal situations often force morally good institutions such as the government to accept less than ideal solutions.

Kantian ethics. Immanuel Kant (1724–1804) was a German philosopher who developed a secular deontological theory of individual rights. A right is a person's entitlement to something such as truthful information and, in a commercial context, the right of a purchaser to receive what is paid for is balanced by the right of a seller to be paid for the goods. Wary of the possibility that his theory could become overly individualistic, Kant developed the concept of the categorical imperative. The categorical imperative has two elements: first, a person should act in such a way that her action could become a universal law and this person should be willing for anyone to carry out the same action in similar circumstances. Second, the person should never treat an individual or a group as a means, but always as an end by never exploiting another human being.

The logic of the categorical imperative would not allow a mortgage securitizer to quickly move mortgage-backed securities containing subprime mortgages in advance of a market implosion, by taking advantage of the ignorance of a naïve customer to the customer's detriment and the seller's advantage. Such a transaction would violate the categorical imperative because the buyer would be used as a means to garner a profit for the seller, and not as a person with a right to be respected and not cheated. Kant's theory leaves no doubt that it is morally wrong to deceive, manipulate and exploit customers. According to Kant's reasoning, securitizers who in 2007 knew that bundled mortgage products were toxic also likely knew that it would gravely damage financial markets if all firms dumped toxic mortgage-backed securities by unloading them on unsuspecting investors. This knowledge should have prompted securitizers to reason that, if it was unethical for all securitizers to dump toxic inventory on unsuspecting buyers, it would be unethical for one securitizer to do so with one issue.

The principle of universality inherent in the categorical imperative does not provide the answer to the question of why some acts are ethically good and others are ethically wrong, but it does make people engage in what Kant calls practical reason. Practical reason is the capacity of figuring out what one should do in a given situation. Reflection of this kind leads to action because as people reason they come to recognize the need to act in one way or another. Kant's approach to ethics is that people know the difference between right and wrong, have the ability to choose the right course, and experience an impulse to perform moral duties which are incumbent on them. People realize that it is necessary to do one's duty and act in conformity with the moral law as understood through the application of the categorical imperative. When individuals act to fulfill their duties, they act ethically.

Kant maintains that the faculties of knowing and choosing are essential to morality; if someone argues that humans do not possess these faculties, the arguer is inferring that there can be no morality. Kant further postulates that good individuals act out of a good will and do not need to be threatened with punishments in order to do the right thing. He makes an interesting distinction explaining that good persons should not be equated with good citizens, as explained by Ronald F. White, Ph.D.,

> A good citizen does the right thing purely out of fear of getting caught. I chose to pay you back only because I wanted to avoid the pain associated with getting beaten up. Note that if I believed that I could effectively defend myself, or hide from you, I might choose not to pay you back. A society comprised entirely of good citizens requires clear laws, monitoring for compliance, and the effective enforcement of those rules. But a society of good persons

would not require monitoring and enforcement. No one would break promises, steal, or murder. We wouldn't need a police force, judiciary, or prisons.[8]

Politicians, business leaders, journalists, community leaders and other interested parties who advocated for and are still working toward implementation of the Dodd–Frank Act might not employ the same terminology as Kant, but they would agree with his thinking that relying on the good will of good people is insufficient to produce orderly financial markets. Recent history shows us that there are individuals and firms who do not act in morally good ways and will find motivation to do the right thing only through fear of the embarrassment associated with getting caught and/or the punishment associated with being prosecuted. Laws, monitoring and documentation of compliance are necessary to prompt these actors in the financial markets to function as so-called *good citizens*.

The theory of justice. The theory of justice is another deontological approach to ethics; it is associated with John Rawls (1921–2002) who was influenced by Kant and Thomas Hobbes (1588–1679). (Hobbes formulated the concept of the social contract according to which the source of good and evil is the will of the people. He reasoned that it is better for citizens to submit to government than to revert to a state of war and argued that the consensus of the community establishes ethical right and ethical wrong.)

John Rawls was an American philosopher who taught at Princeton, Cornell, MIT and Harvard. Rawls' original contribution to ethics was his suggestion that each person decide principles of justice from behind a "veil of ignorance." By this he meant:

No one knows his place in society, his class position or social status, nor does anyone know his fortune in the distribution of natural assets and abilities, his intelligence, strength, and the like.... The principles of justice are chosen behind a veil of ignorance.[9]

Rawls' veil of ignorance gives rise to the so-called *difference principle* which would allow inequalities in the distribution of goods only if those inequalities benefit the worst-off members of society. Rawls' theory of justice would eliminate preferential treatment based on criteria which have traditionally advantaged people, such as being wealthy, well born or well connected. In the aftermath of the financial crisis there have been countless complaints about the fact that the U.S. government bailed out Wall Street while ignoring the suffering on Main Street. This complaint is a sweeping generalization and ignores the stimulus programs of both the Bush and Obama administrations, the extensions of unemployment insurance, the jobs created through the American Recovery and Reinvestment Act, the 2011 payroll tax holiday, and other less well known government initiatives targeted to assist U.S. citizens. The fact is that if the government did not act to prevent the failure of big banks and AIG, whose misdeeds caused economic chaos, a worldwide depression likely would have happened and everyone, advantaged and disadvantaged alike, would have faced the likelihood of being wiped out. Accordingly, if government and financial leaders in the United States followed Rawls' advice and acted from behind a veil of ignorance they would have enacted policies that benefitted the disadvantaged and, in the process, stood by while the structures of capitalism disintegrated.

In a noncrisis atmosphere Rawls' theory has more to recommend it. Justice is advocated because it requires fairness in transactions and concern for those at the margins of society. Rawls says that people should achieve human goals cooperatively by adhering to mutually acceptable regulatory principles. Ironically, in the aftermath of the financial crisis, wherein regulatory oversight and sanctions for wrongdoing were largely lacking, the political atmosphere in the United States is extremely polarized with outspoken opposition to government regulation and a large and vocal minority which is challenging the need for government altogether.

Moral rights theory. Approaching ethics through a consideration of human rights began with John Locke (1632–1704), an English philosopher, and continued with John Rawls, whose theory we just considered. Thomas Jefferson, author of the Declaration of Independence, studied Locke's writings and incorporated Locke's ideas of equality and reference to the inalienable rights to life, liberty and the pursuit of happiness into the founding document. Locke's political theory was organized around the idea that human nature is characterized by reason and tolerance and he said that people establish a social contract through which they determine how to govern themselves and resolve conflicts in a civil way. One of the primary goals that incline people to gather together and form a government, according to Locke, is the protection of private property and Locke is noteworthy for his explication of property rights.

Moral rights theory is correctly termed a type of deontological ethics because the correlative of a moral right is a moral duty, and deontological ethics are concerned with ethical duties. On the one hand, a person has a right to possess something or pursue some goal; the counterpart of this right is the duty or obligation of another to actively assist the person in securing his right. Rights can be positive rights or negative rights. In regard to positive rights, an individual or society is obligated to fulfill the right. In regard to negative rights, there exists only the obligation not to interfere in the individual's pursuit of the right. Libertarians stress negative rights and egalitarians are apt to argue for at least some positive rights.[10] Ayn Rand (1905–1982) was a philosopher who provides us with a libertarian perspective in regard to moral rights. She taught that people should pursue self-interest and that the free market should function without external controls.

Locke's concern with property rights and the role of government in protecting the rights of people who own property can be understood in two ways. The first way is that people inherit property or work to purchase property; the property they acquire is theirs, and the government should provide services such as police and firefighters to prevent intrusions on private property or its destruction from catastrophic events. Property owners pay taxes to governments at all levels and these various levels of government should, in turn, spend tax revenue on what is necessary to protect private property.

The second way to understand Locke's approach to private property is to question his approach as perhaps contributing to the establishment of an underclass because it allies government with property owners and distances government from people who do not own property. Government-sponsored projects to build affordable housing frequently have trouble gaining traction because homeowners in the area protest; there are programs to assist low-income individuals and families to become homeowners but the reality is that few poor or working poor actually do own their own homes. Is this because the function of government is as Locke envisioned it 300 years ago, and there is no reason to move beyond that vision, or is it because Locke's ideas need to be nuanced, but the will to do so is lacking? This philosophical question needs to be addressed. In the 1990s politicians advocated for home ownership as an essential part of realizing the American dream. Beginning around 2002 subprime mortgages were issued to borrowers who, in many cases, did not understand the terms to which they were agreeing. Whether or not they understood the terms, they stood little to no chance of holding on to the property they were buying. They were caught up in a frenzy and, for a brief time, experienced the satisfaction of home ownership. Then everything unraveled and foreclosure and eviction turned satisfaction into chaos, both for individuals and communities. What role did Locke's theory of property rights and the role of government play in the subprime crisis and subsequent bailouts? Government agencies failed poor and lower middle class people who secured subprime mortgages. Oversight over the transactions they entered into was lacking and the role of government vis-à-vis the property of subprime owners turned out to be minimal at best. (The Federal Reserve is charged with supervision of banking and taking steps to stop harmful practices. That the Fed did not carry out these responsibilities during the years when subprime mortgages were being issued is clear.) That Locke's theory at the beginning of the American nation favored property owners is understandable in the context of the times; that the concept of owning property and rights correlative to such ownership has not expanded and developed over time may be a flaw in U.S. culture.

Divine command theory. In the Judeo Christian tradition actions are considered wrong if they violate God's rules, generally derived from the Ten Commandments. Muslims locate rules in the Quran. Defenders of divine command theory maintain that God or Allah would not require submission to irrational rules and that moral goodness is attained by aligning one's conduct with divine commands. While many individuals set their ethical compass according to divine command theory, the influence of this theory in the marketplace is negligible because the marketplace, as well as government, society and the media are secular in nature and carry out functions without reference to theological premises. In addition, not all major religions evaluate ethical conduct as right or wrong within a divine command framework. Buddhism and Hinduism contain sophisticated ethical systems but their theories are not organized around obeying divine laws.

Virtue ethics. Virtue ethics dates from the Greek philosophers and is consistent with the natural law approach, described above. Aware of her goal to be a good person, an individual acts in such ways as to bring about the desired result. It is morally good deeds which will bring contentment and personal integrity. By good deeds, consistently performed, people complete and perfect themselves, becoming the ethically good persons that they are meant to be. Good people are balanced, finding the mean between two extremes; in other words, they act reasonably and are not characterized by excesses. In the task of perfecting their nature, virtuous people perform morally good actions on a consistent, predictable basis. Their ease in performing these actions becomes second nature; the name by which we call this predictability and ease is *virtue*. Such virtues as truthfulness, dependability, courage, generosity, patience, prudence and a host of others characterize morally good people. Virtue ethics is considered deontological because human nature requires effort in order to be perfected; persons understand this requirement as a rule of nature that they have a duty to fulfill.

Virtue based theories tend to elevate community and deemphasize individualism. They focus on character development within harmonious communities.[11] Role models who have lived virtuous lives are held up by the community as exemplars for their contemporaries as well as for succeeding generations to emulate. Vision and hope are two virtues that characterize American self-identity. The story of the financial crisis is a record of lack of wisdom, lack of prudence, absence of good judgment and presence of deceit and greed. These negative attributes are vices – the opposites of virtue. In order to recover from the crisis people need to recommit themselves to the democratic vision and hopeful confidence that characterized the United States in past generations.

In addition, citizens need to understand that wise people exercised courage and spoke truth to power during the run up to the crisis. The fact that the warnings of these individuals were not heeded does not take away from the fact that they spoke out and tried to prevent economic catastrophe. A case in point is the efforts of Brooksley Born, Chairperson of the Commodity Futures Trading Commission, who advocated in the late 1990s for regulation of over-the-counter derivatives, including credit default swaps. She rightly predicted that, if unregulated, these complex instruments could lead to the destabilization of financial firms and undermine the entire economy. The fact that her warnings were rejected by powerful government officials including Alan Greenspan, Fed Chairman (1987–2006), Robert Rubin, Secretary of the Treasury (1995–1999) and Larry

Summers, Deputy Secretary of the Treasury (1995–1999), becoming Secretary of the Treasury (1999), reveals that government and society need to act on well-informed warnings and resist the temptation to dismiss them. Further, both government and civil society need to hold up courageous individuals such as Brooksley Born for emulation.

Moral sense theories. Intuitionism and subjectivism are not so much systems for doing ethical reflection as unsystematized ways by which people make moral decisions. Moral sense theories are not classified as teleological or deontological because ethical decisions are not made in light of a goal and because objective rules do not function as the rationale for action.

Moral sense theories originated in the writings of Anthony Ashley Cooper (1671–1713). Cooper located moral goodness in the proper balance between the natural kindly or generous affections and the unnatural affections of hatred and hostility. Humans, having a moral sense, are able to distinguish between kindly and hostile feelings and follow a moral reflex (or sense) in making decisions about ethical choices.[12]

Moral judgments are reached without recourse to supporting rationale or argumentation. Accordingly, with intuitionism people follow their hunches and say things like "I have a hunch that this candidate will be a good banking regulator. She seems conscientious and I think she is very smart. Let's stop interviewing candidates and hire her." Thus, an extremely important decision about the qualifications and experience of a government banking regulator could be decided on flimsy grounds, i.e., what a decision-maker's instincts dictate. Ironically, people who reach ethical judgments based on intuitionism generally do not grasp the fact that this approach is subjective and arbitrary.

Subjectivism is another superficial and arbitrary approach to ethical decision-making. With subjectivism the criterion for deciding what is morally right or what is morally objectionable is one's feelings. We are as likely to hear a subjectivist judge proclaim, "I feel that this family should get foreclosed on," as to say, "I do not feel that this family should get foreclosed on." What is missing from these two decisions is an answer to the question "Why?" which would provide evidence of the judge's carefully evaluating the foreclosure documents submitted by the lender and considering any special circumstances of the family which ought to be explored before a decision is reached.

A fault common to intuitionism and subjectivism is that neither of these ways of doing ethics is capable of providing an objective basis for resolution of ethical problems. Since factors internal to the decision-maker (hunches or feelings) determine the moral rightness or wrongness of actions, there is bound to be disagreement as to what constitutes right or wrong conduct. In the face of such disagreement the way to preserve social harmony is to condemn as few ways of acting as possible, while tolerating the greatest possible diversity. Such actions as theft, fraud and deceitful misrepresentation of financial products are condemned, but on other ethical matters there tends to be a plurality of possible opinions. Moral relativism is thus encountered with great regularity as is the pervasive inclination to believe that one opinion is as good as another. While this situation is understandable, it is also troubling in that, in the aftermath of the financial crisis, a consensus has emerged that we need to prevent something similar from happening in the future. We need to let go of ethical haziness and find a way to regulate orderly markets and prevent excesses that undermine stability.

Tackling a problem in ethics. In order to analyze any dilemma in a systematic fashion, one needs to have a system for problem solving. As we saw above, there are several ethical approaches from which one can choose, either singly or in combination. While each approach has its limits and while actors in the marketplace do not have the leisure of philosophers to work through all the complexities which scholarly reflection requires, there can be no disagreement about a general goal of leveraging the strengths of various approaches to arrive at the most rational and defensible position. It is important to be aware of the essential elements which should be taken into consideration in solving an issue with financial implications. These elements include clarifying the facts pertinent to the case, the ethical issues contained in the case and various ways of resolving these issues. In light of relevant facts, a decision-maker must decide on the best moral solution and provide rationale in justification of this decision.

Eventually the economy will recover and the financial crisis will be history. Philosophers such as Aristotle, Kant and Rawls who understood morality have provided us with ethical systems within which we can consider not only the issues raised by the implosion of 2008 but, also, have provided the opportunity to become aware of principles of ethics which will be of use in many of the dilemmas the future likely holds. The financial crisis, as other daunting ethical issues, is about human nature, institutions, cultural values, diffusion of responsibility and ability to analyze and make decisions. The particulars of the financial crisis are unique, but the task of responding to tomorrow's crisis will require working through it with an awareness that the principles considered herein are similarly applicable.

Conclusion. The decisions we make about ethical issues determine whether or not we become people of integrity. In addition, the ethical standards which our society encourages influence our communal identity, for good or for ill. Therefore, the importance we place on understanding and implementing ethical theory will have profound and far-reaching results. It is time-consuming and intellectually demanding to clarify theoretical presuppositions but, in the long run, both the time and effort expended will come to be seen as worthwhile.

There were countless ethical lapses apparent in the interactions of those who contributed to the economic crisis. If individuals and organizations had taken the trouble to reflect on what they were doing and had summoned the willpower to make ethically appropriate choices, the crisis would not have happened and people would not be suffering its adverse consequences. It is important that we now seize the teachable moment to which Jim Wallis refers and engage in serious ethical reflection with the hope that ethical conduct will lead to the transformation of the economy and the common good. In order to accomplish this goal, the next two chapters will explain how individual ethics and social ethics should inform the road ahead.

Questions for Discussion

1 Do you think that the economic crisis was caused solely by complex financial transactions, or do you think that ethics played a part? What leads you to think as you do?

2 What is ethics? Describe the role (if any) that ethics should play in resolving the systemic issues that caused the economic meltdown.

3 Do you think it makes more sense to be optimistic or pessimistic about the possibility of putting in place effective measures to fix what is broken in the financial system? Explain what leads you to think as you do.

4 In the past people in the United States dealt with major problems and took steps to correct them. Comment on the lessons history holds for people who are dealing with the consequences of the financial crisis.

5 Discuss how following teleological approaches to ethics can lead to ethical judgments.

6 Discuss how following deontological approaches to ethics can lead to ethical judgments.

7 Explain the basis for reaching an ethical judgment using moral sense theories.

8 Discuss how virtue ethics could be incorporated into business practice.

9 If you were the CEO of a major bank and your firm needed to decide whether or not to participate in the market for a novel kind of security, what ethical considerations would you list as important for discussion at the next management meeting?

Case Study: Mortgage Mediation

Some states were hit harder by the subprime mortgage debacle than others. In one of the hard-hit states, in August 2010, one in every eighty-four houses in the state had received a foreclosure notice, 4.5 times the national average. This state created a foreclosure mediation program in 2009 that was designed to help struggling homeowners stay in their homes. The state requires that representatives of banks meet with homeowners who request mediation and try to work out a resolution. This state is unique among the states in that it requires a face-to-face meeting between lender and borrower. Anecdotal testimony from borrowers in other states suggests that it is difficult to get in touch with a representative of a bank on the phone and harder still to reach the same person for follow-up calls, which makes requirement of a face-to-face meeting appear to be beneficial for borrowers.

Ed Samuels, a retired attorney, who initially participated as a mediator in the state program decided to discontinue his involvement because he did not think that banks were giving borrowers a fair hearing. There were hearings, but he complained that bank lawyers showed up for meetings without the required documents and that bank lawyers did not actually negotiate with borrowers, thus getting nothing accomplished at mediation sessions. Having heard that other mediators who complained about the recalcitrance of the banks in the mediation process were removed by the state from the list of mediators, Mr. Samuels decided to voluntarily withdraw from the program. His motivation in joining the program was that he wanted to help people rework their mortgages so they could stay in their homes. He also cared about the communities in his state and the effects on them from high numbers of foreclosed properties. As a senior citizen, Mr. Samuels has little tolerance for frustration and he has begun to agree with his wife that a bad day of golf is better than the prospect of a good day in the mediator's office, a day which will probably never come.

Although he is glad that he was decisive and got out of a bad situation, Mr. Samuels feels uneasy because he wonders how he is helping his neighbors and his community through a rough time.

1 Put yourself in Ed Samuels' position and state what you would do, and why. What insight would likely motivate your decisions?

2 The program described in this case is a good one, but its implementation is problematic. What steps could be taken to improve the program?

3 Who should get involved in strengthening the mediation program to keep people in their homes? What should these parties do? What should motivate them?

4 If you were a homeowner who was delinquent with your mortgage payments, would you participate in a mediation program? Why or why not?

Case Study: Promoting Corporate Interests through Offering Perks

Stephen Jordan is a business reporter for an online news service; he covers the banking sector. The service has experienced exceptional growth in the past few years and its analysis influences stock prices and the public perception of the banking industry. Mr. Jordan is a frequent commentator on cable television shows that focus on finance and he has built a reputation as a well-informed and even-handed journalist. Dan Owens is a senior vice president at a large regional bank that is well capitalized and likely in a strong position to expand by taking over one or more banks that have been weakened by the financial crisis.

Dan calls and invites Stephen, his college roommate, to attend an all-expenses-paid long weekend at a golf resort in Florida.

There won't be many meetings and they won't begin until after 4 p.m. Cocktails at 5:30, so you don't need to worry about falling asleep at breakout sessions. We can play eighteen holes on Friday, Saturday and Sunday. You can fly back with me Sunday afternoon; I'll get you booked on the 4 p.m flight. I can assure you I play better now than when we were undergrads, but you'll probably still beat me.

Stephen genuinely likes Dan Owens and he could use a few days of golf and sunshine. He knows that he will learn some things about the bank that he doesn't know and that he will get an idea about its future plans at the scheduled presentations. But he is conflicted because he suspects that by accepting an expensive break he will be obligating himself to the bank and this sense of obligation will interfere with his ability to be objective, and perhaps negative, in his coverage of the bank. Further complicating his thinking is his friendship with Dan; Stephen wants to enjoy time with Dan and regrets that it has been so long since they have been together. And Stephen worries that it will look bad for Dan if he declines the invitation because he feels sure that Dan told his superiors that he knew Stephen and, "If anyone can get him to come, I can."

1 Should corporations invite reporters to expensive junkets and wine and dine them? Why or why not?
2 Should Stephen accept Dan's invitation? Why or why not?
3 How much should Stephen's concern for Dan's feelings and Dan's job security influence his decision?
4 What ethical considerations does this case raise?

Case Study: Don't Worry About it; We Have No Skin in the Game

A college professor is trying to explain to her students how a financial instrument as elementary as a residential mortgage could be at the bottom of what caused the financial crisis. She writes a step-by-step script that she hopes will clarify elements of the crisis for her students.

There is a meeting in April 2005 in the office of a mortgage lending company. The meeting is between the manager and a mortgage broker. The manager who approves the mortgage says, "Don't worry about it; we have no skin in the game," to the mortgage broker who voices reservations that the borrower will be able to repay the liar loan she is requesting.

As a formality, the manager tells the managing director of the mortgage lending firm's regional office about the broker's reluctance. The managing director says, "Don't worry about it; we have no skin in the game," to the manager of the local office. "Hurry up and keep sending mortgages because they are selling like hotcakes."

When a caution is voiced by a senior employee of the lending firm during a conference call about subprime mortgages, the CEO shrugs off the note of caution and replies, "Don't worry about it; we have no skin in the game."

The buyer for an investment bank calls the CEO of the lending firm and says, "We need all the mortgages you can get for us; I've never seen such a dynamic market."

The CEO of the investment bank says, "Don't worry about it; we have no skin in the game," to senior bank managers at a staff meeting when they question the soundness of the subprime mortgages that are being bought and securitized.

Just to be on the safe side, the CEO of the investment bank discusses the composition of the MBS with the securitizer.

The securitizer says, "Don't worry about it," to the CEO; "We're selling this stuff; it's not staying in-house. We don't need to abide by the risk standards that we use when we write mortgages that are going into our own portfolio. We aren't keeping these mortgage-backed securities, we're passing them on. And we're being paid well for our labors."

The CEO of the investment bank also decides to talk to the firm's expert in real estate. "What's going to happen to our portfolio and the stuff we haven't securitized if the housing market crashes?" he asks. "Don't worry about it; the worst that will happen will be a soft landing – a drop of 10% max. Nothing to lose sleep over."

Investment banks are not worrying because they are selling CDOs to hedge funds, government enterprises, pension plans and other investors. Their clients are happy because the MBS-CDOs pay higher interest rates than Treasuries.

Hedge funds that buy these products don't worry because they hedge their bets by also buying CDS.

Issuers of CDS don't worry because CDOs are AAA solid, according to ratings agencies

As the process unfurls, the meaning of the initial transaction in the chain is lost; what is happening is not about individuals obtaining financing to purchase a home; investors have entered the picture, along with those willing to insure the investors' investments; two complicated securities known as CDOs and CDS have taken shape; and institutional risk takers have embraced the residential real estate market with the sole intention of making lots of money.

1 What should the initial borrower have worried about?
2 What should the mortgage broker have worried about?
3 What should management of the mortgage lender have worried about?
4 What should the investment bank have worried about?
5 What should the securitizer have worried about?
6 What should the credit rating agencies have worried about?
7 What should the buyers of CDOs worried about?
8 What should the issuers and buyers of CDS worried about?
9 What parties, not mentioned in 1 to 7, ought to have been worried?
10 What is the significance of having no skin in the game?
11 Who, if anyone, should take the punch bowl away before the party is over?

5

INDIVIDUAL ETHICS

We have seen media coverage of well-known people whose misconduct became public knowledge. The athlete or politician or movie star or CEO holds a news conference and says, "I'm sorry. What I did was wrong. I apologize to this individual or that group that I hurt by my actions. I will do whatever I can to make things right. I feel terrible; I will have to live with myself for the rest of my life."

As we watch, we have mixed feelings. We know that the person in the hot seat feels guilty and is going through a hard time. We empathize because none of us is perfect and we understand the weight of the burden the shamed individual is bearing. But we also tend to be critical, to ponder the lines between right and wrong conduct; we know that those who cross the line need to suffer consequences because of the harm they have done.

When a celebrity apologizes, the focus turns predictably to the topic of ethics, with a view to imparting lessons during a teachable moment. In light of the financial crisis, the question is clear: what lessons does ethics have to teach us? In regard to individual conduct involving borrowing, lending, securitizing, selling securities, regulating, rating investment products and related practices, it turns out that ethics has a lot to say.

The financial crisis was a multilayered, complicated phenomenon, but the individual misdeeds that caused economic havoc are not very difficult to enumerate. The financial crisis occurred because people behaved badly by committing fraud, lying, finding a way to get around regulations and/or prudent management practices, and acting to fill outsized wants. The ethical lesson to be learned from the financial crisis can be as simple as "Do not do these things." If individuals were to make rational decisions, act with integrity, and behave virtuously, the free market, subject to reasonable regulations, would work to the benefit of all segments of society. In following ethical guidelines individuals who work in finance as well as those who conduct business with them would make morally appropriate choices that would not destabilize the economy. In adhering to ethical standards, employees of credit rating agencies as well as government and industry regulators would direct their efforts to truthful analysis and rigorous enforcement of fair regulations and would thus contribute to market stability and prosperity. Granted, the capitalist, free market system within which the United States economy functions is not perfect and it would be unrealistic and utopian to expect perfect, or near perfect, compliance with ethical standards on the parts of all the varied actors in the system. That being said, there is no question that the unethical actions of many individuals left the financial system in tatters and that ethical conduct is needed to usher in the recovery.

It was with the ethical dimension in mind that Phil Angelides, Chairperson of the Financial Crisis Inquiry Commission, dismissed the notion that the failure of Bear Stearns in March 2008 was some sort of system failure that happened because technical market forces collided with adverse market conditions. Mr. Angelides contended that Bear Stearns failed because the firm's risk management was flawed and inadequate. Angelides said that people, wanting to avoid blame for what happened, were wont to suggest that the financial crisis was "an immaculate calamity." The FCIC Chairperson rejected the concept of an immaculate calamity and blamed the demise of Bear Stearns and the collapse or near collapse of other firms on human misconduct. Over-leveraging, imprudent risk-taking, poor balance sheet management and over-exposure to scratch-and-dent subprime mortgages caused financial chaos. Mr. Angelides said that poor business decisions, many of which emanated from poor ethics, caused the economic implosion.[1] Having witnessed the effects of the financial crisis, it makes sense to consider the lessons ethics can teach us so that we learn how to better conduct affairs going forward.

As we gathered from our review of ways to approach ethics in Chapter 4, there are several options. In order to proceed rationally and be coherent, individuals who make ethical decisions need to adhere to one approach or another. In general, the approach taken in this chapter is deontological. The contention that individuals are required to fulfill moral obligations is taken as self-evident and the fact that the U.S. legal system is deontologically based stands as an endorsement of this approach. According to natural law, the goal for individuals is to reach human completion, or integrity. The need for humans to act with integrity and follow conscience is thus easily grasped. Immanuel Kant counsels us well when he challenges us not to exploit one another and to act in such a way that what we choose to do could become a universal law. John Rawls' insight that individuals should decide what to do from behind a veil of ignorance would, if accepted, lead to more humane and just business and social policies. As we shall see in this chapter, ethical theoreticians have much to teach us as we proceed with our consideration of individual ethical conduct.

There are rules that bind everyone. Ethical rules are standards that people accept and that they agree should govern their behavior and the behavior of others. Ethical rules are considered reasonable and people tend to accept them without argument. There is general agreement that, if people follow reasonable rules, their conduct will be good and those with whom they associate will benefit. When a mom and a dad bring a child into the world they are expected to follow the fundamental rule that requires that parents take care of their children, provide for them and see to their education. If they follow this rule, parents, children and society prosper. If parents neglect their responsibilities, their unethical conduct causes distress to them, their children and others. Even parents who do not take care of their children agree with this rule and acknowledge that they should have followed it. The point is that there are objective standards, or rules, which are binding on people and rational people agree with this fact. Across cultures and across the ages the responsibility of parents to care for their children has been acknowledged. Similarly, people have agreed that it is wrong to murder, to steal, to cheat, to rape, to drive drunk, to commit arson and to sexually abuse children. Societies have enacted laws and set punishments for individuals who do these kinds of wrongs.

It is important to understand the universal applicability of some moral rules because there is a tendency for people to think, "It all depends on where you are coming from and how you see things. Something could be wrong for you, but right for me. In different cultures there are different practices and different rules, so there are no ethical rules that bind everyone everywhere." While there are cultural differences and changes in thinking from one generation to the next, it has never been considered ethically right to steal from a client and it never will be. Neither has murder been allowed or rape been accepted. Stealing, murder, rape and parental neglect of children are ethically wrong and all societies penalize people who commit these wrong actions.

In the aftermath of the financial crisis, it is clear that many individuals acted unethically and that their unethical actions brought incalculable harm to the U.S. economy. There is no question that we need to acknowledge that there are moral rules which should have been followed and that the validity of these rules needs to be acknowledged.

Rule #1: deal fairly in carrying out financial transactions. In its investigation into the financial crisis, a U.S. Senate committee analyzed practices at Washington Mutual Bank (WaMu) in order to present a case study of how actions by some banks contributed to the implosion. The committee cited the typical way in which WaMu loan officers approached people who were applying for mortgages in 2007 as a vivid example of how an irresponsible attitude toward fair dealing and a willingness to take advantage of clients set the stage for disaster.

> In 2007, WaMu adopted a plan to pay "overages," essentially a payment to loan officers who managed to sell mortgages to clients with higher rates of interest than the clients qualified for or were called for in WaMu's daily rate sheets. The plan stated: "Overages ... [give a] Loan Consultant [the] [a]bility to increase compensation [and] [e]nhance compensation/incentive for Sales Management."[2]

Loan officers acted unethically if they exploited borrowers in order to increase their compensation and they violated the rights of borrowers to be treated fairly. So did mortgage brokers who arranged subprime mortgages for people who obviously lacked the ability to make payments. Likewise, borrowers who provided false data to lenders in order to get approved for loans which they could not repay did not deal fairly with lenders. Those who engaged in these transactions set the stage for the economic crisis that hurt people throughout the world.

Everyone who is involved in borrowing and lending will not act fairly. This is why oversight exists and regulations are in place to make the marketplace fair and stable. Government regulators who failed to stop the dangerous practices that were occurring in banking and mortgage lending did not meet their responsibilities. The hedge fund managers who bet against the market to make quick profits, and traders who bought and sold obtuse investment products that turned out to be toxic did not care about the consequences that would be suffered by those whose livelihoods and savings were ruined when the market imploded. Neither did personnel at credit rating agencies who evaluated unsound mortgage-backed securities as AAA, and mortgage brokers who arranged mortgages for clients who failed to properly document their incomes manifest ethical concern. The actions of these individuals were unethical and imperiled the free market.

An example of individual wrongdoing is contained in the complaint issued on April 10, 2010 by the Securities and Exchange Commission against Goldman Sachs and its trader Fabrice Tourre. The complaint alleges in item #18 that the investment bank knew that the market for collateralized debt obligations backed by mortgage-related securities was turning negative and that "the cdo biz is dead (and) we don't have a lot of time left [sic]."[3] Emails sent by the trader Fabrice Tourre, a twenty-eight-year-old, to his girlfriend disclose Tourre's discomfort with what he was doing. Tourre worked to assemble Abacus CDOs and he understood that Abacus was inherently flawed; he likely thought that selling this investment product was unfair to potential buyers. Portions of an email sent by Tourre on January 23, 2007 stated:

More and more leverage in the system. The whole building is about to collapse anytime now ... Only potential survivor, the fabulous Fab(rice Tourre) ... standing in the middle of all these complex, highly leveraged, exotic trades he created without necessarily understanding all of the implications of those monstruosities!!! [sic].[4]

In view of what he knew about the toxic mortgages he was bundling into CDOs, what should Fabrice Tourre have done? What should managers who supervised his department, and risk managers who oversaw Tourre and his managers have done? In retrospect, the answer is obvious; that is why the SEC is prosecuting this case. Just as the local grocery store needs to remove contaminated produce from its shelves, so the investment bank ought to remove toxic securities from its sales inventory. If a trader, realizing that an investment bank does not have much time left before investors become aware of the perils in the subprime market, comes to work and faces a choice of selling toxic junk or refusing to do so, what should he do? Survive (and thrive) like the Fabulous Fab(rice Tourre) tried to do, or refuse to participate in selling "monstrosities"? The ethical answer is to deal fairly with clients and not find a way to exploit their vulnerability.

Part of fair dealing is telling the truth. What does it mean to be truthful and to tell the truth? This means that people should speak the truth and be sincere in their words, attitudes and actions. Telling the truth should be an implicit part of financial transactions. But this was not the case at the height of the subprime mortgage debacle; *liar loans* proliferated and those who sought and granted these loans mocked the very notion of truth. Liar loans are a category of low-documentation or no-documentation mortgage that have been abused to the point that the loans have come to be referred to by this disparaging term. In both the granting and procuring of liar loans individuals did not deal fairly with each other.

In order not to miss out on big profits being made by mortgage companies in the heyday of subprime by issuing mortgages that were unlikely to be repaid, Angelo Mozilo, CEO of Countrywide, overcame his personal misgivings and directed his firm to deal in this market. Mr. Mozilo expressed his ambivalence in an email:

> "In all my years in the business I have never seen a more toxic product," Mozilo told (Countrywide President) Sambol in an e-mail on April 17, 2006. He was referring to the so-called 80/20 subprime loans that let borrowers borrow 100 percent of a home's value by borrowing 80 percent in the primary mortgage and then 20 percent in a secondary loan. "There has to be major changes in this program," Mozilo wrote [*sic*].[5]

Not only did Angelo Mozilo not face the truth about the toxic nature of subprime mortgages, against his better judgment he allowed his firm to engage in the market. Mr. Mozilo is faulted more, however, because he misled investors about Countrywide stock. Mozilo was accused by the Securities and Exchange Commission of making fraudulent disclosures and these mistruths led to his being barred from ever again serving as an officer or director of a publicly traded company. From 2005 through 2007, Mozilo and other senior executives (David Sambol and Eric Sieracki) were accused of misleading the market by falsely assuring investors that Countrywide was primarily a prime quality mortgage lender which had avoided the excesses of its competitors. Countrywide's Forms 10-K for 2005, 2006 and 2007 falsely represented that Countrywide "manage[d] credit risk through credit policy, underwriting, quality control and surveillance activities," and the 2005 and 2006 Forms 10-K falsely stated that Countrywide ensured its continuing access to the mortgage-backed securities market by "consistently producing quality mortgages."[6] At the time, the public was misled by these statements, but, in July of 2008 when Countrywide was taken over by Bank of America, there was no mistaking the misrepresentations that had characterized Countrywide's reporting. Countrywide was not a viable company; it was on the brink of dissolution.

Although the SEC charged Mozilo, Sambol and Sieracki with securities fraud for deliberately misleading investors about the significant credit risks being taken in efforts to build and maintain the company's market share[7] the case was settled without a trial. Mozilo and the other executives settled with the SEC without either admitting or denying the charges against them. Mozilo paid fines totaling $67.5 million, the largest ever paid by a public company's senior executive.[8]

Commenting on the settlement, SEC Director of the Enforcement Division, Robert Khuzami, said:

> Mozilo's record penalty is the fitting outcome for a corporate executive who deliberately disregarded his duties to investors by concealing what he saw from inside the executive suite – a looming disaster in which Countrywide was buckling under the weight of increasing(ly) risky mortgage

underwriting, mounting defaults and delinquencies, and a deteriorating business model.[9]

The issue of dealing fairly by being truthful also arose during the foreclosure crisis when some of those involved in carrying out the process went as far as making false statements. A newspaper account about an attorney acting in behalf of several banks and making false statements, Steven J. Baum, provides an example:

> New York judges are trying to take the lead in fixing the mortgage mess by leaning on the lawyers. In November (2010), a judge ordered (a law) firm to pay nearly $20,000 in fines and costs related to papers that he said contained numerous "falsities." The judge, Scott Fairgrieve of Nassau County District Court, wrote that "swearing to false statements reflects poorly on the profession as a whole."[10]

During the lead up to the financial crisis there were instances of people who saw signs of grave danger and spoke out about these signs but they were not heeded. In these cases, the ethical lapse lies with responsible parties who refuse to listen. In this regard, consider the following excerpt from the U.S. Senate report on the financial crisis:

> At one point in 2004, (James) Vanasek made a direct appeal to WaMu CEO (Kerry) Killinger, urging him to scale back the high risk lending practices that were beginning to dominate not only WaMu, but the U.S. mortgage market as a whole. Despite his efforts, he received no response: "As the market deteriorated, in 2004, I went to the Chairman and CEO with a proposal and a very strong personal appeal to publish a full-page ad in the *Wall Street Journal* disavowing many of the then-current industry underwriting practices, such as 100 percent loan-to-value subprime loans, and thereby adopt what I termed responsible lending practices. I acknowledged that in so doing the

company would give up a degree of market share and lose some of the originators to the competition, but I believed that Washington Mutual needed to take an industry-leading position against deteriorating underwriting standards and products that were not in the best interests of the industry, the bank, or the consumers. There was, unfortunately, never any further discussion or response to the recommendation."[11]

Those who sell financial products have an obligation to truthfully represent what they are selling and, if the products are misrepresented, the misrepresentation constitutes both a violation of ethics and a violation of securities law. In 2007, as the housing market was crashing and collateralized debt obligations were losing value, JPMorgan Chase marketed Squared CDO 2007-I, without telling investors that a hedge fund that helped select the assets would gain if the investment lost value. Obviously, had investors been aware of the hedge fund's role, they would not have bought the CDO. Failure to disclose this information resulted in SEC action against the bank and a settlement of $125.87 million which made investors in that product whole.[12]

In another instance of deception, Morgan Keegan, an investment firm that sold mutual funds, some of which were made up of mortgage-backed securities, was penalized for exaggerating the value of the products it was selling. The SEC alleged that Morgan Keegan misled customers and exacted a $200 million penalty against the firm. Finra, the Financial Industry Regulatory Authority, which cooperated with the SEC in the investigation, reported that Morgan Keegan sold shares in a fund from January 2006 to September 2007, "using sales materials that contained exaggerated claims, failed to provide a sound basis for evaluating the facts regarding the fund, were not fair and balanced and did not adequately disclose the impact of market conditions in 2007 that caused substantial losses" to the fund's value.[13]

If top management at Washington Mutual had not instructed its sales force to exploit borrowers and the bank had heeded James Vanasek's warnings, if Goldman Sachs and its employee Fabrice Tourre had not misled investors in the Abacus CDOs, if liar loan applicants had told the truth, if Countrywide executives had not misrepresented the firm's condition on disclosure forms, if lawyers did not falsify foreclosure documents, and if firms such as Morgan Keegan had not deceived investors about the value of mutual funds, it is safe to say that the devastation of the financial crisis would have been much less. If individuals had dealt fairly in financial transactions, the daunting crisis would not be as grave and widespread as it is. Individuals did not deal fairly in carrying out financial transactions and the results of their collective unethical conduct sent shock waves throughout the U.S. economy.

Rule #2: don't be naïve and assume fair dealing from actors in the financial marketplace; supervise and regulate so that the marketplace functions efficiently. The United States and other first world countries are capitalist nations. The economies of capitalist nations function through production, sales and purchase of goods and services. These activities – producing, buying and selling – are carried out by the so-called *private sector*; government intervenes by issuing regulations that limit or restrict activities in the interest of a stable marketplace. Capitalism, as an economic system, has positive and negative aspects. When capitalism is functioning well there is prosperity and people are able to earn wages and obtain the goods and services they need to live decent lives. When major components of a capitalist system become dysfunctional, such as the housing and financial sectors, hardship and suffering follow.

The regulatory role that government rightly exercises in capitalistic nations is an important and necessary one. Proponents of capitalism argue for the virtues of the free market, a system in which government regulation is minimal. In regard to the financial crisis of 2008, however, it is apparent that the free market did not regulate itself. Some individuals focused on the short term to the detriment of the big picture and others engaged in deceit and fraud, undermining the functionality of the free market. Government regulation of the actors in the market was so ineffective that irresponsible practices proliferated, with dreadful consequences. Individuals behaved badly and management looked the other way; credit rating agencies did not issue accurate ratings; and government regulators failed to intervene and stop the madness. Ayn Rand's idea that the free market should be left on its own without government intervention was proved to be fatally flawed. She was wrong when she declared, "Government 'help' to business is just as disastrous as government persecution ... the only way a government can be of service to national prosperity is by keeping its hands off."[14]

Capitalism, while a good system, is far from perfect and needs to be restrained in the interests of the common good. The financial crisis of 2008 stands as rationale for the need of government to regulate the private sector and to represent the interests of all members of society. In order for government to be an effective regulator it is necessary that it function independently of the market and that its regulators maintain appropriate professional distance.

A good example of failure of the government to exercise its regulatory role is found in the case of the government-sponsored enterprises. Fannie Mae and Freddie Mac were taken over by the Federal Housing Finance Agency on September 6, 2008. This step was taken because the management of these firms had pursued profit over stability and the companies were on the verge of insolvency. As the reason for the takeover became public knowledge people learned that the government regulator which was charged with oversight of the GSEs had done a very poor job. This regulator was the Office of Federal Housing Enterprise Oversight (OFHEO).

The collapse of Fannie Mae and Freddie Mac did not happen overnight. While the failure of the subprime mortgage market was the immediate cause of the firms' insolvency, the actions of management over more than a decade set the stage for the crisis. Top executives at the enterprises pursued activities designed to get favorable treatment from regulators that would enable these executives to earn outsized salaries. The way the executives generated large profits was by engaging in high risk transactions while maintaining an inadequate capital cushion. How could enterprise executives implement such a destructive business model? As we shall see, it was possible to do this by getting lawmakers to enact enabling legislation and hoping that a weak regulator would go along with questionable practices rather than putting a stop to them.

Jim Johnson was CEO of Fannie Mae from 1991 until 1998. During his tenure at Fannie Mae, Johnson worked closely with legislators who were in the process of creating a new regulator for the company.[15] Fannie Mae spent large sums on lobbying and cultivated legislators in order to get the kinds of laws that would allow it to operate to the advantage of its senior management and not necessarily with the well-being of the nation's economy as a priority. Jonathan G.S. Koppell, a former OFHEO employee who became a Yale professor, explains: "Fannie Mae was able to design its regulations. The government sponsored enterprises control their own controllers."[16]

Banking regulations require that banks maintain a capital reserve of 10 percent; Fannie and Freddie were able to get the OFHEO to set their capital requirement much lower, at 2.5 percent.[17] When Fannie and Freddie faced huge losses due to extraordinarily high leverage against meager capital reserves, the public was on the line for bailouts which could amount to as much as $124 billion through 2014.[18] Jim Johnson and his successors at Fannie Mae, as well as top management at Freddie Mac, were able to get OFHEO to do what suited them and not what was best for the marketplace. Politicians, who received hefty campaign contributions from the enterprises, were complicit with people like Jim Johnson to the detriment of tens of millions of people in the United States and around the world. One creative way in which

Johnson enticed politicians to go along with his plans was through establishing fifty-five Partnership Offices in cities throughout the United States. The ostensible purpose of these offices was to assist low-income people to become homeowners. In actuality, the offices provided photo-ops for ribbon-cutting celebrations for members of Congress and local officials and "supplied jobs for relatives and former staffers of elected officials."[19]

It is unethical to disregard the common good in order to promote practices that undermine the general welfare, but, in the interplay among the enterprises, politicians and regulators such disregard is all too apparent. Needless to say, without government officials acting independently and in the best interests of the society and regulators acting with professional competence and appropriate distance from the firms they regulate, the market will not function ethically and efficiently.

During September 2008, the collapse of American International Group (AIG) was a major destabilizing event. AIG was the largest insurance company in the world, and most of its component businesses functioned properly, but tactics adopted by AIG Financial Products (AIGFP) and AIG Securities Lending Corporation brought the company to the brink of insolvency and required rescue by the U.S. government.

In the case of AIG we find that regulatory arbitrage turned out to be bad for the economy, bad for AIG, and an example of an ethical failure whose financial costs are staggering. Regulatory arbitrage is the practice of capitalizing

on loopholes in regulatory systems in order to circumvent unfavorable regulation. Arbitrage opportunities may be accomplished by a variety of tactics, including restructuring transactions, financial engineering and geographic relocation. Regulatory arbitrage is difficult to prevent entirely, but its prevalence can be limited by closing the most obvious loopholes and thus increasing the costs associated with circumventing the regulation.[20]

At the approach of the millennium, AIG was the largest insurance company in the world and, like many other large corporations, AIG wanted to operate with a minimum of government regulation. In order to be as little regulated as possible, in 1999 AIG bought a small thrift (savings and loan bank) in Delaware and, as owner of a thrift, AIG was eligible to be regulated by the Office of Thrift Supervision. The OTS was viewed as more compliant than the Federal Reserve or the Securities and Exchange Commission (AIG's other options), and so executives at AIG took the steps necessary to reclassify the firm as a thrift. How competent was the OTS to regulate AIG? In 2007, as the subprime crisis was exploding, the Government Accountability Office criticized the OTS, noting a "disparity between the size of the agency and the diverse firms it oversees." Among other things, the GAO report noted that the entire OTS had only one insurance specialist on staff – and this despite the fact that it was the primary regulator for the world's largest insurer.[21]

In March 2009, Scott Polakoff, Acting Director of the OTS, admitted that the agency was not capable of fulfilling its role with regard to AIG and that it "did not sufficiently assess the susceptibility of highly illiquid, complex instruments," to ratings downgrades. Mr. Polakoff admitted, "In hindsight, OTS should have directed the company to stop originating credit-default swap products before December 2005."[22] C.K. Lee expanded on Polakoff's testimony when he said, "We missed the impact" of the collateral triggers. Mr. Lee ran a little-known team in the OTS, which oversaw AIG's finance unit. He said the swaps were viewed as "fairly benign products" until they overwhelmed the trillion-dollar company.[23] Simply put, the job of the OTS was to make sure AIG did not take on too much risk and to assess the overall risk environment for the company and other global financial companies it oversaw.[24] OTS was not up to the job; executives at AIG knew as much and decided to game the system in order to be free to operate with minimal interference. Officials at the OTS were likely uncomfortable in their role because they knew that they lacked the expertise and sufficient personnel to do an adequate job regulating AIG. In addition, OTS officials may have suspected that AIG was gaming the system. The OTS is overseen by the Department of the Treasury, a large and powerful agency of the U.S. government. OTS management should have informed the Treasury that OTS was hampered by a lack of personnel and expertise in the unit that regulated AIGFP, and asked that this deficiency be corrected. Of course, this did not happen and the U.S. government wound up spending $185 billion of taxpayer dollars to keep AIG from imploding and to prevent chaotic repercussions for its counterparties.

Executives at AIG should have been concerned about two things, risk management in terms of the solvency of the corporation and whether or not practices engaged in by units such as AIG Financial Products were in line with prudent business and ethical standards. They seemed to be concerned about neither. Martin Sullivan was President and CEO of AIG from March 2005 through June 2008. In testimony before the Financial Crisis Inquiry Commission, Sullivan admitted that in 2005 he was unaware of the tripling of risk through the issuance of credit default swaps by AIGFP. "My first knowledge of the super senior credit-default swaps portfolio was sometime in 2007," Sullivan said at a hearing of the Financial Crisis Inquiry Commission in June 2010. It was swaps that fueled losses that forced AIG to take a government bailout in 2008.[25] The insurer's outside auditor (PricewaterhouseCoopers) said Sullivan didn't hold his staff accountable for financial reporting matters; Sullivan said that he was aware of the totality of what went on at the Financial Products unit and was not alerted to the specific trades that contributed to the firm's near collapse. "I never recognized that portfolio, and there were no issues raised in that correspondence that would have given me cause for concern," Sullivan testified.[26] People can sympathize with Martin Sullivan and excuse his ignorance about the high risk practices at AIGFP, or people can evaluate his lack of oversight as the failure to do his job and insure his firm's stability. In view of the role of counterparty that AIG assumed in respect to innumerable financial and other institutions, and in view of the fact that the collapse of AIG could have triggered a worldwide depression, taking a benign view of executive ineffectiveness does not constitute a reasonable option. The facts that internal management did not prevent the huge losses that brought AIG to the brink of insolvency and that its regulator failed to put a halt to its derivatives business underscore the need for effective regulation.

Joseph Cassano was the head of AIGFP and it was under Cassano's leadership that AIG's exposure to credit default swaps took shape and led to the firm's downfall. In May 2010, we learned that the U.S. Justice Department did not find sufficient evidence to charge Cassano with a crime but this does not mean that Joseph Cassano carried out his responsibilities in an ethically upright manner. The due diligence that AIGFP should have performed on the complex securities on which it wrote credit protection simply did not take place. Assuming that Cassano was a rational individual, it is fair to assert that, had he been aware of the poor quality of the mortgages that comprised the underlying assets of the CDOs, he would not have authorized the issuance of insurance on them. Failure to meet the responsibilities of one's position constitutes a significant ethical lapse. Mr. Cassano never directed AIGFP to test the likelihood of a scenario whereby AIG would be downgraded by the major credit rating agencies, requiring that the firm post additional collateral to those holding its debt, and, perhaps, triggering a liquidity crisis. As it happened, just such a crisis caused the firm's implosion and all fingers point to Cassano as having caused the debacle. The failure of Joseph Cassano and those he supervised to measure and manage risk contributed significantly to the failure of AIG. This omission constitutes a serious ethical failing.

As head of AIGFP Joseph Cassano promoted and sold a financial product which played a pivotal role in undermining AIG. *Time Magazine* named him one of the twenty-five people responsible for the financial crisis.

Before the financial-sector meltdown, few people had ever heard of credit-default swaps (CDS). They are insurance contracts – or, if you prefer, wagers – that a company will pay its debt. As a founding member of AIG's financial-products unit, Cassano, who ran the group until he stepped down in early 2008, knew them quite well. In good times, AIG's massive CDS-issuance business minted money for the insurer's other companies. But those same contracts turned out to be at the heart of AIG's downfall and subsequent taxpayer rescue. So far, the U.S. government has invested and lent $150 billion to keep AIG afloat.[27]

In the heyday of subprime mortgage securitization and issuance of credit default swaps Joseph Cassano seemed to think that AIG would never have to pay claims and that the profit margins from the derivatives was sufficient to justify taking the risks associated with them. (In 2005 the profit margin was 83 percent.) In 2007 he boasted that his company worked with a "global swath" of top-notch entities that included "banks and investment banks, pension funds, endowments, foundations, insurance companies, hedge funds, money managers, high-net-worth individuals, municipalities and sovereigns and supranationals."[28] He explained:

We're sitting on a great balance sheet, a strong investment portfolio and a global trading platform where we can take advantage of the market in any variety of places. The question for us is, where in the capital markets can we gain the best opportunity, the best execution for the business acumen that sits in our shop?[29]

Should we admire Cassano for his ability to market a novel unregulated product and take advantage of an opportunity? Or should we evaluate what he did as destabilizing and destructive? AIG failed in 2008; the terms of the bailout decimated AIG shareholders but saved its trading partners in order to save the international financial system. If we fault Joseph Cassano for taking advantage of market conditions in order to make a lot of money for himself ($300 million) and his 377 coworkers at AIGFP, we are saying that individuals should not do certain things because they cause grave harm. We are also likely concluding that the OTS should have halted trading credit default swaps on collateralized debt obligations because these instruments had the potential of bankrupting AIG and sinking the international economy.

Martin Sullivan was probably in over his head at AIG; he did not know the extent of the firm's exposure to credit default swaps and did nothing to rein in AIGFP. Meanwhile, Joseph Cassano and his subordinates at AIGFP went full throttle in selling CDS without regard for the downside should the housing market deteriorate. In the absence of internal controls in the executive suite and at the subsidiary, controls should have been imposed from AIG's regulator, the Office of Thrift Supervision. But officials at the OTS appear to have been as unaware as Martin Sullivan of what was going on. The failure of several individuals to do their jobs resulted in the collapse of AIG and trauma to the U.S. economy.

A similar tale resides in the saga of Fannie Mae and Freddie Mac. Jim Johnson and other executives at the government-sponsored enterprises enticed members of Congress (by political contributions) to get laws passed which would enable the firms to over-leverage by maintaining a capital cushion of only 2.5 percent. These executives also arranged to be regulated by a government agency that would not apply rigorous controls. In so doing, Fannie Mae and Freddie Mac implemented a disastrous business model which resulted in short-term profits but caused long-term trauma so severe that it is difficult to calculate.

This section began with the common-sense rule: don't be naïve and assume fair dealing from actors in the financial marketplace; supervise and regulate so that the marketplace functions efficiently. This rule was clearly broken by the OTS and

AIG executives as well as by Jim Johnson and regulators at the OFHEO.

Rule #3: act rationally and do not allow greed to dictate choices. What is greed? What harm does greed cause? Greed is a disorder which is manifest in an excessive desire to possess more money or material things than one needs or deserves. Greed motivates people to steal, to gamble excessively, to act in fraudulent ways and even to manipulate financial markets in view of a temporary benefit without regard for long-term consequences. In the analysis that followed the events of 2008 most commentators agreed that key players in the financial markets were motivated by greed and circumvented rational restraints in order to make large sums of money. This is the thesis at the heart of the book *Reckless Endangerment*. The book is comprised of case studies. One of them focuses on the CEOs of Fannie Mae and Freddie Mac, such as Jim Johnson, Franklin Raines and Daniel Mudd (Fannie) and Richard Syron (Freddie). Authors Gretchen Morgenson and Joshua Rosner argue that these individuals devised strategies aimed at over-leveraging the firms and took unjustifiable risks in order to enrich themselves and others in senior management. In so doing, the U.S. government was forced to take control of the firms in 2008 at a cost of $160 billion, with a worst-case projected cost of $1 trillion.[30]

During Mr. Johnson's tenure at Fannie Mae, one-third of the firm's profits were kept in-house, to be dispensed to executives and shareholders, and used for lobbying activities. Johnson claimed that Fannie passed along every penny of its cost savings to home buyers in the form of lower mortgage rates. Morgenson and Rosner dispute the truth of this claim:

> It wore the claim (of lower mortgage rates) like a coat of armor, protecting itself from critics' slings and arrows. Only later would it emerge that the company kept billions of dollars – at least one third of the government subsidy – for itself each year. This money it dispensed to its executives, shareholders, and friends in Congress.[31]

Morgenson and Rosner say hubris and greed triggered the beginning of the end for Fannie and Freddie.[32] They cite Franklin Raines' incident at Fannie as "the first of many times that heads of organizations accused of improper conduct were not held accountable for the damage they did to shareholders and, later, to taxpayers." (Franklin Raines succeeded Jim Johnson as CEO of Fannie Mae. In 2004 Fannie Mae was accused by the SEC of numerous accounting irregularities and Raines resigned.) Mr. Raines' compensation in 2003, including $3 million in stock options, totaled about $20 million.[33]

Individual executives at Fannie Mae and Freddie Mac engaged in practices that allowed them to get rich while destabilizing the housing sector of the economy. In 2008, when Fannie and Freddie were taken over by the government, Mr. Mudd's earnings were $12.2 million and Mr. Syron's just shy of $20 million.[34] Jim Johnson was Chairman and CEO of Fannie Mae from 1991 until 1998, and his total compensation was more than $100 million.[35] It is not possible to state with certainty the extent to which these individuals were motivated by greed because no one can be sure about the intentions of another human being. What can be reliably stated, however, is that the principal executives of Fannie Mae and Freddie Mac, whose firms dominated mortgage finance before and during the crisis, enacted policies that enriched them and undermined the housing market and the entire economy. Testifying at a hearing of the Financial Crisis Inquiry Commission on April 9, 2010, Armando Falcon, former director of the Office of Federal Housing Enterprise Oversight, stated that the cause of the failure of the enterprises was the greed of their management:

> The failure of Fannie Mae and Freddie Mac will be a case study in business schools for decades. How do you operate a business with the most generous government subsidies possible, which confer very powerful market advantages, and run the business into the ground? Ultimately, the companies were not unwitting victims of an economic

down cycle or flawed products and services of theirs. Their failure was deeply rooted in a culture of arrogance and greed. I should be clear that this was a failure of leadership.[36]

Money is the means of barter used in modern society. People need to have money to buy the things they require to sustain life. The way people meet many of their obligations, or bills, is by paying money to those who provide services. Money can also be given to charities that use the money to assist the needy. Prudent people save money for their retirement years so that they will be able to take care of themselves and they will not be a burden to their children or to society. It is not wrong to approach money in these reasonable ways. However, obsessing over money and always wanting more than one reasonably needs leads to trouble. The statement, "He who loves money never has money enough," rings true because it affirms the fact that an emotional attachment to money undermines an individual's balance. If people are happy with modest increases in the value of their homes; if executives are content with a good wage and do not engage in destabilizing practices in order to inflate their earnings; if union workers cooperate with management to produce cars that are affordable and make concessions so that union benefits do not bankrupt auto companies, the economy will benefit. If traders and investors are satisfied with reasonable gains and do not engage in high risk practices that have the potential to bankrupt firms, the economy will benefit. Individuals such as executives at Fannie Mae and Freddie Mac contributed in large part to the financial crisis of 2008; had these individuals not sacrificed sound business practices in order to gain outsized compensation the United States would not be dealing with a prolonged economic downturn.

Follow your conscience. People make decisions. Faced with an issue that requires their attention, individual human beings choose from among alternatives to do something or to forego action. If the decision involves whether to make a deposit at a

bank or an ATM, the choice is not a big deal and it is not morally significant. If the decision is to forego the check of an applicant's FICO score prior to granting a loan, or to sell a client
mortgage-backed securities without honestly answering the client's questions about the risks of the product, the decision is a
big deal, with significant ethical ramifications. Likewise, if the
issue is to cast one's vote in Congress to satisfy a contributor to
one's campaign, rather than in the interest of the common
good, then the decision is a big deal.

There is general agreement that individuals have the ability
to do the right thing and reject the wrong thing. Society
imposes penalties on people who choose to do the wrong thing
and inflict harm on themselves and others. Consider, for example, the penalty society enacted against Todd Joyce who was
found guilty of mortgage fraud, sentenced to eighteen months
in jail, and ordered to make restitution to the bank he
defrauded. In 2006, Joyce applied for an $800,000 construction
loan to build a "spec home" in the Stonegate subdivision
located in Hurricane, West Virginia. In support of his loan
application, Todd Joyce submitted to United Bank a 2005 tax
return in March 2006, indicating that he and his wife earned
nearly $450,000 in income for the previous year. Less than a
month later, in April 2006, Joyce filed a 1040 tax return to the
Internal Revenue Service indicating that he made zero dollars
in 2005. United Bank relied upon Mr. Joyce's representations
and invalid tax return information in making the construction
loan. The defendant defaulted on the construction loan.[37]

How do people who need to make decisions figure out in
what the ethically correct decision consists? Fortunately, we
human beings have a unique capacity that enables us to use our
rational powers and come to ethically sound decisions. This
capacity is called conscience. It is the subjective element we are
aware of as we struggle to reach a moral decision. When a
dilemma is resolved and a plan to deal with it is adopted an
individual is apt to defend the chosen action or course of action
by referring to conscience: "I am carrying out the dictates of my

conscience. I thought this matter over, and this is what my conscience told me to do. I have a clear conscience." Alternatively, "I had a guilty conscience. I had to admit that what I did was wrong. I need to get this off my conscience."

Conscience is the human capacity most utilized in the process of ethical decision-making and the actual carrying out of moral conduct. Children of five or six usually discover that they have a conscience when they find themselves aware that they should not do something wrong like tell a lie, throw their food on the floor, or take something that doesn't belong to them. They don't make their conscience, they discover it. It is subjective; it is within them. Their conscience affirms general rules or standards which they have appropriated at home and in school settings.

Conscience is a power of the mind and will. The mind or intellect enables a person to reason as to what the right action is and the will provides the capacity to carry out the decision. To go against one's conscience is to diminish one's integrity and lessen one's goodness. Conversely, by following one's conscience, one grows in integrity and goodness.

Conscience is a specifically human capacity so that we do not think of nonhumans as exercising conscience. Just as humans are complex and have many levels of competence, so the way they exercise conscience is reflective of these realities. In order to act on their consciences, persons need to be sane, mature and capable of self-discipline. It follows, therefore, that people who are mentally impaired or incapable of self-control cannot be expected to form or act on conscience. We don't expect people who are suffering from Alzheimer's disease to reach decisions of conscience. And we do not incarcerate the criminally insane but, rather, hospitalize these individuals because medical science has educated us to the fact that, because of mental impairment, they lack the capacity to distinguish between right and wrong.

We want business leaders to have a conscience and deplore the lack of conscience that was manifest during the financial crisis. A blogger on the Motley Fool website makes this point when commenting on a story about the movie *Inside Job*. The movie details the actions of executives who caused the financial crisis and laments the fact that they did not go to jail.

> If these executives had any sort of a conscience at all they would resign, like Japanese executives did back in 2009. Unfortunately honor and integrity are qualities rarely found in the US business realm; we prefer cutthroats and underhanded tactics.[38]

We need to question the blogger's assertion that "we prefer cutthroats and underhanded tactics." The financial crisis was replete with unethical behavior in which individuals harmed others by unfair dealings but, in the aftermath of the crisis, as we try to move on, a key to recovery is that we reject cutthroats and underhanded tactics.

In response to some wrong acts such as taking advantage of people by steering them into mortgages with high rates of interest when the people qualify for lower rates, a question can be raised as to whether or not there are loan officers who have no conscience. This is a hard question to answer, but some elucidation is possible. People can have *a blind spot* which means that they can do ethically questionable things without realizing that they should not be doing these things. In regard to the hypothetical loan officer, the person might be well intentioned in that she considers authorizing the loan a good thing because the commission it brings will increase her income and help her provide better for her family. If this is what motivates her, the loan officer fails in her responsibility to deal fairly with the customer. Her blind spot is not seeing the harm she is doing; she rationalizes and fails to acknowledge that truthfulness and fair dealing are professional responsibilities.

Some people never grow up ethically. They never get to the point where they realize that they are responsible for what they do and, instead, operate from an inclination to blind obedience, that is, to do whatever they are told. With blind obedience ethical conduct takes place only if the boss gives the morally correct order. But an employee would actually do the wrong thing if he followed an unethical order. Consider, for example, a researcher for a credit rating agency who is told to gather information about an investment product and formulate a rating. The process requires that the researcher carry out analysis and submit the results to his manager. Based on knowledge of weaknesses in components of the investment product, the analyst determines that the rating should be negative and this is his recommendation. The manager, on learning of the researcher's rating and the reasons for it, tells the researcher to rework his analysis and to value the product as AAA, the highest rating possible. "We do a lot of business with that firm, and, if we go negative on what they put together, they'll pull their account. Let's keep them happy and keep the business coming." The researcher, who thinks that doing the right thing consists in doing what he is told, changes his analysis and rates the product AAA. In the long run, no one is well served by the researcher's blind obedience and complicity.

Sometimes people do wrong things from misguided motivation. They have a conscience and they try to do the right thing, but they experience an impediment in following through on their convictions. Consider the case of the manager who enjoys a friendship with a subordinate. They generally take breaks together and their families sometimes socialize. The manager's recommendation determines his friend's pay increases, bonuses and promotions as well as those of others in the department. Production and revenue are down in the department and the manager knows that his subordinate's job performance has fallen short. Others in the department have stepped up and compensated for his friend's shortcomings. The manager can act on what he knows and write a negative evaluation. Or he can be vague in his evaluations of this specific subordinate and the others in the department. If he is vague, his friend will keep his job and the exceptional performance of others in the department will go unnoticed. The manager manifests misguided motivation and acts contrary to conscience when he decides, "I can't let my friend down; I'm going to write a passing evaluation because this is what friendship requires." Misguided motivation prevents him from separating professional responsibilities from personal feelings and keeps him from doing the right thing. Lack of professional distance kept members of Congress from legislating for the good of society and, instead, prompted them to write laws requested by their friends at Fannie and Freddie.

Even in view of the factors which can keep people from acting in accord with their consciences, it still happens that most people, under most circumstances, are capable of following conscience, making the living of an ethical life a realistic possibility. How does one go about reaching a decision of conscience in complex circumstances? We need to begin by brainstorming to elucidate the facts particular to the situation as well as the moral standards and principles by which we choose to live. Next, we should try to see the situation we are dealing with in the context of the total picture: what came before, what else is going on and what can be expected to happen as a result? Then we need to try out different solutions and ask ourselves which hypothetical solutions make sense and which ones do not, and why. At this point it would be appropriate to confer with respected advisers, share with them what we have been thinking, and ask their advice. It is also good to confer with someone who found herself in similar circumstances and to ask for whatever advice she can offer. We may want to do some research in terms of societal and ethical leaders and their thinking in regard to similar dilemmas so as to have considered as many opinions as possible. Having done all this, we will be ready to make our decisions and we should feel secure in the knowledge that it is the very best that we could do.

It should be clear by now that conscience is an ability of the intellect that an individual possesses and uses to deliberate about what to do when faced with an ethical dilemma. Even though this is the case, people are still inclined to identify conscience with the little voice that tells them what to do and what to avoid. Why is it incorrect to think of conscience as a little voice? Simply because in exercising conscience people go through a challenging rational process in which they consider various courses of action that are open to them and, ideally, they choose the correct course because their reasoning tells them that this specific choice is the one that honors objective standards and will advance their good, their client's well-being, the interests of the firm, and the good of the broader society.

It was Sigmund Freud who formulated the theory of the *superego*, the subconscious appropriation of the mores of one's parents or social group. This psychological phenomenon prompts us to perform actions we have been socialized to do because parents or society consider them appropriate. Saying thank you when receiving a gift, not interrupting conversations, and covering one's mouth when one yawns or coughs, are actions prompted by the superego. If we act counter to the promptings of the superego in social situations, we tend to feel that we did something wrong. We have; we have violated social conventions. However, the type of subconscious prompting that facilitates acting correctly in social situations does not equip us to resolve the challenging ethical dilemmas that we encounter in finance, commerce, politics or other parts of life. The little voice is a learned, automatic response mechanism in contrast to the workings of conscience which are deliberative and take into account complex matters that require resolution.

Act with integrity. The right of a person to follow conscience is associated with the notion of personal integrity. By integrity is meant the quality or state of being of sound moral principle; uprightness, honesty and sincerity.[39] The concept of integrity is aligned with the notion of wholeness, implying that a person would compromise or violate himself by performing unethical actions. To be a person of integrity requires honesty and a commitment to doing the right thing, no matter how difficult this might be. A person of integrity is unselfish and recognizes a responsibility to act in behalf of the common good. Although the term integrity tends to be bandied about and its use has been cheapened over time, its real meaning, to do the right thing even when no one is watching you and if it costs you personally,[40] merits consideration as we try to recover from this economic crisis. The authors of *Reckless Endangerment* speculate that Jim Johnson, former CEO of Fannie Mae who instituted policies and practices at the firm that contributed in large part to the financial collapse, was regretting his own lack of integrity when he quoted George Bernard Shaw in a graduation address at Augsburg College in Minneapolis in 2002: "The man I miss most is the man I could have been." The authors hypothesize:

Invoking (his mother) Adeline, his father, Alfred, and his Norwegian emigrant grandparents, Johnson urged the graduates to pursue their careers with integrity and honesty. Just months after a rogue energy company called Enron had hurtled into bankruptcy, faith in corporate America and the nation's markets had been shaken. Avuncular, professorial, and attractive, Johnson delivered a reassuring message: "Good ethics are good business."

It was the kind of advice to be expected from a man who just three years earlier had presided over Fannie Mae, one of the world's largest and most prestigious financial institutions. Johnson had then gone on to serve on the boards of five large and well-known public companies, including the mighty investment bank, Goldman Sachs. "What we want from friends – honesty and integrity, energy and optimism, commitment to family and community, hard work and high ethical standards – are the same qualities we need from American business," he told the graduates.

But as he wound up his speech, the fifty-nine-year-old Johnson struck a wistful tone. Just before George Bernard Shaw died, Johnson said, the playwright had been asked to name a famous deceased man – artist, statesman, philosopher, or writer – whom he missed the most.

Johnson recounted Shaw's reply: "The man I miss most is the man I could have been."[41]

It would be next to impossible to find a CEO, manager, board member or regulator who would speak *against* integrity. Actions, however, speak louder than words, and putting in place a corporate culture that insists upon and supports integrity is what is needed if economic recovery is to have an ethical foundation. The topic of integrity needs to be given more than a nod in college ethics courses, graduation speeches or at corporate workshops. The indisputable value of committing oneself to acting with integrity should be held up as a standard to embrace for a lifetime.

An author on ethics, J. Patrick Dobel, writes that the key to ethical behavior is personal integrity. According to Dobel, personal integrity "demands consistency between inner beliefs and public actions."[42] Integrity requires that people understand their beliefs and values and make a commitment to honor these beliefs and values by their actions. Integrity also means that individuals are unified in their roles and commitments (professional, public, family, private, etc.) and their values. "Personal integrity resembles a network of roles and promises all held together by a central web of values and commitments."[43] It would not be a manifestation of integrity to tell the truth to one's family while concealing the truth from one's clients, or to meet one's obligations to one's clients and neglect one's obligations to one's spouse. Integrity demands holding oneself to high standards in all aspects of one's life.

Practice virtue. Because becoming a good person entails becoming a person of virtue, one way of approaching ethics is by examining the nature of virtue and acquiring the underlying attitudes that facilitate virtuous behavior. A virtue is a good habit that a person becomes proficient in because of repetition. For example, people can develop the virtue of punctuality by always holding themselves to the standard that they be on time. People can develop the virtue of generosity by volunteering and regularly contributing to worthy causes.

Greek philosophers cited four virtues which they considered the foundations of the moral life: prudence, justice, fortitude and temperance. They called these four virtues *cardinal virtues*. *Cardinal* means hinge: the philosophers contend that all other virtues hinge on, or develop from, these four virtues.

Because these virtues directly impact personal attitudes, it is important to understand their meanings as well as the ways in which the practice of these virtues enables people to develop into good human beings. What is prudence? Prudence is the virtue that motivates individuals to figure out what constitutes the ethical choice in each situation and to choose the right means to bring it about. Prudence is not timidity or fear; it is not duplicity or dissimulation. Prudence is a foundational virtue because it needs to accompany other virtues in guiding action. It is through exercising prudence that people make reasonable judgments about specific choices. Prudence enables people to apply moral principles to particular cases and come up with solutions. The virtue of prudence enables people to know how to act in the particular circumstances and situations that make up each and every human life. For example, prudent parents would know how harmful it would be to their family if they went into debt greater than they would be able to repay. This knowledge would incline them to live within their means and not place an unsustainable financial burden on their family.

Prior to the heyday of subprime mortgages, mortgage lenders abided by prudent standards. These criteria were known as the four Cs: capacity to pay; credit history; character; and collateral. The borrower's income, her credit history, her standing in the community, and the value of the property on which a mortgage might be issued were the criteria that guided the lender. When lenders abandoned these prudent standards, economic calamity followed.

While it does not use the term "prudence," the Financial Crisis Inquiry Commission pointed to the lack of this virtue as a direct cause of the financial crisis. The failure of key people in government, finance, investing, insurance and related fields to act prudently resulted in the economic implosion. Consider this statement from the Commission *Report*:

> We conclude this financial crisis was avoidable. The crisis was the result of human action and inaction, not of Mother Nature or computer models gone haywire. The captains of finance and the public stewards of our financial system ignored warnings and failed to question, understand, and manage evolving risks within a system essential to the well-being of the American public. Theirs was a big miss, not a stumble. While the business cycle cannot be repealed, a crisis of this magnitude need not have occurred. To paraphrase Shakespeare, the fault lies not in the stars, but in us.[44]

Prudence also requires that individuals who appoint officials to carry out specialized tasks choose appointees who have the skill set and expertise necessary to do the job. Harry Markopolos, a money manager who recognized that Bernard Madoff was running a ponzi scheme and who over a period of nine years frequently contacted the SEC to explain that Madoff could not be on the level, makes this point:

> The five commissioners of the S.E.C. are securities lawyers. Securities lawyers never understand finance. They don't have the math background. If you can't do math and if you can't take apart the investment products of the 21st century backward and forward and put them together in your sleep, you'll never find the frauds on Wall Street.[45]

Justice is the second of the cardinal virtues. Justice is a constant and firm commitment to give to others what is their due. By practicing justice people show respect for the rights of others and a commitment to establish in human relationships the harmony that promotes the common good. The word justice has different meanings for different people.

Some think justice has to do primarily with the legal system, with crime and punishment. Others believe that justice has to do with people using power in the right ways, or with having the right procedures in place to protect people's rights and freedoms. Justice can also be approached as fairness in transactions: giving a customer the correct change, or returning to the cashier extra money inadvertently handed over. All interpretations are correct. But, there is also another way to understand justice, in an altruistic sense, according to which justice requires that people give to those in need what they require in order to live in a decent fashion. The scope of altruistic justice is much larger than the notion of fairness which applies to contracts or the idea of meting out a reasonable punishment. Altruism mandates caring for the poor and vulnerable and making sure that the needs of the unemployed are met.

The Financial Crisis Inquiry Commission reports on how a lack of commitment to transactional justice which requires fairness in dealings led to the economic crisis. Their report documents that major financial institutions ineffectively sampled loans they were purchasing to package and sell to investors. The Commission asserts that firms suspected that a significant percentage of the sampled loans did not meet their own underwriting standards or those of the originators. Nonetheless, they sold securities containing those loans to investors. The Commission's review of many prospectuses provided to investors found that this critical information was not disclosed.[46] This nondisclosure constituted a serious ethical lapse.

At the time of writing unemployment in the United States stands at 8.2 percent and there is general agreement that it will remain high for the foreseeable future. High unemployment may even be the so-called *new normal*. In providing assistance in the form of unemployment insurance, members of Congress need to be aware that they should use the power of the purse in the right way, distribute taxpayer money fairly, and apply altruistic justice as called for by the needs of the unemployed.

Fortitude is the third of the cardinal virtues. Fortitude is the virtue that ensures firmness in difficulties and constancy in the pursuit of the good.[47] Life usually lasts a long time and, unbidden, problems crop up. Moods change, so that sometimes people feel energetic and positive, and, at other times, angry, depressed, lethargic or negative. The virtue of fortitude enables people to stay the course, and persevere in living a good life even in the face of temptations and threat. Fortitude is a necessary virtue for people to practice as they ride out the difficult days following the Great Recession. Staying positive and engaged and working for systemic change are important when one step forward is followed by two steps back. For people whose work requires that they evaluate potential business, accepting viable opportunities and rejecting those that are not solid, the virtue of fortitude comes into play. This was especially true for an employee of a credit rating agency who needed to say "No" to the request to issue a positive rating on a CDO made up largely of subprime mortgages. It would have been easier to say "Yes" and give a favorable rating, but it would have been dishonest. Refusing to go along to get along requires fortitude.

Temperance is the fourth, and last, cardinal virtue. Temperance moderates the attraction of pleasures and provides balance in the acquisition and use of things. Temperance ensures the will's mastery over instincts and keeps desires within the limits of what is reasonable. A temperate person directs her appetites toward what is good and maintains a healthy balance in life. The Greek philosopher Aristotle observed that animals are ruled by instinct; human beings, in contrast, possess the ability to reason and the capacity to choose. Using reason and choosing wisely, a temperate person knows the meaning of enough; the good things of life, such as food, drink and leisure activities should be enjoyed in moderation. Money is good for the good it can do; of itself it has no intrinsic value and the hyper pursuit of money is folly. The point of temperance is to use, but not abuse, what we find pleasurable so that we retain moral equilibrium and do not devote our lives to the quest for pleasure. While it is not easy to achieve ethical balance, striving for it is worth the effort because temperance brings contentment.

Bethany McLean and Joe Nocera co-authored the book *All the Devils Are Here*. Their engaging account of the individual misconduct that resulted in the financial crisis includes commentary on a retreat for top Washington Mutual sales personnel that was held in Maui in 2006. During that meeting employees performed a rap skit called "I like big bucks." The lyrics are an example of mindless intemperance:

> I like big bucks and I cannot lie
> You mortgage brokers can't deny
> That when the dough rolls in like your printin' your own cash
> And you gotta make a splash
> You just spend
> Like it never ends
> 'Cuz you gotta have that big new Benz.[48]

Ethics in financial transactions. We reviewed three rules regarding ethics in financial transactions: first, that we should deal fairly, second, that we should not be naïve and assume fair dealing from actors in the financial marketplace. Supervision and regulation are needed so that the marketplace functions efficiently. And, third, we considered the advice that we should not be ruled by greed. We then looked at the role of conscience in making right choices, but realized that conscience is the mechanism, it is not a collection of answers about what to do or avoid doing. Engaging in introspection and asking oneself what kind of person one wants to be is critically important to ethics, but a commitment to integrity provides the motivation for ethical living, not the steps to be taken to set things right. By being prudent and temperate and practicing justice and fortitude people develop ethically and strengthen themselves in advance of making hard decisions related to restoring our nation to financial soundness.

There are specific ethical guidelines that supplement the general ethical information just reviewed. Following these guidelines would restore the health of the economy and insure the common good. These guidelines are fundamental components of individual ethics and people who work in finance and related fields as well as consumers need to follow them.

Exercise fiduciary responsibility. A fiduciary is a manager of money. The fiduciary manages money for individuals or groups. Alternatively, a fiduciary can be a trustee of a for-profit corporation or not-for-profit institution such as a university or hospital; in such instances the fiduciary is not managing money but, instead, overseeing asset management in order to keep the assets secure.

Money managers have a fiduciary responsibility to honor the trust of those whose money they manage. Money managers are also duty bound to exercise due diligence and act with high professional standards. Employees of mutual funds and professional money management firms control 70 percent of the shares of large public companies. In view of this market share, these firms wield considerable influence over corporate America. Investors trust money managers to make investment choices for them because the managers are seen as *experts*. One lesson of the financial implosion was that a lot of money managers did not meet their obligations as fiduciaries. John C. Bogle, founder of Vanguard Group, speculates as to how money managers contributed to the financial collapse by failing to live up to the trust of their clients:

the trust we have placed in these agents is undeserved ... the agents have failed to serve their clients – mutual fund shareholders, pension beneficiaries and long-term investors; instead, the agents have served themselves.

Consider fees. Charges levied on mutual fund investors are much higher than those that the identical firms exact on pension clients, for example. The three largest money managers ... charged an average fee rate of 0.08 percent to pension customers. This compares with 0.61 percent charged to fund shareholders.

Money managers also haven't done the kind of due diligence that might have protected their investors from titanic losses. "How could so many highly skilled, highly paid securities analysts and researchers have failed to question the toxic-filled, leveraged balance sheets of Citigroup and other leading banks and investment banks?"[49]

At the time Mr. Bogle made this statement he was not aware that Citigroup would go on to pay a fine of $285 million. In a press release dated October 19, 2011, the SEC stated:

The SEC alleges that Citigroup Global Markets structured and marketed a CDO called Class V Funding III and exercised significant influence over the selection of $500 million of the assets included in the CDO portfolio. Citigroup then took a proprietary short position against those mortgage-related assets from which it would profit if the assets declined in value. Citigroup did not disclose to investors its role in the asset selection process or that it took a short position against the assets it helped select.

Citigroup has agreed to settle the SEC's charges by paying a total of $285 million, which will be returned to investors.[50]

(Commenting on the fine, Thomas Friedman, op-ed writer for the *New York Times*, wrote: "It doesn't get any more immoral than this." Mr. Friedman went on to advocate meaningful transparency, regulation and oversight of the banking industry in order to achieve the ethical objective of fiduciary responsibility.[51])

Since the fiduciary responsibility of money manager to client entails a significant ethical dimension, restoring the viability of the U.S. economy necessitates that managers recognize this duty and act in light of it. Fiduciary responsibility requires that the client's privacy be respected, and that the money manager act to insure the client's best interests. The trust that the client places in the manager requires that the client's interests are primary, not the manager's. In serving clients, fiduciaries are not allowed to enter into relationships or transactions that represent a conflict of interest or to profit from their position by engaging in actions that bring profit to the money manager at the expense of the client. Lest there be a reservation about the ethical (and legal) obligation to exercise fiduciary responsibility, the Dodd–Frank Act spells it out, giving the SEC the authority to impose a fiduciary duty on brokers who give investment advice: the advice must be in the best interest of their customers.

Refuse to pursue personal benefit in situations of conflict of interest. A conflict of interest is a situation in which a person has a private or personal interest sufficient to influence the objective exercise of his or her official duties as a professional.[52] People who are faced with conflicts of interest in their professional lives act unethically when they engage in transactions to benefit themselves to the disadvantage of their clients. When faced with a conflict of interest, a professional should do one of two things: refuse the advantageous opportunity or disclose the opportunity to the client and cease representing the client in order to accept the opportunity. It would be dishonest and a violation of integrity to benefit from a transaction that harms clients to whom an individual bears a fiduciary responsibility.

Of the many ethical lessons contained in the financial crisis, there are more than enough involving conflicts of interest. These lessons should present us with the insight we need to avoid similar lapses in the future and contribute to the foundation for an ethical recovery. Accounting means that one states what one has; it means to give a clear and transparent picture of assets and liabilities. By taking derivatives off the books of investment banks and large commercial banks, these banks appeared to be in better shape than was, in fact, the case. Concealing exposure to MBS-CDOs was an accounting gimmick that contributed significantly to the economic meltdown. As the market for mortgage-backed securities disintegrated, management and accountants were likely conflicted about presenting complete financial disclosure because such disclosure would show how bad the situation was. In resolving the conflict in favor of so-called *creative accounting* rather than full disclosure, those who participated deceived the public. "Widespread off-balance sheet accounting arrangements ... allowed large financial firms to hide trillions of dollars in obligations from investors, creditors, and regulators."[53] These arrangements allowed public companies to fail to adequately disclose the risks posed by off-balance sheet arrangements to investors.[54]

Credit rating agencies are made up of individuals whose work entails reaching judgments about the creditworthiness of securities. If an investor is considering buying a security, the investor wants to know what the chances are that the interest and principal will, or will not, be paid. The yield, or rate of interest, is determined by the creditworthiness of the issuer and the nature of the debt. Credit rating agencies estimate the probability that securities like CDOs will be repaid when they come due and that regular interest payments will be paid along the way. A credit rating agency has a two-fold responsibility, to honestly evaluate the investment instrument for the company that employs it and to truthfully present an evaluation of the instrument for potential investors. The best rating that agencies can give to an investment product is AAA.

In order to get a rating from a credit rating agency, the issuer of a security pays the agency a fee to evaluate the product and attach a rating to it. This arrangement allows for a conflict of interest to occur. Clients bring business to rating agencies and rating agencies need business in order to be profitable. If a client is not pleased by the rating an agency gives to its product, it may take its business to another agency. This simple fact caused credit agencies to give inflated ratings to investment products in order to keep client business. By so doing the rating agencies did not meet their obligations to investors who were misled by inflated ratings. The personnel who participated in this unethical conduct also diminished their integrity; they played a big part in the unraveling of the U.S. economy. This role was in contravention of the ethical requirement that they engage in truthful analysis and accurate reporting.

Traders can face conflicts of interest. The conflict for the trader is between taking a conservative course with moderate profit and making a big bet which may or may not pay off. If the pay of the risk taker designing the trade is based on current year profits, her bonus may strike her as more important than the firm's long-term financial well-being. If she acts to enrich herself and does not concern herself with long-term consequences for the firm and its shareholders, this hypothetical trader does herself and her employer a disservice. This is because greed, and not prudence, dictates the course that she takes. This is not an ethical way to proceed.

Mortgage brokers who arranged subprime mortgage loans for borrowers often engaged in conflicts of interest. They knew from their interviews with borrowers and the information that borrowers provided that the borrowers would not be able to make payments on the subprime mortgages they were applying for, but they went ahead with the transactions in order to earn commissions. Alternatively, mortgage brokers recommended mortgages that were better for the broker than the customer based on the commission brokers would receive. They steered trusting customers into more costly mortgages rather than mortgages with lower rates that the customers qualified for. In both these scenarios, mortgage brokers were not honest brokers; they chose benefits for themselves instead of meeting their professional obligation to act in their clients' interests.

Politicians are elected to serve the people and act in behalf of the common good. Politicians who take campaign contributions from businesses and subsequently legislate in behalf of those businesses in order to stay on their good side are guilty of a conflict of interest. Politicians who secured cut-rate loans from Countrywide may also have compromised their ability to act independently. These politicians include former Senator Chris Dodd (D, Ct), Senator Kent Conrad (D, ND) and Barbara Boxer (D, Ca) as well as Donna Shalala, former Secretary of Health and Human Services.[55] As we have seen, government regulation of the financial industry was lacking and this lack facilitated practices that resulted in the economic crisis. To the extent that elected and appointed government leaders aided or abetted misconduct, they are guilty of having violated the public trust. Going forward, attention needs to be paid to elected officials who act to benefit the interests of their friends in finance or their campaign contributors; they should not be returned to office.

Conflicts of interest situations frequently arise for mortgage servicers. A servicer is an agent who works for investors in a mortgage-backed security or for a bank or other entity which holds a mortgage. The servicer's job is to collect payments from borrowers, take a preset fee for the specific service rendered, and transfer the remainder of the payments to lenders. When homeowners are in arrears, servicers initiate and carry out fore-closure proceedings. Adam Levitin and Tara Twomey, in a White Paper on mortgage servicing, explain how conflicts can happen:

> Servicers' compensation structures create a principal–agent conflict between them and MBS investors. Servicers have no stake in the performance of mortgage loans, so they do not share investors' interest in maximizing the net present value of the loan. Instead, servicers' decision of whether to fore-close or modify a loan is based on their own cost and income structure, which is skewed toward foreclosure. The costs of this principal–agent conflict are thus externalized directly on homeowners and indirectly on communities and the housing market as a whole.[56]

In many cases, based on fees generated, it is more advantageous for servicers to foreclose on properties rather than engage in loan modifications. In some cases, it benefits servicers to apply payments to a first or second mortgage because *that* mortgage is held by the bank that employs the servicer. (Legally, the first mortgage should get paid before a second mortgage.) In many cases it suits servicers to make it difficult for homeowners to contact them and to engage with them in mortgage modifications. Mortgage modifications are labor intensive and not financially profitable.

What needs to be done to bring mortgage servicing in line with ethical standards? First, servicers need to appreciate the human dimensions of the work that they do. Yes, mortgages are legal documents; they are pieces of paper, but they are also much more. The people who entered into these legal contracts need shelter for themselves and their families. This need should weigh more heavily in motivating decisions to modify mortgages or to foreclose on homeowners, rather than desire for fees to be earned by one set of procedures or another. In addition, servicers and those who employ them should be willing to engage openly with regulators to institute transparent procedures and to outlaw egregious practices that bring harm to homeowners, investors and the broader community. If a home equity line of credit and a first mortgage are both in arrears, servicers should follow established guidelines in dispersing payments. To clarify, if a servicer works for a bank that issued a home equity loan, and payments are late on both the HEL and mortgage, the servicer should adhere to the recognized standard that the holder of the first mortgage receives payment before the holder of the HEL. It would be an unethical conflict of interest to contravene procedures to benefit the servicer's employer and act to the detriment of a mortgage holder who is legally first in line to receive payment.

Accept rational limits in the use of credit. We need to pay for the things we buy and it is easy to do so using a credit card. It is also easy to obtain a credit card because card issuers aggressively market these handy plastic devices. Each and every item we purchase on a credit card goes on a bill and the bill comes due every month. If the balance is not paid in full, interest is added to the balance, and the card user owes more money. When we reach the maximum on one credit card, we can open a new account and get another credit card. This process can be repeated again and again. Some credit cards allow users to get cash advances and others allow for overdrafts. These features add to the bill. Most people who use credit cards complain about small print, terms and conditions of which they are not aware but which cost them money because unexpected charges turn up on their bills. The way people use and pay off their credit cards determines their FICO score, and this score is used by mortgage lenders and others to decide on whether to lend money to borrowers as well as the terms of the loans.

In the past few decades people in the United States have become increasingly dependent on credit cards and have tended to spend more than they can reasonably afford. They have gone into debt, borrowing to pay for things they need as well as things they could do without. Many people with large credit card debt took out home equity loans to pay off their credit cards and reorganize their finances. For those who became unemployed or suffered other financial reversals, paying off credit cards and home equity loans became impossible and they faced foreclosure and/or bankruptcy. The lesson to learn about credit cards is fairly straightforward: we should impose rational limits on how much we charge because we need to pay the bills when they come due. All the cardinal virtues play a role in this regard. It is not prudent to use credit to obtain something we cannot afford or do not need. It would be unjust not to pay the credit card company the money we owe; the company paid the merchant for the products we bought and it is only fair that we meet our obligations to the credit card company. Living on a budget in a consumerist culture is difficult, but fortitude demands that we do difficult things and deny ourselves stuff that we want but cannot afford. Temperance teaches us to strike a balance in life; applying this balance to purchasing goods and services is required of mature ethical people.

Listen to the whistleblower and encourage whistleblowing. If you see something, say something. In the post-9/11 world, each of us is encouraged to keep our eyes open for those who might want to do us harm and to let law enforcement officials know when we suspect that something dangerous might be happening.

In the aftermath of the economic meltdown, how many times did you hear people ask, "Didn't anyone see this coming?" As it turns out, a lot of people knew about problems with subprime mortgages, but their knowledge did not become general knowledge and attempts to comprehend the implications of problems in the housing sector were lacking. While there is no guarantee that in the future whistleblowers will be taken seriously, it needs to be stated that they represent one of the best hopes we have for avoiding another financial disaster. In regard to an individual who witnesses practices that endanger a financial system, or the political system, the media or the economy, that person should consider himself responsible to inform appropriate authorities by detailing what he knows. If the authority to which he reports dismisses his claim, he should take it a step further. It may be necessary to write letters to the editor or to post information online. The point is that it is important to disseminate accurate information so that people know what is happening.

In addition to calling for whistleblowers to speak up, it is essential that society show respect for these people. To marginalize them or dismiss them out of hand would be an act of disrespect and would undermine the value of the free exchange of information in a democratic society.

Ilya Eric Kolchinsky, an executive who oversaw the ratings process for CDOs at Moody's, followed the ethical script and pointed out shortcomings in the process. He also sent a fourteen-page memorandum about ratings on two investment products to the company's compliance group. The issues raised by Kolchinsky were not corrected by Moody's and, instead, Kolchinsky was transferred to a different department. Subsequently, Kolchinsky was suspended. He is currently suing the firm and claims that he has been blacklisted based on derogatory statements about him from Moody's which have circulated within the financial community.[57] Mr. Kolchinsky spoke up, followed up and tried to make an important change in a dysfunctional system. Unfortunately, his advice was not heeded and he experienced retaliation. Nevertheless, he did the ethically right thing and he merits respect for doing so.

What about a few people who see what is coming and can use this information for their advantage by short selling stock or buying credit default swaps? Would this be an ethical option? In an individualistic society wherein it is each person for herself, the answer would be to take advantage of the opportunity and resist the impulse to feel guilty. If one views humanity as interconnected and interdependent, however, the idea of profiting ahead of other people's misfortune and the collapse of the economy would be evaluated as immoral. From an ethical perspective, the few who see what is coming should accept the role of whistleblower and warn those who do not perceive the dangers that lie ahead.

Acknowledge the value of simplicity and reject the mindlessness of conspicuous consumption. The dawn of a brighter day still seems some distance away. But when it comes, will we step into it older and wiser or merely older and poorer? When recovery takes hold, will we allow ourselves to be lured back into debt by ads for state-of-the-art knick-knacks, designer everything, and houses with more bedrooms and baths than we need? Or will we strike a healthier balance between living for the moment and planning for the future? There are signs that a more sober mindset is emerging. The consulting firm Strategic Business Insights refers to it as "conspicuous conservation." We're weighing risk against reward now. We're placing a greater emphasis on value (instead of glitz) when we go shopping, opting for the functional over the flashy, the rational over the reckless. Most profoundly, we're remembering what our parents taught us: that money isn't everything. In a recent Merrill Lynch survey, more than half of retired respondents said that if they could do it all over again, they'd focus more on "life goals" and less on "the numbers."[58]

A research study of changes in consumer attitudes following the economic collapse states:

> Downturns are stressful and typically increase people's desire for simplicity. Even prior to the downturn, many consumers were feeling overwhelmed by the profusion of choices and 24/7 connectivity and were starting to simplify. This trend will continue to accelerate through the recovery into the long term. Unlike consumers in previous recessions, who greeted the return of financial stability with a buying spree, consumers will continue to buy simpler offerings with the greatest value.[59]

This report, from a marketing expert, is instructive for its ethical implications. As a consequence of the economic collapse, many people lost money in their investment and retirement accounts and they have had to learn to make do with less. The unemployed are trying to get by on a lot less. It would be insensitive to say that it is good to have less and spend less and make do with less. For many people there is real and profound suffering and this fact cries out to be acknowledged. It is also true, however, that during the past few years people have thought about the value of simplicity and have come to reject the mindlessness of conspicuous consumption. Stuff is just stuff; it does not make us happy; it is not fulfilling. It is very important to get the economy going again, to get the unemployed back to work, and to restore the housing sector to viability. But when these reasonable goals are achieved it should not be an occasion to go out and splurge, buying things we neither need nor want. Learning this lesson will be a positive outcome of this bleak financial season.

Conclusion. Ethics is about doing the right thing and rejecting the wrong thing. Conscience is the human ability to figure out what constitutes the right choice in a given situation. By following time tested rules like dealing fairly in financial transactions and not allowing greed to dictate one's choices, people will act in an upright way and contribute to a prosperous society. Admitting the need for government regulation of the free market and insisting that rational limits be imposed on individuals and corporations will aid in the recovery. Working at becoming virtuous is much more important than working to become wealthy and valuing integrity makes more sense than valuing material possessions. When individuals in the finance and mortgage industries resolve to carry out fiduciary responsibilities in an ethical manner, to avoid conflicts of interest, and heed the valid warnings of whistleblowers, society will have turned a corner. When citizens learn to be restrained in their use of credit and value simple things, we will be well on our way to recovery.

Questions for Discussion

1 Do you agree with the statement that there are rules that bind everyone? Why or why not?
2 State two examples of dealing fairly in carrying out financial transactions.
3 Why is it necessary for government agencies to regulate the financial marketplace?
4 What is wrong with greed?
5 Describe the role played by conscience in the process of reaching a moral decision.
6 What is integrity and why should individuals strive to become people of integrity?
7 List the cardinal virtues and provide an example of how each of these virtues should be practiced in an economic context.
8 Describe the ethical responsibilities that accompany fiduciary responsibility to a client.

9 What should an individual who works in finance or government do when confronted with a situation that constitutes a conflict of interest?

10 What lessons does ethics teach consumers concerning the use of credit cards?

11 Explain how emphasis on consumption can undermine an individual's and a society's stability.

12 Most people are reluctant to take on the role of whistle-blower. Speculate on why this is the case and suggest ethical reasons to counter this inclination.

Case Study: Conflict over Executive Compensation

The executive compensation committee of a large investment bank is meeting to discuss the package that should be offered to the next CEO of the corporation. The former CEO resigned unexpectedly because of a serious health issue; a nationwide search was undertaken and there is widespread agreement that the candidate chosen, from within the company, has the requisite skill set and deportment to do an excellent job.

The committee decides that lessons learned from the financial collapse should be applied in arranging the pay package for the next CEO. Accordingly, they agree that the CEO's salary should be at the low range of salaries for chief executives of investment banks and settle on a figure of $8 million. In order to discourage excessive risk-taking by bank personnel, the committee decides to attach strings to the CEO's bonus, which will be keyed to the bank's overall performance. He will be allowed to take home only 30 percent of his bonus (half in cash and half in stock) and payment of the remaining 70 percent will be dependent on the bank's bottom line over the next three years. If the bank loses money in any of those three years, a proportionate amount of the bonus will be forfeited. In regard to the 30 percent bonus that the CEO is scheduled to receive yearly, there will be a clawback provision that requires that he repay part or all of that amount if the bank does not operate in the black during his tenure.

When the candidate is informed of the pay proposal, he rejects it out of hand. He says that he will assume the position of CEO and accept the annual salary set by the committee, but he insists that his bonus be paid in cash and in full each year, with no clawback provisions. He is not willing to accept stock in lieu of cash. He knows that he has many options and he says that he intends to explore them if the committee does not meet his terms.

1   What should the committee do: stick to its plan or meet the demands of the candidate? What prompts your reply?
2   Will deferring bonuses and including clawback provisions in pay packages discourage excessive risk taking and benefit financial stability? What leads you to answer Yes or No?
3   Is the candidate acting in an ethical manner by refusing the pay package proposed by the committee? What leads you to your conclusion?
4   What might the financial industry do about this issue? Should there be a council that sets compensation guidelines? What would be the advantages and disadvantages of such a council?
5   What responsibilities do members of the executive compensation committee have as they decide on compensation amounts?
6   How should shareholders contribute to decisions about executive compensation?
7   Is public backlash against excessive executive compensation justified? Why or why not?

Case Study: Credit Check Brings Bad News

Cameron Stone applied for a job for which she considered herself well qualified. She was pleased when she got a call to come in for an interview and, in her opinion, the interview went well. Then she went home and waited for a call, hoping that she would be hired.

Cameron had been out of work for close to a year and it had been a difficult time for her. The unemployment compensation she received did not come close to covering her expenses. Her credit card payments were overdue and her landlord had begun eviction proceedings. Her family lived in a different area of the country and Cameron, who was used to living on her own, had decided that she would not return home to save on expenses. Instead, she would try to hang on where she had established herself after college graduation.

Things had never been as bleak for Cameron as they were now. A self-confessed shopaholic, she was finally becoming convinced of the need to live within her means and was resolved to begin a rainy-day fund as soon as she started collecting a paycheck. Cameron was ready to take to heart the sound advice that her parents had given her when she was growing up and she resolved that her financial affairs would be in better shape in the future.

After waiting several days to hear from the interviewer, Cameron was becoming anxious and so she decided to call and ask about the job. She felt the interview had gone very well and that she had established a good rapport with the interviewer. "I'm sorry," the woman told her, "but we will not be able to extend an offer to you." Cameron pleaded with the interviewer to tell her why she was rejected, and her plea was granted. "I should not tell you this," the woman replied, "but we checked your credit history. We don't hire people with poor credit scores and there is no question that yours meets this definition. I'm afraid our decision is final."

1 Is a company justified in denying employment to a qualified applicant on the basis of the person's credit score? Why or why not?
2 In view of the hardships people are suffering from the recession, should employers disregard the recent credit scores of job applicants? Why or why not?
3 How should Cameron react to the fact that she was denied a job because of her credit score?
4 What lessons does this case study contain?

Case Study: Running for Office and Financing the Campaign

Marla Winters is a 58-year-old high school civics teacher who has always been interested in politics. She believes that citizens should be actively involved in government and considers herself an Independent. Marla has not joined a political party because she has reservations about each party's platform.

When her school district institutes an early retirement program, Mrs. Winters decides to avail herself of the program. Following her retirement she becomes more interested in politics and, when a special election for the U.S. Senate is scheduled because of the untimely death of a sitting senator, Marla Winters decides to run as a third-party candidate for the office. She is a virtual unknown to everyone in the state with the exception of acquaintances in her local community. But Marla is confident because the person who agrees to be her campaign manager "knows everybody" and also because he knows how to get things done. In addition, if it ever makes sense to be an Independent, this is the time because of the record low approval ratings of the major parties.

Marla defines her stands on the issues of the day. One of her positions is strong opposition to allowing credit default swaps on collateralized debt obligations. Marla knows that, even in the new regulatory climate, it will be next to impossible to completely eliminate trading in CDOs, but she reasons that, if investment banks and hedge funds cannot hedge against CDOs, the market in these potentially problematic asset-backed securities will not grow huge.

Surprisingly, Marla's candidacy goes well, largely because one of her opponents has been hurt by the revelation of a personal scandal and because her other opponent does not communicate effectively.

Marla's campaign manager schedules a meeting with her. He is delighted and tells her that she has a good chance of winning. But she needs more exposure, better name recognition. He tells her that he has been contacted by lobbyists for financial firms and that these corporations are prepared to make large contributions to her campaign which will allow her to purchase air time; media exposure will put her over the top. "Why do they want to give me money?" Marla asks. "Because you could be a good friend to them," her manager answers.

1 Should Marla accept campaign contributions from these firms and tacitly agree to be their friend? Why or why not?

2 Since politics is the art of the possible, should Marla be flexible in her policy positions in order to get elected and do some good in Washington? Why or why not?

3 If Marla loses the election, should she give up her interest in politics? Why or why not?

4 If Marla wins the election and enters the U.S. Senate, how willing should she be to accommodate contributors by voting for legislation that favors them?

5 Describe the role you think corporate money should play in U.S. elections?

6

SOCIAL ETHICS

Individual ethics is directed to people; we take in the instructions of individual ethics and act on them. We learn: you have a conscience; you should honor objective standards in making decisions; you are responsible for your choices; cultivate good habits and take care to value things that are truly worthwhile. Do unto others as you would have them do unto you. We expect individuals to do the right thing and we punish individuals who do the wrong thing.

Social ethics differs from individual ethics in that it emphasizes the well-being of the community and the kinds of practices, policies, regulations and culture that produce justice and prosperity for everyone. Social ethical behavior is carried out by corporations, government and the media, rather than by individual actors. Business ethics is a subset of social ethics. Questions for social ethics such as "how should society be structured in order to protect human rights and what should be done to bring about just institutions and promote the common good?" arise in the context of business ethics. These questions prompt government officials and corporate leaders to examine how they need to conduct themselves in order to uphold ethical standards and promote prosperity. While business ethics involves individual moral choices, to a large extent protecting human rights and promoting the common good depend on the policies of corporations and government.

In light of the financial crisis, just as the question for individual ethics is fairly straightforward, so, too, is the question for social ethics: what lessons does social ethics have to teach us? In regard to borrowing, lending, rating, investing, determining risk-reward parameters and regulation of financial markets, social ethics has a lot to say. Commitments to ethical conduct by the financial industry, credit rating agencies, government and U.S. society are indispensable components of economic recovery.

As with Chapter 5, this chapter will proceed from a deontological premise which assumes that there are obligations that corporations and government need to acknowledge and act upon. These obligations are not optional; they are mandatory and failure to meet them constitutes negligence. In addition, these obligations are not open to negotiation and there is general consensus that it would be wrong not to meet them. We begin with ten imperatives that need to be implemented to promote prosperity.

Ten ethical imperatives to promote prosperity. Banks, hedge funds, mutual funds, clearinghouses, stock brokers, ratings analysts and others, such as mortgage brokers, enter into financial transactions which have far-reaching consequences, for good or for ill. These transactions are carried out to make money or provide information, and the firms which are involved in the transactions need to conform to standards that support the financial market and not act in ways that imperil the market. It is wrong to think that anything goes to make money. There are objective ethical standards that need to be acknowledged and a crass negativity to ethics needs to be rejected. These standards are deontological in nature, meaning that they are moral obligations that bind entities such as government, business and the media and these obligations are readily affirmed by rational people. The U.S. legal system punishes crimes such as fraud, theft, failure to disclose pertinent information, and insider trading, and citizens agree that such acts are unethical and illegal.

First. Contribute to the common good. The common good is achieved when individuals and groups act to bring about the well-being of everyone.

The common good is a notion that originated over two thousand years ago in the writings of Plato, Aristotle, and Cicero. More recently, the contemporary ethicist, John Rawls, defined the common good as "certain general conditions that are ... equally to everyone's advantage." The Catholic religious tradition defines it as "the sum of those conditions of social life which allow social groups and their individual members relatively thorough and ready access to their own fulfillment." The common good, then, consists primarily of having the social systems, institutions, and environments on which we all depend work in a manner that benefits all people.[1]

In order to bring about the common good financial institutions need to broaden the perspective from which they evaluate transactions. In addition to how transactions and policies affect the firm, its employees, shareholders and clients, financial institutions need to take into account the effects on other businesses and the public. If financial institutions appreciate how interconnected the economy is and that shared prosperity is better for everyone, self-interest might not be the sole motivation for carrying out transactions. If a commitment to the common good were to be part of a firm's strategy, some money-making prospects likely would be rejected in the interests of the stability of the financial system. During the heyday of the housing boom, the strategy of pursuing profits without regard to consequences backfired, causing economic hardship for everyone, including mortgage brokers who lost their jobs and those who saw a precipitous drop in their earnings.

Policies that focus solely on profits and exclude ethical considerations are short-sighted and, ultimately, carrying out business in this way is not ethically appropriate. Former Senator Bob Graham (D, Fl), a member of the Financial Crisis Inquiry Commission, posed a rhetorical question that is meant to drive home the fact that some financial products should not even exist because of their potential for harm: he asked if speculative bets such as naked credit default swaps and synthetic collateralized debt obligations held any social value for the U.S. economy.[2] By his question Senator Graham sought to make the point that the common good of the entire economy should be taken into consideration by those whose transactions affect the economy.

Archbishop Rowan Williams, the Anglican Archbishop of Canterbury, urges people in corporate governance to promote the common good through the policies they put in place:

> We find ourselves talking about capital or the market almost as if they were individuals, with purposes and strategies, making choices, deliberating reasonably about how to achieve aims. We lose sight of the fact that they are things that we make. They are sets of practices, habits, agreements which have arisen through a mixture of choice and chance. Once we get used to speaking about any of them as if they had a life independent of actual human practices and relations, we fall into any number of destructive errors. We expect an abstraction called "the market" to produce the common good or to regulate its potential excesses by a sort of natural innate prudence, like a physical organism or ecosystem. We appeal to "business" to acquire public responsibility and moral vision. And so we lose sight of the fact that the market is not like a huge individual consciousness, *that business is a practice carried on by persons who have to make decisions about priorities* – not a machine governed by inexorable laws.[3] (Emphasis added.)

We learn from Archbishop Williams that firms need to enact policies that will promote the common good and that this will not happen without consciously putting policies in place that support the economic well-being of everyone, an important aspect of the so-called *common good.*

Second. Act according to corporate conscience. Just as we expect individuals to use their conscience to determine the ethical choice, so we expect corporations to acknowledge a corporate conscience and to act in accordance with it. A corporate conscience entails determining what principles a corporation stands for and conforming corporate practices to those principles. A firm's tradition plays a role in the formation of its corporate conscience; values handed down from past generations are honored by contemporary management and workers. Analysis of current conditions and discussion of how morally right strategies and practices should contribute to a corporation's identity should take place. Ideally, a broad spectrum of a corporation's stakeholders should play a role in the discussion and should support the conclusions. Adherence to the dictates of corporate conscience should be required whether such adherence results in profit or loss. For corporations, as for individuals, compromising principles and violating integrity should not be options.

An example of financial institutions that stood by their principles and weathered the financial crisis is found in local banks. Kim Nelson relates that community bank mortgage lending is leading the financial recovery of residential finance as a supportable business model. She notes that many lenders were forced to restrict their lending or shut their doors, but community bank lending has remained relatively strong. Why? Ms. Nelson attributes the reason to the fact that, as a general rule, community banks did not abandon prudent lending standards and dabble in the subprime product; thus, they were not imperiled by liquidity issues and were able to maintain stability during the recession.[4]

Third. Honor corporate codes of ethics. A corporate code of ethics is a policy statement that defines ethical standards for conducting business. In writing these statements, many people typically offer input: the founder, the CEO, board of directors, management, workers, consultants and lawyers. Codes of ethics address workplace issues and workplace rights; they also describe business practices that are allowed and those that should be avoided. Corporate codes of ethics are strong statements written from a deontological perspective. Activities such as those likely to cause conflicts of interest are listed and forbidden. Implementation of codes of ethics is carried out by management. To the extent that corporate codes of ethics are words on paper that read well and are filed away, they are worthless. It is obvious that this should not be the case because a corporate code of ethics that plays a central role in the way a business is run provides education to employees about what is right and what is wrong. More importantly, the corporation's adherence to the code provides reassurance to workers that when they make a difficult choice that is the ethically right choice they are meeting the firm's expectations.

An ethical culture takes hold in a company that lives by its code of ethics. According to the Ethics Resource Center, establishing an ethical culture is the single biggest factor in deterring misconduct, and, as we have seen in regard to the financial crisis, wrong actions by even a small number of employees can jeopardize a company. At the current time, when public anger has created an opportunity for fixing problems, we have an ethics bubble, but the opportunity is unlikely to last so firms need to act promptly to review and, if necessary, revise corporate codes of ethics. History tells us that when times are tough, ethics improve. According to the Ethics Resource Center, when business thrives and regulatory oversight eases, ethics erode.[5]

Fourth. Carry out appropriate government relations. Business and government are two of the major institutions that make up society. Businesses exist to fulfill their particular missions and to make money. Governments exist on the local, state and national levels to keep order in society, provide services, and assist those who lack the ability to care for themselves. One of the services provided by agencies of state and federal governments is the regulation of business practices so as to promote the common good and prevent practices that are harmful to society. In order to fulfill this function, government needs to operate at arm's length from corporate management and needs to act independently to prevent abuses in the so-called *free market*.

There is an obvious tension between business and government: business executives do not want their enterprises hampered by government regulations that outlaw profitable activities that benefit the corporation and its shareholders. Executives tend to question the analysis that leads to government regulations and claims are often made by business leaders that the government is misinformed and should not be regulating one practice or another. Government officials push back by defending their policies as well thought out and unbiased and they argue that they do their job when they act in behalf of the common good.

Life is complicated and so is the maze of possible business practices, regulations and regulatory authorities. In view of this complexity and out of self-interest, it is not surprising that financial corporations contribute to political candidates and hire lobbyists in order to get laws and regulations passed that allow the business practices that enable the corporations to make money. This is the current state of affairs but it is ethically problematic because, if government rules and regulates in favor of financial institutions instead of in favor of the common good, the public is not served and questionable practices that may undermine the stability of the economy may be allowed.

Corporate boards and senior management need to recognize that it is wrong to influence government in order to get regulations that help businesses but will likely harm the overall economy. Business needs to respect the rightful role of government and work to insure the impartiality of those elected to office as well as appointed regulators. When the finance industry agrees to cease making political contributions and hiring lobbyists the public will have reason to believe that a needed change is in place. Until that day comes, pressure has to be put on government officials to be independent and not beholden to special interests. And people have to advocate for full disclosure of contributions to politicians as well as to political parties. This information will not prevent abuses but it will make it more difficult, and, perhaps, less beneficial, for campaign contributions to influence public policy.

Another way in which it would be unethical for financial firms to operate is by resorting to regulatory arbitrage. This practice entails the purposeful evasion of regulations in pursuit of higher profits.[6] For example, American International Group engaged in regulatory arbitrage when it selected the U.S. Office of Thrift Supervision (OTS) as its regulator because AIG knew that the OTS was the regulatory agency least likely to restrict its practices. This strategy was beneficial in the short term for profits but, ultimately, cost the company and the economy an incalculable amount. A lesson to be learned about regulatory arbitrage is that the practice may create a temporary advantage, but, long term, the advantage can morph into a catastrophe.

Fifth. Observe due diligence. Financial institutions perform specialized tasks related to securitizing, trading and investing in financial products. Lay people, for the most part, often lack the information and expertise to make accurate evaluations of these products. Due diligence is a responsibility of financial institutions and it requires that those who sell products investigate what they are selling and evaluate the products before offering them for sale. Information produced describing what is being sold needs to be clear, complete and truthful. In terms of arranging a mortgage loan for a potential home buyer, due diligence requires that information about the borrower's source of income, credit history and other pertinent factors be investigated and an application not accepted unless the information is true. In respect to credit ratings agencies, due diligence requires that personnel examine all parts of a collateralized debt obligation and issue an accurate assessment of the security. In financial firms, management is ethically obliged to put in place systems to require that due diligence be done and that information learned from conducting due diligence be properly utilized. To the extent that credit rating agencies and investment banks allowed computer modeling to take the place of human judgment in evaluating and designing financial products, these institutions made a serious error. A lack of due diligence at multiple junctures undermined the economy and the financial system will not recover unless management corrects this problem.

The Financial Crisis Inquiry Commission (FCIC), appointed by President Barack Obama to study the causes and context of the economic meltdown, understands the role played by lack of due diligence; hence, the Commission specifically listed "the quality of due diligence undertaken by financial institutions"[7] as contributing to the crisis. The Commission conducted research and hearings on this subject as part of its inquiry into what caused the economic implosion. During the time that banks were securitizing mortgages, the banks employed Clayton Holdings to do due diligence on the mortgages it was buying. Keith Johnson, President of Clayton from 2006–2009, told the FCIC in testimony in 2010 that the banks waived through 39 percent of the mortgages that Clayton classified as deficient Grade 3 loans.[8] It was apparent to Mr. Johnson as well as to the members of the FCIC that banks that ignored the results of due diligence and securitized mortgages that they knew were toxic junk acted unethically. Likewise, it would be wrong to skip the due diligence step and bundle products such as mortgages without concern for whether or not the items were creditworthy.

Sixth. Do not engage in moral hazard. Policies that are tolerant of moral hazard allow high risk financial gambles because the likelihood is that the firm will benefit and, even if things get out of hand, the firm will probably survive with help from the government. The firm will live to wager another day. The client, the investor, the counterparty and the taxpayer will lose; some might be wiped out, but the firm will survive. Tolerance or encouragement of high risk practices that cause financial harm to others is unethical. It is the responsibility of corporate management to manage the risk its employees take both for the sake of the stability of the institution and its fiduciary duty to clients and counterparties. Boards of directors should select executives who balance intelligence and creativity with humility and restraint. By so doing they will insure that corporate leaders, motivated by hubris and greed, who take big risks with the expectation of big gains will not have control of the executive suite.

As we have seen, mortgage-backed securities and collateralized debt obligations were complicated products and it is not surprising that some investors bought them without understanding what they were buying. To the extent that financial firms took advantage of the ignorance of investors and profited from markets that lacked transparency, they acted unethically. To the extent that they built up bigger and bigger portfolios of MBS in order to ride the crest of the market and make greater and greater profits while ignoring the possible downside, they engaged in moral hazard and wrought incalculable financial harm. Further, to the extent that they gamed the system by buying insurance – credit default swaps – to protect themselves against losses, their dealings were ethically questionable. Going forward, it is imperative that corporate codes of ethics address moral hazard and forbid its practice.

In this regard, J. Kyle Bass cautions that the marketplace is not a perfect world and that it is unrealistic to expect that the systemic changes that are being put in place as a response to the financial crisis will eliminate moral hazard. For this reason, Mr. Bass argues that the result of moral hazard should be bankruptcy because, "Capitalism without bankruptcy is like Christianity without hell."

Tom Armistead questions whether the true nature of moral hazard is that it occurs when a firm engages in too much risk while thinking that the government will intervene to prevent it from failing. He disagrees with limiting the definition to this way of thinking and says:

> The true moral hazard is created by a financial system that permits a small band of manipulators to make leveraged bets in favor of negative outcomes in situations where they have no other stake in the matter. . . . There is no requirement (that manipulators have) an insurable interest. The problem this creates is that speculators buy (credit default

swap) protection on a company's debt and then put out rumors or distortions while shorting the stock. The results lately have been devastating. I regard it as the financial equivalent of arson for profit.[9]

Mr. Armistead's observation enlarges the concept of moral hazard considerably and makes it a subject of regulation both for individual financial firms and for the government which must exercise control over the marketplace. What should government do to counter moral hazard created by manipulators who act to profit from the financial chaos they are able to cause by buying credit default swaps (CDS), bashing the stock they insure against, and then shorting it? The obvious role for government is to forbid sales of CDS to those who do not own the stock or securities they are insuring against, and to forbid naked short selling.

Seventh. Reject a wagering mentality and enforce rigorous risk management. Major investment and commercial banks, and Fannie Mae and Freddie Mac were brought to brink of collapse because they engaged in a high degree of leverage without having sufficient capital to back them up. When the market for mortgage-backed securities became illiquid, firms that needed to sell these securities were unable to do so. They could not get rid of their risk; they were stymied by it. Because they could not raise cash by selling MBS, they could not pay creditors. They were insolvent because a worst-case scenario played out and they did not have the capital needed to meet their business obligations. They had engaged in too much risk; their activities bore more resemblance to placing bets than to carrying out reasonable trades; institutional policies that allowed taking on too much risk set the stage for a disaster. The ethical mandate, going forward, is that boards of directors and senior management institute rigorous risk management policies and insist that these policies be followed so that those who work in financial firms transact trades with rational limits that do not have the potential to drive firms into bankruptcy. The pursuit of profit must be constrained by an awareness that excessive leverage is destabilizing and will not be tolerated. If financial firms elevate the status of risk managers so that these personnel have equal status and compensation with revenue producers, such a policy change will go a long way toward producing the desired result.

On October 21, 2009, the Senior Supervisors Group of the Financial Stability Board of the Bank for International Settlements commented on risk management in light of the crisis of 2008. Their comments reveal the complex and multilayered reality that risk management consists in as well as the role played by corporate governance in its implementation.

> Some of the changes that firms have made are among the more easily achievable enhancements, such as organizational efforts to improve the coordination and interaction between the treasury function, the risk management function, and the business lines. The extent to which such changes are formalized into policies and procedures – and more important, ingrained into the corporate culture – will determine their sustainability and effectiveness. Other structural changes – such as improvements to firms' liquidity reports, collateral management practices, and funds transfer pricing – are more resource- and time-intensive. Concerted discipline and commitment on the part of boards of directors, senior management, and supervisors will be required to undertake the IT infrastructure investments needed to support these changes and to continue to improve the robustness of these liquidity risk management systems.[10]

Eighth. Make compensation systems fair. The CEO of an investment bank should make more than the mailroom manager, but how much more? This question came to the fore in the aftermath of the financial crisis. In 1980, the average CEO made forty times as much as the average employee. In 2008 the multiple was 319.[11] Top level executives of financial services firms are paid significant salaries which are supplemented by large bonuses and stock options. Executive salaries are easier to accept when the companies they lead contribute to the economy but, when these companies are at the center of an economic tsunami, it is hard to justify them.

Shareholders and members of the compensation committee of the board of directors need to curb egregious executive compensation, not only because it looks bad for the firm, but because the firm's profits should be more widely distributed. Rewarding successful executives with company stock that cannot be sold for several years, rather than cash, may motivate them to take a big picture view when they are making decisions. This and other strategies that are designed to keep executives from engaging in high risk activities with quick payoffs can contribute to a more ethical marketplace. One such strategy is to rethink the wisdom of multi-year guaranteed contracts which provide security for executives but do not allow the penalty of termination to act as a check on the executive's decisions. Finally, institutional policies which stipulate clawback provisions are ethically appropriate. Executives who have clawback clauses in their contracts face being penalized by being required to return stock or money to the firm if, in the future, the firm learns that erroneous reporting or improper trading activities took place.

Ninth. Take short- and long-term consequences of actions and policies into account. Each financial institution has a culture and this culture consists of many aspects. The culture is communicated to new hires by those who have worked at the company for some time. Management refers to the corporation's culture in verbal and nonverbal ways. Employees learn the way things are done and they realize that, in order to succeed, they need to conform to the culture. Because so much of what is done is influenced by the corporate culture, it is important for management to explicitly communicate that gaining short-term advantages at the expense of long-term disadvantages is not acceptable. Two horizons should be taken into account when transactions are contemplated: the short-term horizon and the long-term horizon. Whenever short-term gain places long-term viability at risk, short-term gain should not be pursued. This principle constitutes good ethics and good business.

Tenth. Be sensitive to the social context in which business operates and be open to dialogue about the social context. In the summer of 2010 a movement began in New York City called Occupy Wall Street. In the months following people joined this movement and organized in other U.S. cities and in capitals around the world. The Occupy Wall Street movement involves demonstrations by protestors who are dissatisfied with the way the financial system operates. They are troubled by the consequences of the Great Recession and pose the question: is it fair that those who suffer the most from such downturns have their safety net cut, while those who generated the volatility are bailed out by the government?[12] Demonstrators are angry about the bailouts, the foreclosure crisis, the unemployment situation, and political contributions from the financial sector that result in favorable legislation from politicians. They contend that the playing field is not level and that the average citizen is at a disadvantage. In order to make their voices heard, demonstrators employ a variety of tactics including stopping traffic, staging rallies, marching on upper-class neighborhoods, posting online, and talking to the media. They camp out at protest sites and, at the time of writing, seem committed to continue indefinitely.

Occupy Wall Street states its mission on its website:

Occupy Wall Street is a leaderless resistance movement with people of many colors, genders and political persuasions. The one thing we all have in common is that We Are The 99% that will no longer tolerate the greed and corruption of the 1%. We are using the revolutionary Arab Spring tactic to achieve our ends and encourage the use of nonviolence to maximize the safety of all participants.

This OWS movement empowers real people to create real change from the bottom up. We want to see a general assembly in every backyard, on every street corner because we don't need Wall Street and we don't need politicians to build a better society.[13]

The Occupy Wall Street protesters are correct in stating that the vast majority of people in the United States do not enjoy the privileges and standard of living of the top earners on Wall Street. They also make a valid point when they call for change in the corporate and political realms so that a better society emerges. Are the protestors right in asserting that the country does not need politicians or the existing financial system (dubbed Wall Street) in order to build a better society? This suggestion is a radical one; it implies dismantling the capitalist system on which the nation functions and does not propose an alternative. Perhaps the protesters think that the alternative will take shape at backyard general assemblies, but this does not seem like a proposal which should be naïvely embraced.

What should happen? What changes should come from the Occupy Wall Street movement? To begin, the protesters need to stop demonizing every worker on Wall Street and admit that the vast majority of people who went to work there in the lead up to the financial crisis as well as in the years following acted reasonably and did not contribute to the collapse. In truth, most workers on Wall Street are in the 99 percent of everyday citizens, not members of the 1 percent elite. For their part, top managers on Wall Street who make major decisions and out-sized earnings should not dismiss the protesters and refuse to listen to their complaints. Wall Street firms hurt themselves by their tolerance for insane risks, but these firms also undermined their standing in the nation by embracing a radical version of the free market ideology without concern for the consequences attendant on adherence to this ideology. The nation narrowly avoided a depression.

The questions Occupy Wall Street raises should not be addressed by public relations firms representing major banks and other financial institutions. The questions should be engaged by chief executive officers, chief financial officers, others in upper management and members of boards of directors. A radical rethinking of how Wall Street operates may be in order and, as the protest is a bottom-up movement, so the response needs to be top-down.

Just as Occupy Wall Street is highly critical of financial firms, so the movement is negative toward politicians. It decries the cozy relationship between Wall Street firms and elected officials, considering this relationship a fundamental reason why a system exists that favors political contributors and leaves all others beyond the concern of lawmakers. Peter Gelling suggests that the primary goal of Occupy Wall Street may be reform of campaign financing:

> Central to the frustration of Occupy Wall Street demonstrators is corporate influence on politicians, which, they say, has led to most of the other concerns on their list, such as deregulation of the financial sector, unequal distribution of wealth and environmental destruction. Campaign-finance reform, some Occupiers believe, would address the root of the problem.[14]

It stands to reason that just as business executives should take the agenda of Occupy Wall Street seriously and should engage in constructive dialogue with a willingness to change, so too should U.S. politicians. In terms of the politicians, citizens actually can play a meaningful role: if politicians are not willing to govern with the common good in mind and are not willing to reject contributions from special interests, voters can act to put them out of office or reject their initial candidacy.

In summary, the implementation of these ten ethical imperatives by financial institutions would bring changes in the way business is done and would result in a better climate for business and improvement in the overall society. To be sure, had these social-ethical imperatives guided the actions of the financial industry during the first eight years of the new millennium, the crisis would not have happened. There is likely to be general agreement about the importance of these imperatives; however, in order to resolve the foreclosure crisis and stabilize the housing sector, banks, other lenders and government officials need to grapple with thorny ethical conundrums in order to attain stability. Let us consider the roles of mortgage lenders and government in addressing the present state of the housing crisis.

Ethics and the role of banks and mortgage lenders in resolving troubled mortgages. Banks need to make a profit to stay in business. A major problem faced by banks is that their portfolios of residential real estate contain subprime mortgages that are unlikely to be repaid. If homeowners become delinquent and stop paying their mortgages, banks can foreclose; in this situation, the bank owns the home and needs to sell it. If underwater buyers walk away from their homes, the houses will be empty and banks will be forced to sell them. According to a third scenario, people can declare bankruptcy. They move out of the house and the bank becomes the owner of a property which it then needs to sell. In each of these cases, banks have problems because there are few home buyers in the market and because, in order to sell the properties, banks would likely have to sell for less than what is owed and sustain a loss.

The economy is disrupted by people who do not pay their mortgage loans and banks or other lenders that hold subprime mortgages are in a no-win situation. A generous ethical strategy for the bank would be to renegotiate the mortgage, extending the length to lower monthly payments and forgiving late fees and penalties. This approach would enable some people to stay in their homes and would cut down on blight in neighborhoods with many abandoned homes. It would probably also be a better option for the bank than being the owner of houses that might stay on the market indefinitely and that would likely sell for less than the amount of the existing mortgage. Asking banks to bear this burden is not an ideal solution but, given the situation, where applicable, it might be the best practical alternative available and the most ethical.

Whatever decisions banks come to regarding renegotiating payments with distressed borrowers, there will still be a lot of residential real estate in foreclosure. Mortgage lenders own foreclosed properties. What should mortgage lenders do to maintain these properties? How should they price these properties in order to get them sold? In the interest of the common good, banks or mortgage lenders that own foreclosed properties should not neglect maintenance so as to promote stability in neighborhoods. The answer to the pricing question is not simple. Trying to resell the house for the amount owed on the mortgage is probably unrealistic because home values have fallen. Pricing the houses at less than the amount owed translates into a loss for the lender. While it is not fair that a lender not be repaid in full the amount that is owed, plus interest, with each foreclosure, home abandonment or bankruptcy, lenders must face this reality. They need to act to salvage as much for themselves and their shareholders as possible, and also take into consideration the needs of people for shelter and communities for stable housing prices and occupied residences. The policies of banks and mortgage lenders who own foreclosed properties should reflect their understanding of the leadership responsibilities they bear in communities where they transact business.

As far as policies in regard to foreclosures are concerned, it is morally imperative that banks that foreclose on properties observe scrupulous adherence to the legal procedures governing these transactions. Well-trained personnel should document each step of the process and shortcuts should be avoided so that mistakes, which result in wrongful evictions, do not occur. In cases wherein banks have mistakenly foreclosed on people who were current on their mortgages as well as in cases wherein banks have not followed proper procedures in issuing foreclosures, banks are morally required to make things right.

Ethics and the role of government in resolving troubled mortgages. As we saw in Chapter 3, the government program HAMP (Home Affordable Modification Program) is not working and the number of homes that have been foreclosed, are presently being foreclosed, or likely will be foreclosed is estimated to reach as high as thirteen million. The fact that the government's mortgage modification program did not work does not excuse the government from failing to undertake new initiatives. This situation represents an urgent human problem and the government should use its resources to aid in rebuilding the troubled housing sector.

After financial firms embrace rational ethical policies and mortgage lenders and government institute strategies designed to stabilize the housing market, a great deal of progress will have been made in achieving economic recovery. The task, however, still will not be complete because ten additional social ethical goals need to be met. Let us consider each in turn.

First. Understand the causes and context of the crisis. The Financial Crisis Inquiry Commission was appointed by President Barack Obama to learn about the complex and interconnected transactions carried out by financial and other industries and determine how those practices caused the financial crisis. A bipartisan group of ten highly qualified people was charged with analyzing what happened and issuing a report to inform the American people. There is no question that it is ethically appropriate for the president to appoint a bipartisan group and charge this group with getting to the bottom of things. Data gathering is the first step; making wise decisions based on this information and implementing new policies are needed follow-ups. It is important that an ethical recovery rest on a well-informed foundation. Originally, the Commission report was scheduled to be released on December 15, 2010; because of controversy about how to assign responsibility for the crisis as well as the enormity of the their task, the Commission announced on November 17, 2010 that it would delay issuance of its report until the end of January 2011.[15] The final report

consisted in three separate opinions: the majority (six Democratic members) authored a long and detailed report; three
Republicans joined in a report which dissented in some ways
from the majority report; and Peter Wallison, a Republican,
issued a separate dissenting view to which he was the lone signa-
tory. (Details of the Commission's work are available at www.
fcic.gov/.)

By reading this report as well as the testimonies of key people
involved in the financial crisis which are found on the FCIC
website people can come to comprehend the complicated ideas
and actions that resulted in the financial crisis.

Second. Restore public trust. A survey conducted by the Pew
Foundation from March 11–21, 2010 of more than two thousand adults revealed a marked decline from earlier in the millennium in regard to trust in government. "A perfect storm of
conditions associated with distrust of government – a dismal
economy, an unhappy public, bitter partisan-based backlash,
and epic discontent with Congress and elected officials"
resulted in negative attitudes toward government and fear that
government lacks the ability to do its job.[16] This finding is
alarming because it suggests that citizens think that two systems
are broken, government and the financial industry, and they do
not trust those in authority to fix these systems. This constitutes
a major problem because the U.S. economy is a fragile entity
that depends on consumer confidence to prosper. The optimism that characterized consumer behavior until the recession
began in 2007 has been replaced by fear and pessimism. People
who fear losing their jobs, their homes or their savings have
turned against elected officials; they do not believe these men
and women have the knowledge or skill set to right the ship of
state.

Restoring trust is an ethical mandate. What steps can
government take to achieve this goal? It is essential that government officials stop taking contributions from special interests so
that questions about their loyalties are put to rest. The regulatory changes stipulated in the Dodd–Frank Act need to be

implemented and enforced. The extreme partisanship that pits one political party against the other and results in gridlock is unproductive and discouraging. Elected officials need to learn to act as adults and work together to bring about the common good. If these and other steps are taken to restore trust in government, citizen attitudes will likely improve.

Third. Respond effectively to the unemployment crisis. People started losing their jobs in large numbers in 2008, and job losses continued for the next two years. In spite of the fact that monthly job losses declined in 2009 and 2010, close to 9 percent of Americans are unemployed. Many long-term unemployed stopped looking for work, and were not counted in this number; neither were those who settled for part-time work but who want to work full-time. At a debate by Republican candidates for their party's presidential nomination, Jim Cramer asked Mitt Romney, "Do corporations have a social responsibility to create jobs, or do they exist solely to maximize profits for shareholders?" Governor Romney's answer was that "The right thing for America is to have profitable enterprises that can hire people," and his thinking is that tax policies and lack of government regulations will facilitate corporate profitability.[17] There are those who would disagree with Romney and argue that corporations, as well as government, should take initiatives to put people to work. This argument is likely to be rejected by corporate leadership, however, because this leadership sees the corporation's functions as directed toward profits for shareholders, not jobs for the unemployed.

It is not clear what the government's role in fostering employment should be: some argue for putting people to work clearing land and building parks as was done during the Great Depression of the 1930s. Others say the government should offer incentives to small businesses to facilitate hiring workers. Some want the government to provide job training and others think the government should penalize U.S. corporations that employ people overseas rather than in this country. Still others advocate that the federal government give money to the states so the states can hire public employees or so that struggling states can keep public employees on the payroll.

The downside of government spending to promote employment is that this spending adds to deficit spending and increases the national debt. Both the deficit and the debt are staggering sums and there is little appetite on the part of politicians to add to these totals. So, unemployment constitutes a conundrum which is not easily solved and the high rate of unemployment contributes to public distrust in the government's ability to work with the private sector to bring about prosperity.

The ethical reasons for government leaders to take a major role in enacting policies to bring unemployment down and put people back to work are that meaningful work contributes to each individual's sense of self-worth and earned wages allow workers to support themselves and their families and provide stimulus for the economy. A sustained economic recovery will not take hold until the unemployed go back to work and there will be little trust in government until officials come up with a plan to get people off unemployment. This is both a pragmatic and an ethical mandate.

Fourth. Reinforce the safety net. The unemployed need unemployment insurance; the poor need food stamps, Medicaid and housing assistance. Schools, health care facilities and social service agencies in disadvantaged and middle-class areas have more needs and fewer resources during hard times and require more assistance, not less, from government. Even as government officials struggle with regulatory issues, the housing crisis and job creation, it would be ethically wrong to ignore the needs of the unemployed, and the poor. Government must supply what is needed to keep the safety net intact. This is an ethical obligation, not an option.

Fifth. Implement measures so that regard for the common good takes hold. Americans value their individual rights and the myth of the rugged individual, and these are worthwhile aspects of our culture. We are more than individuals, however;

we exist in communities and our communities depend upon the participation and contributions of all members in order to thrive. The common good sometimes requires that some people contribute more than others and that some make sacrifices for others. For example, in corporations the salaries of executive management are higher than those who hold lesser positions and people accept that this is the way it is. Should a corporation experience a crisis that forces severe cuts in order to stay solvent, management has within its discretion to terminate workers to achieve this goal. Mindful of the common good of the corporation and the morale of those who work there, however, management may decide instead to cut its own pay or work without compensation for a period of time so as to avoid firing people. A decision of this type would be entered into "for the common good" and would be a praiseworthy decision.

Commitment to the common good emphasizes the values, resources and traditions people share and requires helping the disenfranchised find their way into the mainstream. The common good is not attained until the basic needs of all are met and conditions established that allow people to engage in pursuits that are compatible with their human dignity. In the context of a society that has experienced an economic collapse and is struggling to put in place programs and policies that will result in recovery, sentiments which focus on self-satisfaction to the detriment of the group should be exposed as deficient. Americans need to appreciate the fact that we exist as social creatures, that we are our brother's and sister's keepers, and that it would be ethically wrong to think, "I'm okay and I don't care whether or not you're okay."

Sixth. Acknowledge the limits of capitalism. Capitalism is defended as the system that has brought the United States the highest levels of prosperity, education and comfort in the history of the world. There is no question that capitalism has strengths, but it also has weaknesses. Monopolies or practices that undermine the entire economy should not be tolerated. Capitalism, if it stands for greed and an unrestricted quest for profits, is not an ethical system. Capitalism needs to be modified by controls that prevent it from getting out of hand and destabilizing society. Government regulations need to outlaw harmful capitalistic practices, and businesses need to reflect on their ethical identities and conform their practices to rational limits.

Seventh. Confront the ethical limits of consumerism. In the context of the aftermath to the financial crisis consumerism can be seen as a two-edged sword. Those who obtained subprime mortgages and then took out home equity loans on the same property so that they could finance big ticket purchases were the worst kinds of consumers. Their practice of consumerism started the events that snowballed into an economic implosion. On the other hand, many people are now sitting on the sidelines, unwilling to buy real estate, invest in stocks, go on vacation or buy a new car. These people have the means to make these purchases, but their level of confidence in the economy is so low that they do not want to spend money. These consumers are not providing stimulus for small businesses and are hampering efforts to get the economy moving again.

Economic growth will be accomplished when society finds a middle path between consumer-driven debt and confident consumers who spend money on useful and pleasant purchases. Learning if, when and how to spend is a valuable lesson for consumers and its ethical aspects are self-evident.

Eighth. Affirm the dignity of the human person. Americans are familiar with the Declaration of Independence and its assertion about rights to life, liberty and the pursuit of happiness. Ethically sensitive people realize that this list should be expanded to include basic economic rights to employment, decent working conditions, wages and other benefits sufficient to provide individuals and their families with a standard of living in keeping with human dignity, and to the possibility of property ownership.[18] These ideas about employment, working conditions, just wages, benefits like health care and a pension, and home ownership represent many of the economic needs of ordinary people who work in order to earn money to meet basic human needs. U.S. society has a moral responsibility to stand behind policies that allow for these good things that promote human dignity.

Social ethics demands that meaningful steps be taken to assist the poor. People will be able to overcome poverty when they can take control of their own lives. Therefore, paternalistic solutions should be rejected and, instead, effective public policies to deal with poverty should be put in place. The best remedy against poverty is a healthy economy. In addition, self-help programs among the poor should be fostered, and there should be improved educational opportunities and access to job training programs. Poor people must expend personal initiative if they are to climb out of poverty, and this initiative should be supported by the broader society.

Ninth. Make a commitment to work for social justice. A commitment to work for justice can only take hold in a society that is committed to the common good. Working through the minutiae of regulating the financial industry will entail a great deal of stress as regulators try to comprehend the likely consequences and unintended outcomes of various proposals. Against this backdrop there needs to be a commitment to work for justice so that each and every player in the economy is treated fairly and with respect and so that the public and private sectors understand that standards of justice exist to which they need to conform their actions.

Tenth. Argue for the necessity of politics. The reason for politics in democratic societies is to represent the views of the majority and institute policies that will result in conditions of peace and order. This rationale contends that through the political process citizens elect representatives who are selected because of the belief that they will work together to bring about the common good. After what the United States experienced in the lead up to the financial crisis, its unfolding and its aftermath, there can be no question about the need for politics to fulfill its mission. Politics is necessary to operate as government and to oversee and regulate the economy in the interest of safeguarding the common good. The political sector needs to exercise its authority over the financial sector for the common good; the political sector cannot function if it is a pawn of the financial sector and not the independent overseer of the financial sector.

Citizens are skeptical about politicians and politics because government did not prevent the financial crisis and has not been able to ameliorate the human suffering that resulted from it. Citizen dissatisfaction is understandable but the rational response to this dissatisfaction is neither anarchy nor a return to an unregulated free market. The rational response is to improve the political process through campaign reform and to insist on representative government by intelligent, independent, ethical people who are committed to act in behalf of the common good.

Conclusion. The well-being of the community depends on a commitment to social ethics. The practices of the financial industry need to take into account the common good of the broader society. Government should regulate to promote the well-being of citizens regardless of whether or not these regulations are agreeable to the financial industry. The foreclosure crisis is a daunting one, but government authorities and mortgage lenders need to be proactive in working for a resolution. The needs of the unemployed and the poor have to be taken into account and there must be a commitment to meet these needs. Cultural attitudes need to change so that respect for human dignity and regard for the common good take precedence over self-centeredness and individualism. As the United States embarks on the road to economic recovery, the insights of social ethics must illuminate the path.

Questions for Discussion

1 What is social ethics? How does social ethics differ from individual ethics?
2 What is the common good? What practices should corporations and government institutionalize in support of the common good?

3   How did lack of due diligence contribute to the financial crisis? Going forward, how should financial firms, insurance firms and credit rating agencies conduct due diligence?

4   What can citizens, government and corporations do to prevent tolerance for moral hazard from taking hold?

5   Are there ethical limits on how much individuals should be paid? Explain the reasoning for your answer.

6   Describe how people who work in industries related to mortgage lending can assist in bringing about economic recovery.

7   Suggest policies and practices to counter unemployment and provide ethical reasons for why it is necessary to deal effectively with unemployment.

8   What is human dignity and how should a commitment to uphold human dignity motivate society to meet the needs of the poor during difficult economic times?

9   What changes are necessary in order for politics to serve the common good?

Case Study: Public Employee Pensions and Renegotiation of Benefits

Jared Cooper is forty-nine years old and has been employed by a state department of education for twenty-four years. He intends to retire at age fifty-five and collect his pension. He plans to set up a home-based small business after he retires and he hopes to supplement his pension checks with future earnings.

In 2011 Mr. Cooper's state elected a new governor who sounded alarms about the condition of the state's finances. When he took office, the state was getting by on reduced tax revenues by continuing its practice of deficit spending and increasing its overall debt burden. If this practice continued, in a few years, the default of the state government on its debt seemed a realistic possibility. The pension fund was a particular concern; it was underfunded by tens of billions of dollars;

payments from the state to the fund had not been made in several years; and the value of the fund declined significantly due to poor investment performance during and after the financial collapse. A bipartisan commission, appointed to study the condition of the pension fund, agreed that it was a major problem which needed to be dealt with immediately. Public opinion polls of state residents revealed that more than two-thirds agreed with the governor that drastic cuts in benefits to state employees were necessary to reverse the decline in the state's financial condition.

In view of the grim fiscal situation, the governor recommended a proposal to the state legislature: raise the retirement age for current employees to sixty-five, reduce pension payments for current and future retirees, and institute a new benefits system for future employees with significant reductions in pensions and other benefits. Going forward, the governor said, the state could not continue to afford to maintain the current level of funding. There were also recommendations to raise taxes on gasoline, alcohol and tobacco, and to raise tolls. There would be strict limits on hiring of state workers and many positions would be eliminated by attrition.

Jared Cooper is alarmed by these developments. He is a union member and he does not want to see his future plans disrupted by the governor's policies. He decides to become an activist, to write letters, attend demonstrations, make phone calls and keep his co-workers informed about what is going on. Mr. Cooper contends that the state is ethically required to keep its promises to its employees and that it would be wrong of the state to take away pension benefits that were agreed to in the past. He says that public employees should not be singled out to suffer the consequences of the state's fiscal negligence in not properly funding the pension plan. And he thinks that the value of the pension fund, which declined during the financial collapse, will likely make up what it lost in better times, so the state should not be using the fund's temporary negative performance to permanently punish employees.

1   Evaluate Jared Cooper's argument against the governor's
     pension proposals and discuss the strengths and
     weaknesses of the argument.
2   When a state government faces a shortfall like the one
     discussed in this case, what steps should the executive
     and legislative branches take to resolve it?
3   What ethical insights and principles should motivate indi-
     viduals and government officials as they try to resolve def-
     icits?
4   How should consideration for the common good moti-
     vate the interested parties in this case?

Case Study: Free Tuition – A Change to College Policy

Dr. Susan Wilson is president of a medium-sized private college,
Central College, located in a state that has been hit hard by the
recession. Central College is near the public university, but the
two institutions of higher learning do not collaborate on a regular basis. Central College's significant endowment lost little
money in 2008 because the endowment was very conservatively
invested. Central's enrollment has stayed stable because students tend to be from affluent families who continue to be able
to pay tuition, residence costs and fees. The school is fortunate
to be in much better shape than many institutions of higher
education.

The situation at the public university, Public U, differs mark-
edly from that of Central. There have been massive cutbacks in
state aid which have forced Public U to cancel a lot of classes.
Students at the school find themselves in limbo because they
cannot get into the classes they need to graduate; hence, their
lives are on hold. These students know all about the high unemployment in their state but they also know that they need to
finish their coursework, get their degrees, and begin trying to
find work. As things stand, they feel discouraged and frustrated.
They are worried about themselves and their families.

Aware of the plight of students at Public U, and wanting to
help them, Dr. Wilson proposes to the board of trustees that

Public U students be allowed to take classes at Central College free of charge, provided that the credits would be transferrable and that there are seats available. She explains that she wants to extend this offer only to seniors and only if there is space available. "At times like this, we should pitch in and help these young people."

The chairperson of the board of trustees is taken aback by Dr. Wilson's idea and argues that it would be hard for her to justify giving away credits that Central College's students pay a lot of money to purchase. Brief time is allotted to discussion of the proposal and a decision is made to come back to this matter at the next meeting. Members of the board say they need to consider both the president's suggestion and the chairperson's objections.

1　What ethical values are at stake in this case?
2　Whose position makes more sense, the college president's or the chairperson's? Why?
3　What issues, not referred to in this case study, likely lurk beneath the surface?
4　What steps could Public U take to respond to the needs of students who cannot get into the classes that they need for graduation?

Case Study: Rebuilding the Corporate Brand

Sheila Stockton has just been appointed CEO of one of the largest banks in the United States. After an extensive search, Ms. Stockton was chosen from among a group of four finalists. She was the only one of the four with experience in several fields, having held elective office, worked as an executive in Silicon Valley, been VP of a hedge fund, and freelanced as a media commentator. Ms. Stockton is an excellent communicator and a decisive leader. Her appointment comes with vigorous encouragement from the board of directors to do "whatever it takes" to rebuild the bank's corporate brand, which was badly damaged from fallout over the financial crisis.

During the interview in which she was offered the position, Ms. Stockton asked the board, "Am I hearing you right? Are you giving me a blank check?" She was reassured by their response that they were willing to place their confidence in her to restore both the bank's profitability and reputation and that she would have the final say on how to deploy resources in achieving this goal.

Ms. Stockton begins her tenure by meeting with senior executives and brainstorming about how to move the firm forward. She quickly learns that there are competing interests among the division heads. The traders, money managers, mergers and acquisitions people, risk managers and IT personnel, to name a few, defend their key importance to the firm and argue for bigger slices of the profit pie. All seem taken aback by Ms. Stockton's suggestion to increase the budgets for public relations and community outreach. Negative comments about her competence and proposed strategy fill the rumor mill. She is in a difficult position and realizes that her reputation and future with the firm depend on the consequences of the policies she needs to implement.

Sheila Stockton sits in front of her computer screen and composes an email that reads as follows:

> I have just completed my first month at this firm and it has been a busy and challenging time. When the board hired me, I was charged with turning this business around, restoring its reputation and profitability. According to projections, this year and next, approximately 20% of budget expenditures will be discretionary. Since fixed costs must be met before discretionary spending takes place, we are fortunate to have this cushion and our stockholders will be pleased.
>
> How are we going to proceed with discretionary spending? I am going to recommend to the board that for the next two years bonuses not exceed 10% of salary and that our community outreach and public relations budgets be

significantly increased. The public suffered as a result of the financial shenanigans of the subprime era; our bank needs to take responsibility for our role in the calamity and help communities to recover by providing support for job retraining programs. This is an ethical mandate and one that this bank embraces. I count on you to support me in the necessary task of rebuilding our brand by strategic publicity and positive action. Two years from now we will be a stronger and better institution and I will revisit the bonus policy at that time.

1   Should Sheila Stockton hit send?
2   How are recipients of Ms. Stockton's email likely to react? Is there an ethically right or wrong way to react? Describe the characteristics of an ethical response.
3   Discuss whether or not Sheila Stockton neglects her responsibility to the bank's employees when she directs that more of the bank's profits go to community outreach and public relations than to their bonuses.
4   Senior executives who oversee many of the bank's departments do not agree with the direction the CEO is taking. Comment on her motives, and theirs, both practical and ethical.
5   Do you think key producers will leave the bank as a result of the bonus policy? Should the CEO's decisions be based on likely moves by key personnel? Why or why not?
6   List and discuss points to be emphasized in public relations efforts to rebuild the bank's brand.

NOTES

INTRODUCTION

1 http://c0182732.cdn1.cloudfiles.rackspacecloud.com/fcic_final_report_ full.pdf.

1 WHAT WENT WRONG?

1 www.freddiemac.com/corporate/buyown/english/mortgages/what_is/.
2 www.fdic.gov/bank/analytical/fyi/2005/021005fyi.html#foot1.
3 www.fcic.gov/hearings/pdfs/2009–0917-CommissionerStatements.pdf.
4 The accounts of IndyMac borrowers were insured by the FDIC for $100,000; amounts greater than $100,000 were repaid by the FDIC at 50 cents on the dollar.
5 http://articles.moneycentral.msn.com/Banking/HomeFinancing/ CountrywideTheMortgageMessAndYou.aspx.
6 www.nytimes.com/2011/07/06/business/06bank.html.
7 www.fcic.gov/hearings/pdfs/2010–0602-Transcript.pdf, 9.
8 www.fcic.gov/hearings/pdfs/2010–0114-Bair.pdf.
9 www.fcic.gov/hearings/pdfs/2010–0602-Weill.pdf.
10 U.S. Senate Report, *Wall Street and the Financial Crisis: Anatomy of a Financial Collapse*, April 13, 2011; http://levin.senate.gov/newsroom/support-ing/2011/PSI_WallStreetCrisis_041311.pdf.
11 www.moneyweek.com/investment-advice/how-to-invest/subprime-mortgage-collapse-why-bear-stearns-is-just-the-start.aspx.
12 www.huffingtonpost.com/social/markinaz?action=comments&display= news&sort=newest.
13 http://bonds.about.com/od/derivativesandexotics/a/CDO.htm.
14 www.wired.com/techbiz/it/magazine/17–03/wp_quant?current Page=all.
15 JPMorgan fared better than other investment banks at this time because of lessons learned from losses it sustained in mortgage-backed securities in 2004; these losses prompted management to be leery of this invest-ment and, as a result, JPMorgan had very limited exposure at the time when the market crashed.

By 2008 the CEO of JPMorgan, Jamie Dimon,

> showed himself to be infinitely more prudent than his competi-tors. The bank used less leverage to boost returns and didn't engage in anywhere near the same amount of off-balance gim-mickry. So while other banks began to stumble severely after the

market for subprime mortgages imploded, JP Morgan stayed strong and steady.
(Andrew Ross Sorkin, *Too Big to Fail*, New York: Viking, 2009, 76)

16 "The Story of the CDO Market Meltdown," Harvard Undergraduate Dissertation, Anna Katherine Barnett-Hart, 95.

17 www.fcic.gov/hearings/pdfs/2009–1020-Scott-Taylor-article.pdf.

18 www.wikinvest.com/stock/Citigroup_(C)/Glossary Terms.

19 Michael Lewis, *The Big Short*, New York: W.W. Norton & Company, Inc., 2010.

20 www.fcic.gov/hearings/pdfs/2009–0917-CommissionerStatements.pdf.

21 www.newsweek.com/2008/09/26/the-monster-that-ate-wall-street.html.

22 Ross Sorkin, *Too Big to Fail*, 396.

23 www.nytimes.com/2010/07/18/business/18gret.html.

24 There is a third, smaller GSE, Ginnie Mae. Ginnie Mae plays a similar role in the secondary market for mortgages insured by the Federal Housing Administration and the Department of Veterans Affairs. (www.fcic.gov/reports/pdfs/2010–0407-Preliminary_Staff_Report_-_Securitization_and_the_Mortgage_Crisis.pdf).

25 Ross Sorkin, *Too Big to Fail*, 229.

26 www.consumeraffairs.com/news04/2010/12/six-more-banks-fail-total-for-year-now-157.html.

27 www.calculatorplus.com/savings/advice_failed_banks.html.

28 www.reuters.com/article/idUSTRE50F1Q720090116.

29 http://levin.senate.gov/senate/committees/investigations/.

30 www2.goldmansachs.com/our-firm/on-the-issues/viewpoint/viewpoint-articles/04–13–2011-statement-in-response-to-report-by-senate-perm-sub.html.

31 http://dealbook.nytimes.com/2011/06/06/the-fine-print-of-goldmans-subprime-bet/.

32 www.fcic.gov/hearings/pdfs/2009–1020-Baily-article.pdf.

33 www.marketwatch.com/story/banks-in-the-shadows-brought-down-wall-street.

34 www.riksbank.com/upload/Dokument_riksbank/Kat_publicerat/Ekonomiska%20kommentarer/2009/ek_kom_no3_eng.pdf.

35 Ross Sorkin, *Too Big to Fail*, 14.

36 Ibid., 10.

37 http://s3.amazonaws.com/propublica/assets/docs/fuld_statement_081006.pdf.

38 http://levin.senate.gov/newsroom/supporting/2011/PSI_WallStreet-Crisis_041311.pdf.

39 http://levin.senate.gov/newsroom/supporting/2011/PSI_WallStreet-Crisis_041311.pdf.

40 www.bloomberg.com/news/2010–10–19/greater-risk-management-role-coming-to-securities-markets-francioni-says.html.

41 www.fintools.com/docs/Warren%20Buffet%20on%20Derivatives.pdf.
42 http://c0182732.cdn1.cloudfiles.rackspacecloud.com/fcic_final_report_full.pdf.
43 www.autointhenews.com/bush-auto-bailout-necessary-to-safeguard-american-workers/.

2 WHO IS AFFECTED?

1 www.nydailynews.com/news/politics/2010/08/06/2010–08–06_soc_sec_pay_now_goin_the_wrong_way.html.
2 Ibid.
3 www.irs.gov/newsroom/article/0,,id=232590,00.html.
4 http://money.usnews.com/money/retirement/articles/2011/01/18/4-social-security-changes-coming-in-2011.
5 www.economy.com/mark-zandi/documents/FCIC-Zandi-011310.pdf.
6 www.nytimes.com/2010/09/10/us/10defenders.html.
7 http://articles.businessinsider.com/2011–08–31/wall_street/30013396_1_countrywide-s-ceo-angelo-mozilo-subprime-loans-brian-moynihan.
8 www.ibtimes.com/articles/211652/20110910/bank-of-american-layoffs-profits-banks-moynihan-hsbc.htm.
9 www.wtffinance.com/2011/02/more-losses-for-fannie-and-freddie-how-much-will-it-cost-taxpayers/.
10 www.npr.org/2011/02/15/133777142/End-Of-Fannie-Mae-Freddie-Mac-Will-Affect-Minorities.
11 www.nytimes.com/2007/04/02/business/03lend.web.html?hp.
12 Ibid.
13 www.investopedia.com/articles/07/bear-stearns-collapse.asp#axzz1aOEZkqpw.
14 www.cnbc.com/id/23676915/Half_of_Bear_s_14_000_Employees_May_Lose_Their_Jobs.
15 http://financecareers.about.com/od/insurancecompanies/a/AIG.htm.
16 www.businessinsurance.com/article/20111004/NEWS04/111009971/-1&template=mobileart.
17 www.sec.gov/spotlight/dodd-frank/creditratingagencies.shtml.
18 www.marketwatch.com/story/us-household-stock-ownership-posts-modest-upswing.
19 www.dailyfinance.com/market-news/.
20 www.wikinvest.com/stock/Home_Depot_(HD).
21 www.answers.com/topic/toll-brothers-inc.
22 Will Daly, "Companies sitting on cash, ready to spend it," *The Star Ledger*, August 1, 2010, 3:6.
23 Ibid.
24 www.sba.gov/advo/stats/sbfaq.pdf.
25 www.fcic.gov/hearings/pdfs/2010–0907-Peterson.pdf.

26 In his 2010 book Michael Lewis describes the unusual and very percep-tive skill set of hedge fund directors who did see what was coming and understand the flaws in MBS-CDOs. These individuals traded based on their knowledge and made huge amounts of money. They were in the business of making money and did not appropriate the mantle of whistleblower. Had they been whistleblowers instead of investors, no one knows what the likelihood would have been that they would have been listened to and corrective action taken before the market collapse.

27 www.editorsweblog.org/analysis/2008/11/financial_crisis_a_media_ failure.php.

28 Motoko Rich, "Growth is expected to slow in 2nd half," *New York Times*, July 30, 2010, 5.

29 www.washingtonpost.com/wp-dyn/content/article/2009/04/15/ AR2009041503791.html.

30 www.nytimes.com/2010/08/03/us/03unemployed.html?

31 http://professionals.collegeboard.com/data-reports-research/trends/ studentpoll/economy.

32 www.census.gov/hhes/www/poverty/.

33 www.huffingtonpost.com/marian-wright-edelman/children-need-emergency-h_b_691380.html.

34 Ibid.

35 www.telegraph.co.uk/finance/recession/5025115/RBS-traders-hid-toxic-debt.html.

36 www.nytimes.com/2011/10/10/business/3-countries-agree-on-bailout-of-european-bank.html.

37 www.nytimes.com/2007/12/02/world/europe/02norway.html? pagewanted=all.

3 WHAT NEEDS TO BE DONE TO SET THINGS RIGHT?

1 www.nytimes.com/2008/10/23/business/worldbusiness/23iht-gspan.4.17206624.html.

2 This contention is substantiated in an exhaustive case study issued in the form of a book: Gretchen Morgenson and Joshua Rosner, *Reckless Endan-germent: How Outsized Ambition, Greed, and Corruption Led to Economic Arma-geddon*, New York: Times Books, 2011.

3 www.time.com/time/specials/packages/article/0,28804,1877351_ 1877350_1877322,00.html.

4 Ibid.

5 Ibid.

6 http://business.timesonline.co.uk/tol/business/industry_sectors/ banking_and_finance/article7059719.ece.

7 Ibid.

8 http://news.yahoo.com/s/nm/20100920/bs_nm/us_usa_economy_ nber.

9 http://money.cnn.com/2010/06/09/news/economy/double_dip_recession/index.htm.

10 www.cpa2biz.com/Content/media/PRODUCER_CONTENT/News-letters/Articles_2011/CPA/Sep/DoubleDipRecession.jsp.

11 http://en.wikipedia.org/wiki/Federal_takeover_of_Fannie_Mae_and_Freddie_Mac.

12 George Bush, *Decision Points*, New York: Crown, 2010, 458.

13 On December 16, 2010, Treasury Secretary Timothy Geithner said that, when government-owned stock was sold and debts were repaid by beneficiaries of the program, the $700 billion financial bailout would end up costing taxpayers less than $25 billion.

14 www.federalreserve.gov/bankinforeg/tarpinfo.htm.

15 Bush, *Decision Points*, 464.

16 www.publicbroadcasting.net/kplu/news.newsmain/article/1/0/1712979/KPLU.Local.News/Many.NW.Banks.In.No.Hurry.To.Repay.U.S..Treasury.Infusions.

17 www.nytimes.com/2010/08/27/business/27toxic.html.

18 Ibid.

19 This amount, $250,000, was agreed upon in 2008 in order to calm depositors in the midst of the crisis. In the years leading up to the crisis the amount of deposit insurance had been $100,000.

20 www.fdic.gov/regulations/reform/role.html.

21 www.nytimes.com/2010/09/18/us/politics/18warren.html.

22 www.fdic.gov/regulations/reform/summary.html.

23 www.npr.org/templates/story/story.php?storyId=128752960.

24 Prepayment penalties are undesirable because, if a home owner sells the house before the mortgage expires, he or she will have to pay a predetermined fee in order to satisfy the mortgage. Additionally, if people obtain adjustable rate mortgages and the interest rate increases significantly, they may want to repay or refinance the ARMs. Prepayment fees make this an expensive option.

25 www.financialserviceslitigationmonitor.com/tags/consumer-finance-protection-bu/.

26 http://documents.nytimes.com/supervisory-capital-assessment-program-bank-stress-test-overview.

27 www.fdic.gov/news/news/press/2010/statement_chairman_bair07152010.html.

28 http://banking.senate.gov/public/_files/070110_Dodd_Frank_Wall_Street_Reform_comprehensive_summary_Final.pdf.

29 www.ny.frb.org/aboutthefed/PVolckerbio.html.

30 www.sec.gov/answers/mktmaker.htm.

31 Jesse Eisinger, "The gray areas in proprietary trading," *New York Times*, November 26, 2010, B5.

32 http://c0182732.cdn1.cloudfiles.rackspacecloud.com/fcic_final_report_full.pdf.

33 www.nytimes.com/2010/12/19/opinion/l19derivative.html.
34 www.fdic.gov/regulations/reform/summary.html.
35 www.nytimes.com/2010/12/12/business/12advantage. html?pagewanted=all.
36 www.usatoday.com/money/companies/regulation/2010–06–25-fixed-or-not_N.htm.
37 http://goliath.ecnext.com/coms2/gi_0198–652467/Bank-regulation. html.
38 www.sec.gov/news/testimony/2009/ts120909rk.htm.
39 www.sec.gov/news/press/2010/2010–197.htm.
40 www.sec.gov/news/testimony/2008/ts091808lct.htm.
41 www.fcic.gov/reports/pdfs/2010–0114-EnforcementMeasures.pdf.
42 www.sec.gov/news/press/2010/2010–123.htm.
43 http://blogs.forbes.com/afontevecchia/2010/11/01/echoes-of-abacus-jp-morgan-to-face-sec-probe-over-cdo-transaction-with-hedge-fund/.
44 http://topics.nytimes.com/top/news/business/companies/indymac-bancorp-inc/index.html.
45 www.nytimes.com/2011/03/18/business/18bank.html?_r=1&pagewanted=print.
46 www.law360.com/articles/237026/print?section=topnews.
47 www.reuters.com/article/2011/04/19/mortgage-fraud-farkas-idUSN199639120110419.
48 www.nytimes.com/2011/07/21/business/wells-fargo-to-settle-mortgage-charges-for-85-million.html.
49 www.nytimes.com/2011/07/21/business/countrywide-to-pay-borrowers-108-million-in-settlement.html.
50 www.fcic.gov/reports/pdfs/2010–0114-EnforcementMeasures.pdf.
51 www.washingtonpost.com/wp-dyn/content/article/2010/10/12/AR2010101205604.html.
52 www.ag.ny.gov/media_center/2010/dec/dec21a_10.html.
53 www.nytimes.com/2011/01/08/business/08mortgage.html.
54 www.miamidade.gov/mayor/releases/09–05–06-senate_mortgage_fraud.asp.
55 www.fcic.gov/reports/pdfs/2010–0114-EnforcementMeasures.pdf.
56 www.federalreserve.gov/aboutthefed/mission.htm.
57 Nouriel Roubini and Stephen Mihm, *Crisis Economics: A Crash Course in the Future of Finance*, New York: Penguin, 2010, 153.
58 Ibid., 154.
59 www.newyorkfed.org/markets/pridealers_current.html.
60 www.federalreserve.gov/newsevents/press/monetary/20100810a.htm.
61 www.nytimes.com/2011/01/10/business/economy/10fed.html.
62 www.fcic.gov/hearings/pdfs/2010–0901-Transcript.pdf.
63 www.fcic.gov/hearings/pdfs/2010–0407-Greenspan.pdf.
64 www.reuters.com/article/idUSN2725790820100827.

65 www.reuters.com/article/2011/08/26/usa-fed-idUSN1E77O 1LR20110826.
66 www.nytimes.com/2010/08/18/business/18fannie.html.
67 http://dealbook.blogs.nytimes.com/2010/08/04/for-fannie-stock-even-betting-pennies-is-a-risk/.
68 Ibid.
69 www.nytimes.com/2010/07/18/business/18gret.html.
70 www.nytimes.com/2010/08/10/business/10freddie.html.
71 www.nytimes.com/2010/08/12/opinion/12poole.html.
72 http://thatstoday.com/article/2986289/us-recovers-billions-in-sale-of-gm-stock—new-york-times.
73 www.phonienews.com/14451/general-motors-should-focus-on-selling-cars-to-consumers-who-can-afford-the-vehicles/.
74 www.nytimes.com/2010/08/10/business/10sorkin.html.
75 http://money.cnn.com/2011/07/21/autos/chrysler_government_exit/.
76 www.nytimes.com/2011/07/30/business/forced-marriage-of-fiat-and-chrysler-yields-success.html.
77 www.brockfc.com/stimulus-act-arra-provides-substantial-tax-breaks-for-businesses-and-individuals.html.
78 www.whitehouse.gov/the-press-office/2011/09/08/fact-sheet-american-jobs-act.
79 www.washingtonpost.com/business/economy/lawmakers-white-house-regroup-after-senate-scuttles-obama-jobs-plan/2011/10/12/gIQA6K-fdeL_story.html.
80 http://news.yahoo.com/s/ap/20101218/ap_on_go_co/us_tax_cuts_165.
81 www.miseryindex.us/urbymonth.asp.
82 www.wsws.org/articles/2010/aug2010/jobs-a07.shtml.
83 www.nytimes.com/2011/01/13/business/economy/13econ.html.
84 www.cleveland.com/business/index.ssf/2011/09/ben_bernanke_says_in_cleveland.html.
85 www.nytimes.com/2010/08/06/business/06wall.html.
86 http://dealbook.blogs.nytimes.com/2010/08/06/norris-caveat-emptor-continued/.
87 www.marketwatch.com/story/geithner-eyes-more-common-equity-for-big-banks-2010–08–02.
88 http://dealbook.nytimes.com/2011/01/11/goldman-vows-to-be-more-open-about-its-business/.
89 www.nytimes.com/2010/11/06/business/06fannie.html.
90 www.realtor.org/press_room/news_releases/2009/08/helps_short.
91 www.nytimes.com/2010/12/26/business/26mod.html?_r=1&pagewanted=2.
92 www.nytimes.com/2010/12/05/magazine/05Dimon-t.html?pagewanted=4.

93 www.nytimes.com/2010/12/19/realestate/19mort.html.
94 http://portal.hud.gov/portal/page/portal/HUD/topics/avoiding_ foreclosure/foreclosureprocess.
95 http://foreclosureblues.wordpress.com/2010/11/27/ny-times-gretchen-morgenson-don%E2%80%99t-just-tell-us-show-us-that-you-can-foreclose/.
96 www.southcoastaccidentattorney.com/blog/bank-of-america-wrongfully-forecloses-on-naples-florida-homeowner.cfm.
97 www.nj.com/business/index.ssf/2010/12/borrowers_caught_in_fore-closur.html.
98 www.nytimes.com/2011/01/20/opinion/20kapell.html.
99 www.haas.berkeley.edu/news/20100113_rosenfcic.html.
100 www.nytimes.com/2011/10/03/opinion/foreclosures-are-killing-us. html.
101 www.nytimes.com/2011/01/09/business/09gret.html?page wanted=all.
102 www.post-gazette.com/pg/10301/1098694–84.stm#ixzz13gdrW78i.
103 www.nytimes.com/2010/11/18/business/economy/18mortgage. html?partner=rss&emc=rss.
104 www.nytimes.com/2011/01/07/business/07norris.html.
105 www.nytimes.com/2011/10/01/business/california-quits-states-talks-with-banks.html.
106 www.nytimes.com/2010/12/17/business/economy/17norris.html.
107 www.zerohedge.com/news/us-needs-generate-261200-jobs-month-return-pre-depression-employment-end-obama-second-term.
108 www.theglobeandmail.com/globe-investor/investment-ideas/street-wise/corporate-cash-hoard-in-the-trillions-moodys/article2111286/.
109 www.fcic.gov/report/conclusions.
110 www.nytimes.com/2010/12/19/business/19gret.html.

4 ETHICS AND RECOVERY

1 www.archbishopofcanterbury.org/2324.
2 For further information, cf. Joseph A. Petrick and John F. Quinn (2001), "Integrity capacity as a strategic asset in achieving organizational excellence," *Measuring Business Excellence*, 5:1, pp. 24–31.
3 www.vatican.va/roman_curia/pontifical_councils/justpeace/docu-ments/rc_pc_justpeace_doc_20060526_compendio-dott-soc_en. html#I.%20MEANING%20AND%20UNITY, 163.
4 www.pbs.org/wnet/religionandethics/week1204/perspectives.html.
5 www.sec.gov/comments/s7–08–09/s70809–3779.pdf.
6 http://clipsandcomment.com/wp-content/uploads/2008/10/ greenspan-testimony-20081023.pdf.
7 http://4closurefraud.org/2010/10/07/false-statements-americas-servicing-company-lender-processing-services-wells-fargo-bank-n-a/.

8 http://inside.msj.edu/academics/faculty/whiter/ethicsbook.pdf, 21.
9 http://plato.stanford.edu/entries/original-position/.
10 http://inside.msj.edu/academics/faculty/whiter/ethicsbook.pdf, 22.
11 Ibid., 24.
12 Andrew C. Varga, *On Being Human*, New York: Paulist Press, 1978, 38–40.

5 INDIVIDUAL ETHICS

1 http://fcic-static.law.stanford.edu/cdn_media/fcic-testimony/ 2010–0505-Transcript.pdf.
2 http://levin.senate.gov/404/?CFID=84847642&CFTOKEN=85079798.
3 www.sec.gov/litigation/complaints/2010/comp-pr2010–59.pdf.
4 Ibid.
5 www.sec.gov/litigation/complaints/2009/comp21068.pdf.
6 Ibid.
7 www.sec.gov/news/press/2009/2009–129.htm.
8 Ibid.
9 Ibid.
10 http://stopforeclosurefraud.com/2011/01/11/nytimes-judges-berate-bank-lawyers-in-foreclosures/.
11 http://levin.senate.gov/404/?CFID=84847642&CFTOKEN=85079798.
12 www.nytimes.com/2011/06/22/business/22sec.html.
13 www.nytimes.com/2011/06/26/business/26gret.html.
14 http://orient.bowdoin.edu/orient/article.php?date=2009–02–20&section=2&id=5.
15 Morgenson and Rosner, *Reckless Endangerment*, 27.
16 Jonathan G.S. Koppell, *The Politics of Quasi-Government*, as cited in Morgenson and Rosner, *Reckless Endangerment*, 27.
17 Ibid., 28.
18 http://online.wsj.com/article/SB10001424052970203687504577001653467422674.html.
19 Morgenson and Rosner, *Reckless Endangerment*, 64.
20 www.investopedia.com/terms/r/regulatory-arbitrage.asp#ixzz1cGJeBW2T.
21 www.commondreams.org/view/2009/03/22–6.
22 www.bloomberg.com/apps/news?pid=newsarchive&sid=aDm4OdFvcWUw&refer=home.
23 http://articles.moneycentral.msn.com/Investing/Extra/was-aig-watchdog-not-up-to-the-job.aspx.
24 Ibid.
25 www.bloomberg.com/news/2010–06–30/sullivan-says-he-was-unaware-until-2007-of-aig-credit-swaps-risk-tripling.html.
26 Ibid.
27 www.time.com/time/specials/packages/article/0,28804,1877351_1877350_1877321,00.html.

28 www.nytimes.com/2008/09/28/business/28melt.html?pagewanted= 2&hp.
29 Ibid.
30 www.bloomberg.com/news/2010–06–13/fannie-freddie-fix-expands-to-160-billion-with-worst-case-at-1-trillion.html.
31 Morgenson and Rosner, *Reckless Endangerment*.
32 Ibid., 242.
33 www.washingtonpost.com/wp-dyn/articles/A17241–2004Dec21.html.
34 www.msnbc.msn.com/id/26963309/ns/business-stocks_and_economy/t/can-wild-ceo-pay-be-tamed-probably-not/#.Tp8WBt77i3c.
35 Morgenson and Rosner, *Reckless Endangerment*, 122.
36 http://fcic-static.law.stanford.edu/cdn_media/fcic-testimony/2010–0409-Falcon.pdf.
37 www.loansafe.org/west-virginia-homeowner-convicted-of-mortgage-fraud-and-tax-evasion.
38 www.fool.com/investing/general/2011/04/26/why-so-few-ended-up-in-jail-after-the-financial-cr.aspx.
39 Eileen P. Flynn, *My Country Right or Wrong? Selective Conscientious Objection in the Nuclear Age*, Chicago: Loyola University Press, 1985, 18.
40 http://business.asiaone.com/Business/Office/Learn/Career%2BBuilding/Story/A1Story20100813–231955.html.
41 Morgenson and Rosner, *Reckless Endangerment*, 9.
42 www.imakenews.com/cppa/e_article001267422.cfm?x=b11,0,w.
43 Ibid.
44 http://c0182732.cdn1.cloudfiles.rackspacecloud.com/fcic_final_report_conclusions.pdf.
45 www.nytimes.com/2010/02/28/magazine/28fob-q4-t.html.
46 http://c0182732.cdn1.cloudfiles.rackspacecloud.com/fcic_final_report_conclusions.pdf.
47 www.vatican.va/archive/ccc_css/archive/catechism/p3s1c1a7.htm, 1808.
48 Bethany McLean and Joe Nocera, *All the Devils are Here*, New York: Portfolio, 2010, 126.
49 www.nytimes.com/2009/04/12/business/12gret.html.
50 www.sec.gov/news/press/2011/2011–214.htm.
51 www.nytimes.com/2011/10/30/opinion/sunday/friedman-did-you-hear-the-one-about-the-bankers.html.
52 www.businessethics.ca/definitions/conflict-of-interest.html.
53 www.alston.com/financialmarketscrisisblog/?entry=3905.
54 Ibid.
55 Morgenson and Rosner, *Reckless Endangerment*, 187.
56 http://foreclosureblues.wordpress.com/2010/12/16/servicer-conflicts-of-interest-and-the-principal-agent-problem-findsen-law/.
57 www.nytimes.com/2010/09/14/business/14moodys.html.
58 www.gather.com/viewArticle.action?articleId=281474978480277.
59 www.wbiconpro.com/06-Priya.pdf.

6 SOCIAL ETHICS

1 www.scu.edu/ethics/practicing/decision/commongood.html.
2 www.oea.umaryland.edu/communications/news?ViewStatus=FullArticle &articleDetail=9855.
3 www.archbishopofcanterbury.org/1982.
4 www.loansouth.com/pdf/NelsonRES06111.pdf.
5 www.ethics.org/files/u5/execComp.pdf.
6 Roubini and Mihm, *Crisis Economics*, 80.
7 www.fcic.gov/about/.
8 http://books.google.com/books?id=QIKfTVrhNfMC&pg=PA166&lpg =PA166&dq=testimony+of+keith+johnson+fcic+and+corporate+due+di ligence&source=bl&ots=mya62-TN4w&sig=vtRCeBagyWU400E0cezet4 Ayh2s&hl=en&ei=7ae6TuL8OYrC2wXz5ujCBw&sa=X&oi=book_result &ct=result&resnum=3&sqi=2&ved=0CDkQ6AEwAg#v=onepage&q&f=t rue.
9 http://seekingalpha.com/article/96074-moral-hazard-a-danger-to-our-financial-system.
10 www.financialstabilityboard.org/publications/r_0910a.pdf.
11 www.ethics.org/files/u5/execComp.pdf.
12 www.nytimes.com/2011/11/06/opinion/sunday/worldly-philosophers-wanted.html.
13 http://occupywallst.org/.
14 www.globalpost.com/dispatch/news/regions/americas/united-states/111108/occupy-wall-street-demands-campaign-finance-reform.
15 www.ft.com/cms/s/0/92bbba26-f2a7-11df-8020-00144feab49a. html#axzz15ewuxaYy.
16 http://pewresearch.org/pubs/1569/trust-in-government-distrust-discontent-anger-partisan-rancor.
17 http://swampland.time.com/2011/11/10/what-you-missed-while-not-watching-the-cnbc-oops-debate/?xid=gonewsedit.
18 Ibid.

FURTHER READING

Ahamed, Liaquat, *Lords of Finance*, New York: Penguin Press, 2009.

Barnett-Hart, Ann Katherine, *The Story of the CDO Market Meltdown: An Empirical Analysis*, Harvard thesis, 2010, www.hks.harvard.edu/m-rcbg/students/dunlop/2009-CDOmeltdown.pdf.

Dodd–Frank Wall Street Reform and Consumer Protection Act, http://docs.house.gov/rules/finserv/111_hr4173_finsrvcr.pdf.

Federal Reserve Bank, Timelines of Policy Responses to the Global Financial Crisis, www.ny.frb.org/research/global_economy/policyresponses.html.

Financial Crisis Inquiry Commission, *The Financial Crisis Inquiry Report*, www.fcic.gov/.

Financial Crisis Inquiry Commission, Reports and Fact Sheets; Hearings and Testimony, www.fcic.gov/.

Levin, Carl (Sen., D) and Tom Coburn (Sen., R), *Wall Street and the Financial Crisis: Anatomy of A Financial Collapse*, Majority and Minority Staff Report, April 13, 2011, http://levin.senate.gov/newsroom/supporting/2011/PSI_WallStreetCrisis_041311.pdf.

Lewis, Michael, *The Big Short*, New York: W.W. Norton & Company, 2010.

Lowenstein, Roger, *The End of Wall Street*, New York: Penguin Press, 2010.

McLean, Bethany and Joe Nocera, *All the Devils Are Here: The Hidden History of the Financial Crisis*, New York: Portfolio, 2010.

Morgenson, Gretchen and Joshua Rosner, *Reckless Endangerment: How Outsized Ambition, Greed, and Corruption Led to Economic Armageddon*, New York: Times Books, 2011.

Paulson, Jr., Henry M., *On the Brink: Inside the Race to Stop the Collapse of the Global Financial System*, New York: Business Plus, 2010.

Ross Sorkin, Andrew, *Too Big to Fail*, New York: Viking, 2009.

Roubini, Nouriel and Stephen Mihm, *Crisis Economics: A Crash Course in the Future of Finance*, New York: Penguin, 2010.

Securities and Exchange Commission, SEC Initiatives Under New Regulatory Reform Law, www.sec.gov/spotlight/dodd-frank.shtml.

Wallis, Jim, *Rediscovering Values: On Wall Street, Main Street, and Your Street*, Brentwood: Howard Books, 2010.

INDEX